M000232764

(From a lithograph by Robert Riggs)

False Face Society doctors enter the long house.

MIDWINTER RITES
OF THE
CAYUGA LONG HOUSE

by
FRANK G. SPECK

in collaboration with
ALEXANDER GENERAL
(Deskáheh)

Introduction to the Bison Book Edition
by William N. Fenton

University of Nebraska Press
Lincoln and London

Library of Congress Cataloging-in-Publication Data
Speck, Frank Gouldsmith, 1881–1950.
Midwinter rites of the Cayuga long house / Frank G. Speck; in collaboration with
Alexander General.
    p.   cm.
Originally published: Philadelphia: University of Pennsylvania Press, 1949.
Includes bibliographical references (p.   ) and index.
ISBN 0-8032-9231-7 (pbk.: acid-free paper)
1. Cayuga Indians—Rites and ceremonies.   2. Cayuga Indians—Religion.   I. Title.
E99.C3S6   1995
299'.74—dc20
94-44361   CIP

Reprinted by arrangement with Roy Blankenship.

INTRODUCTION TO THE BISON BOOK EDITION

Frank G. Speck: American Ethnologist (1881–1950)
By William N. Fenton

Of all of Franz Boas's students, Frank G. Speck was the most persistent fieldworker. As his contemporary Edward Sapir once remarked, Speck was forever at it. From the "Dying Speech Echoes of Connecticut," heard as a boy, to the songs of the Eagle Dance sung by the Allegany Senecas to revive him at the brink of the grave, Speck kept an ear to the wind for the voices of remnant Indian bands rising from the hills and swamps of the Eastern Woodlands. No academic appointment, no learned gathering, no university function, took precedence over the visit of an Indian colleague, the summons to a tribal council, or the call to attend a ceremony. Though qualified in every respect, and learned in fields outside of anthropology, Speck did not covet academic honors; he rather valued the good opinions of his Indian friends and esteemed them as colleagues along with academicians.*

In the 1930s no member of the Yale faculty except Sapir had experienced Iroquois fieldwork at first hand. Sapir knew Speck as a fellow teaching assistant at Pennsylvania, and as chief of the Anthropological Survey of Canada, Sapir had employed Speck on contract research. Sapir sent me to see Speck in the spring of 1933, a visit that marked the beginning of a professional relationship and warm friendship of nearly twenty years.

I had glimpsed Speck briefly at a meeting of the American Anthropological Association held in 1931 at Andover Academy, where I went to learn what it meant to be an anthropologist. We did not meet. Speck did not stay for the entire session. I recalled seeing a compact individual with graying hair, a smoker of small cigars, seated on a couch talking with a colleague.

My trip to Philadelphia was to consult Speck before commencing Iroquois fieldwork. On climbing the stairs of College Hall, I found an elf of a man seated with knees drawn up to his chin on a deep window ledge opposite Speck's office door. I remarked that I was hoping to meet Dr. Speck, and the man replied that so was he. My fellow visitor went on to extol Speck's virtues as a field ethnologist: no one had quite the same approach or had comparable success with native Indians. My informant allowed that he too was an ethnologist, John Swanton by name. This indeed was a banner day for a graduate student.

---

*I derive Speck's career from two previous articles, both titled "Frank G. Speck's Anthropology:" the first appeared in *The Life and Times of Frank G. Speck 1881–1950,* Roy Blankenship, ed., University of Pennsylvania Publications in Anthropology, no. 4, University of Pennsylvania, Philadelphia, 1991, pp. 9–37; the second appeared in *Man in the Northeast,* no. 40, 1990, pp. 95–101. By permission.

As we talked, Speck came up the four flights of stairs followed by a graduate student whom he introduced as Loren Eiseley, a Nebraskan. Eiseley and I talked quietly in a corner of Speck's cavernous office while the two eminent ethnologists discussed some problem in Southeastern studies that Swanton had on his mind. But Speck soon demurred that I had come by appointment and suggested that we four go for lunch. Swanton begged off and departed, leaving three of us to cross Woodland Avenue to "the Greek's" where Speck greeted the proprietor in modern Greek. The food was not memorable, but the conversation made up for it.

I had been preparing for fieldwork by reviewing F. W. Waugh's ethnobotanical notes that Sapir obtained from Ottawa. I showed Speck how I proposed to organize them, and he brought in Gladys Tantaquidgeon, whose research on Delaware medicines was quite advanced. They both suggested further collecting to verify Waugh's data, ways to get new information, how to classify and retrieve it. Speck, showering me with pertinent reprints, said "This will get you started."

Then, while recounting his recent collaborative work on Cayuga Longhouse ceremonies, Speck impressed upon me a second research problem: each Iroquois community, much like the Pueblos, probably had its own cycle of ceremonies. Iroquois rituals, group by group, deserved equally just such study before any generalizing on the overall patterns of Northern Iroquois culture. This approach would enable us to establish the annual calendar of ceremonies for each community. To get at the functional groupings of constituent rites, one should ascertain the "time, duration, purpose, and composition of each day's activities in the annual round of festivals." Speck was forecasting the contents of his monograph on Cayuga ceremonies, then in manuscript, while charting the direction of my subsequent research career.

This lead inspired me to test Speck's model during the Green Corn and Midwinter ceremonies at Coldspring Longhouse (Fenton 1936), and to repeat the exercise at Tonawanda (Fenton 1941), both Seneca communities. Somehow Speck found time for his students and those of colleagues. He treated me as a professional from the start.

Speck had learned how to survive in academe, and although he wasted little time at it, he was willing to coach a neophyte in its mysteries. After the war, he encouraged me to advance the idea of an Institute for Iroquoian Research and suggested how to achieve it. The concept evolved as a much less formal affair that after 1945 became the Conference on Iroquois Research, which continues to meet, to attract younger scholars, and to produce significant research without institutional funding.

After the first conference at Red House, four of us went up to Ohsweken on Six Nations Reserve to share fieldwork. Sharing fieldwork with the master and learning how he worked proved both enjoyable and productive. The word that Dr. Speck was in Ohsweken brought the leaders of Sour Springs Cayuga Longhouse to our lodging. Listening to Alexander General (*Deskaheh*), Speck's collaborator in this book, talking for an hour with Speck made it quite apparent that their relationship was something special. Speck treated his visitors as colleagues. His great erudition challenged them, and his humor afforded endless amusement.

Elsewhere I have cited several instances of Speck's field method (1990:97; 1991:13). The ethnologist learns what he knows. Speck brought a vast comparative knowledge of languages and customs to his interviews. Working with fading cultures, he assembled older informants who stimulated each other's memories. He then worked intensively with one or more of them. Of necessity, he made short visits at intervals, rather than prolonged field trips, allowing interest to ferment between sessions. His returns were greeted as manifestations of continued interest in the subject and concern for collaborators. When back at the university, he usually found some literate person with whom he kept up a steady stream of corrrespondence, usually on post cards. These "F.G.S." penny postcards comprise a significant portion of his literary remains.

Persons who knew Speck recall his lifetime interest in natural history, especially his passion for birds (Hallowell 1951: 67), rivaled only by his addiction to snakes. He knew medicinal plants equally. Indeed, Speck was a product of the natural history movement that ran strong at the turn of the century. Collecting was the path to science, and Speck was a collector par excellence.

Speck's affinity to Indians began early. His parents packed off a sick child to rural Connecticut to recover his health among Mohegan-Pequot descendants. This proved a lucky accident for American linguistics, for Speck's flair for languages attracted him as a Columbia undergraduate to J. Dynley Prince's course on ancient languages. When one day Prince drew on Natick, an extinct language of Massachusetts, for illustrations and mentioned some of its defunct cognates, Speck, to the professor's astonishment, volunteered that some Pequots spoke their language and offered some examples. Speck and Prince were soon publishing joint papers on supposedly extinct Algonquian languages (Fenton 1990: 17–18).

From Prince to Boas was a natural progression. Speck came to Boas prepared for the rigors of taking texts in the native language, and he had lived with Indians and learned an exotic language. He soon acquired the elements of linguistic analysis. He was quite prepared to fulfill two of Boas's precepts—texts and fieldwork. He needed to acquire discipline and a sense of problem. For Speck there was never the trauma of crossing cultural boundaries that panics some students. He quickly established rapport with informants.

Having received a Master of Arts degree from Columbia within a year of graduating from the College, Speck was promptly sent by Boas to Indian Territory (now Oklahoma) to do ethnographic fieldwork among the then unknown Yuchi, a people removed from the Southeast. This introduction to the cultures of the Southeast yielded publications on the Creek, Chickasaw, Osage, as well as a dissertation on the Yuchi, which he submitted as a Harrison Research Fellow to Pennsylvania (Speck 1909). More than a standard ethnography, Speck's monograph carried transcriptions of recorded ceremonial music. Here began an interest in ceremonialism, native music, and language that runs as a persistent thread through Speck's later work down to the present book.

Elsewhere I have commented on Speck's major discoveries and listed his major publications. His output was enormous— five to ten papers and monographs a year. Hallowell (1952:72), who knew him best, remarked that the writing was consistently of a high quality and substantiality. The man knew what he was about. Two of his books, besides this one, were long delayed: *Penobscot Man* (1940), and *Naskapi* (1935), although the latter reported more recent work.

Speck followed the thread of music, ceremonialism, and religion from Yuchi to Algonquian studies, thence back to Cherokee (Southeastern Iroquoian), and over the bridge of the Delaware Big House Ceremony (1931) to Cayuga Longhouse ceremonies at Six Nations Reserve, Ontario. We come full cycle to his final major book. Here began the study of local diversity and specific patterning of rites. This brilliant lead was wrong in one respect. Although the longhouse cycles are unique, localized, and different, their identity is with place, a reservation or congregation. They are not tribal ceremonies in a generic sense, as Shimony later demonstrated (1961). Speck would have welcomed Tooker's (1970) synthesis of all these patterns.

Speck undertook the study of the *Midwinter Rites of the Cayuga Long House* in collaboration with Alexander General (*Deskaheh*), the noted Cayuga chief, in 1931. For the Iroquoianist the book is Speck's most important ethnological contribution. Regularly at midsemester Speck went off to Six Nations Reserve to work with Deskaheh and observe the ceremonies that fall at that season. Intensive work at that season only explains why the study does not cover the summer segment of the annual cycle that the Midwinter Festival recapitulates. Between field sessions, back at the university, Speck systematically classified his observations, noted loopholes, and prepared questions for the next session with Deskaheh.

Speck wrote up his field notes while they were fresh. Within three years he had outlined the structure and function of the annual cycle, which he offered me as a model for my own study of Seneca ceremonies at Coldspring Longhouse (1936). By 1939 he had a completed manuscript; but while awaiting a publisher, Speck returned intermittently to the field during the next ten years. He kept revising the manuscript to accommodate new information, added a final chapter of philosophical commentary, which resulted in writing of uneven character and quality. His early observations are crisp, but the later retrospections on Iroquois religion and society are uneven.

What was Speck's method? Like other North American ethnologists, Speck worked intensively with a single informant, coupling interviews with observation of "the doings," in which society participated. But unlike contemporaries among anthropologists, he gave full credit to his native collaborator, Chief Alexander General, with whom he went over the manuscript in minute detail during repeated visits in later years. Regularly, Speck took graduate students with him to the field, encouraged them to pursue independent research, and credited their observations in print.

In later years Speck would turn over an unfinished manuscript to a student, tell him to "fix it up," and then give the student joint authorship. His 1942 monograph on *The Tutelo Spirit Adoption Ceremony* had just such a history.

The reader will find the religious framework of Cayuga culture outlined in Part One, which also includes a chapter on Sour Springs Longhouse, its history, and general symbolism. At the time Speck wrote, great interest centered on the structure and functioning of moieties, their reciprocal action in ceremonies, and the question as to whether they were exogamous like their constituent clans. Speck has them named after their dominant clans, which contradicts Goldenweiser's earlier finding at Six Nations Reserve, and Seneca moieties are nameless. They are simply "the sides."

Speck the naturalist was systematic, classifying phenomena hierarchically, grouping ceremonial acts in tables by time, duration, purpose, function, and composition, thereby demonstrating patterns of sequence (Table 2, pp. 34–36). Speck was the first to show the relationship of people on earth to a hierarchy of spirit-forces that are divided into an upper and lower pantheon and graded upward from earth to sky (Table I, p. 30). Corresponding rites and dances addressed to ranked spirit forces comprise the inventory of ritual acts from sacred to profane (Table 3, p. 37).

Culture is a seamless web of activities. Officials, foods, musical instruments, and other ritual props that pertain to particular ceremonies, or are shared by many, belong together and comprise conceptual units.

A significant part of the Midwinter ceremony proper (Part 2), is composed of the celebrations of the Medicine societies, to which entrance befalls an individual in response to a particular dream followed by a cure. The obligation to fulfill these ceremonial requirements is a powerful force in keeping Iroquois ceremonialism alive. The phenomenon of substitution, as Speck discovered, enables the ceremonies to survive without altering their structure or purpose. Pork for bear meat; beef for venison; canned hominy corn for native maize, etc.

Four sacred ceremonial rites—Feather Dance, Individual Thanksgiving, Skin or Drum Dance, and Bowl Game—make up the core of Iroquois traditional religious celebration. White Dog Sacrifice, on a par with the League and the False Faces as distinctive Iroquois features, has not been celebrated within the memory of living man.

Speck and Deskaheh make a nice distinction in the annual cycle between winter rites associated with men's activities, and a summer series of festivals that mark planting, cultivating, and harvesting the "Three Sisters" (corn-beans-squash), which are women's activities.

Studies of Iroquois ceremonialism have made great strides along the path that Speck and Deskaheh charted fifty years ago. But one could not possibly replicate their study today. The sources no longer exist. The confident savants of Deskaheh's generation have gone the long trail. A new generation of younger Iroquois, unsure of their own culture but eager to restore it, while beset by a fallacy that one must have native genes to appreciate Iroquois culture, have closed the longhouse doors to outsiders who might assist them. They should welcome the republication of Speck's classic. Younger scholars pay heed to the work of a master.

Slingerlands, New York
8 June 1994

REFERENCES CITED

Fenton, W. N.
1936   *An Outline of Seneca Ceremonies at Coldspring Longhouse.* Yale University
         Publications in Anthropology 9. Yale University Press, New Haven.
1990   Frank Speck's Anthropology (1881–1950). *Man in the Northeast* 40: 95–101.
         Albany.
1990   [Same title] *The Life and Times of Frank G. Speck 1881–1950.* Roy Blankenship,
         ed., pp. 9–37. University of Pennsylvania: Publications in Anthropology No. 4.
         Philadelphia.

Hallowell, A. I.
1951   Frank Gouldsmith Speck (1881–1950). *American Anthropologist* 53: 67–87.

Prince, J. D. and F. G. Speck
1903   Dying American Speech Echoes from Connecticut. *Proceedings of the Ameri-
         can Philosophical Society* 42: 346–52. [and two subsequent articles in the
         Anthropologist.]

Shimony, A. A.
1961   *Conservatism among the Iroquois at the Six Nations Reserve.* Yale Univesity
         Publications in Anthropology 65. New Haven.

Speck, F. G.
1909   *Ethnology of the Yuchi Indians.* University of Pennsylvania Museum Anthro-
         pological Papers 1: 1–154.
1917   Medicine Practices of the Northeastern Algonquians. *Proceedings of the Nine-
         teenth International Congress of Americanists*, pp. 303–21.
1931   *A Study of the Delaware Indian Big House Ceremony.* Publications of the Penn-
         sylvania Historical Commission 2. Harrisburg.
1935   *Naskapi: the Savage Hunters of the Labrador Peninsula.* University of Okla-
         homa Press. Norman.
1937   *Oklahoma Delaware Ceremonies, Feasts, and Dances.* Memoirs of the Ameri-
         can Philosophical Society 7. Philadelphia.
1940   *Penobscot Man: The Life History of a Forest Tribe in Maine.* University of
         Pennsylvania Press. Philadelphia.
1942   *The Tutelo Spirit Adoption Ceremony: Reclothing the Living in the Name of
         the Dead.* Pennsylvania Historical Commission. Harrisburg.

1946   Bird Nomenclature and Song Interpretation of the Canadian Delaware: an Essay in Ethno-ornithology. *Journal of the Washington Academy of Sciences* 36(8): 249–58.
1949   How the Dew Eagles Society of the Allegany Seneca Cured *Gahehdagowa*. *Primitive Man* 22(3–4): 39–59.

Tooker, E.
1970   *The Iroquois Ceremonial of Midwinter.* Syracuse University Press. Syracuse.

CONTENTS

PART TWO

THE MIDWINTER CEREMONY

CONTENTS

LIST OF ILLUSTRATIONS

LIST OF TABLES

LIST OF PLATES
(Following page 192)

INTRODUCTION

THE voluminous literature dealing with the culture of the Iroquois has not as yet touched specifically upon the rich ceremonial properties of the Cayuga. The reason for this lies apparently in the disregard for a possible distinctiveness of traits which any single tribe of the Iroquois Confederacy might possess. According to most writers, a long-continued leveling process is supposed to have worked toward reducing any originality of institutions which may have characterized individual Iroquois divisions before their political unification in the sixteenth century. But to the ethnologist who has prosecuted research in eastern North America among non-integrated peoples of Algonkian affinity, Iroquoian uniformity in cultural details is not self-apparent. Attention is called particularly to the differences distinguishing the aspects of Iroquoian civilization as known to have existed among the southern Cherokee, the Tuscarora, the now extinct tribes of Iroquoian affinity in southern Virginia, the Huron, and the Five Nations of the north.

The present study limits itself to consideration of Cayuga cultural history, approached through the treatment of religious rites of the Cayuga of the Sour Springs Long House. The project of which this work is the result was systematically begun in 1931, developing from research on the holy festivals of the Delaware and Munsee of Oklahoma and Ontario to investigation of the ceremonies performed in the Long Houses (religious centers) of the Canadian Cayuga. The extension of research to the Cayuga grew out of the discovery that an association had existed, in early as well as later times, between the Cayuga and members of the before-mentioned Algonkian peoples (the Delaware and Munsee) in New York and Pennsylvania. This association has been intimately maintained by the Delaware-Munsee and the Cayuga now coresident since about 1768 upon the Six Nations Reserve, Brant County, Ontario. The effect of long association and intermarriage between these peoples, radically different in language, suggested the possibility that religious motives and processes might have had as their sources a common functional or historical background. Examination has accordingly brought forth a series of elements common to the tribes of the eastern Atlantic woodland area. These common elements include ideas of cosmogony,

1

as represented by the hierarchy of the spirit forces dominated by the "Great Spirit" as Creator; the complementary functioning of ceremonial groups or "moieties"; the dominance of dreams and visions as motivating forces; the medicinally functioning societal groups; the mask-image rites; the order of ceremonies; the Big House of the Delaware or the Long House of the Iroquois as a shrine; and the sacredness of new fire. What do these homologies in Iroquoian and Algonkian ceremony signify? As a problem the question arose, and a problem it still remains. They do prove that Iroquoian cultural traits are not all exclusive. Comparative studies by other investigators projected under the supervision of Dr. William N. Fenton will later show to what extent they are homogeneous.

The investigation of Cayuga rites was carried out through grants from the Faculty Research Fund of the University of Pennsylvania (Grants Nos. 50, 93, 163, 256, and 300) during the winters of 1932-33, 1933-34, 1934-35 and in January and February, 1936, when summarization was made of the Sour Springs rites and accumulated results checked. Subsequent trips to the Six Nations Reserve were made from 1938 through to 1947 (on Grants Nos. 555, 570, 586, and 594), when parts of the manuscript were gone over with Cayuga informants and additional data incorporated into the body of material.

Contacts were restricted to sessions with Cayuga officers and leaders of the Sour Springs Long House, and observations of rites were made only within this group. The aim was to secure information covering a wide range of possibilities and to bring to the surface those obsolete customs which have been abandoned by the tribe or modified in the evolution of Iroquois festivals since the period described in the writings of the Jesuit missionaries. Efforts were made to see and study under observation as many of the ritual units and ceremonial composites as possible. The Midwinter Ceremony was attended and witnessed in its entirety over the seven-day period in 1933 and in 1936, and in part in 1934, 1935, 1944, and 1945. Some of the dances had been witnessed during earlier visits to the Six Nations, in 1914 and 1925, so that most of the separate dances have been observed, except in the case of those noted as obsolete. The major collaborator on this work, Deskáheh (whose contribution will be discussed later), is conversant with, and is an active leader in, the entire set of rituals of the Sour Springs ceremonial cycle.

A departure has been made from the idea, a tradition promulgated by L. H. Morgan, that the religious practices of the Five Nations are so uniform in history and character as to be treatable through the assembling of sources consulted in any or all of the Iroquois tribes. Such a generalization is apparently not one to be accepted as a conclusion, but held rather as something the relative truth of which can be established only through material deliberately obtained from sources of information among the separate tribes in question. There have been already recorded some variations, additions, and omissions in the ceremonial procedures of Long House devotees among the Onondaga, Seneca, and Oneida whose tabernacles are still attended, and some of the Mohawk of the Six Nations Reserve.[1]

Dr. J. N. B. Hewitt (1918) pointed out the distinct position of the Cayuga in the regime of the Iroquois. He found that the Cayuga had largely repudiated the legend that Dekanawidah was the founder of the League of the Five Nations. The Dekanawidah legend is by them associated with an anonymous character, "The Fatherless Boy" (see pages 127–29 of this paper), who instituted a prototype of the League government among the Cayuga. Hewitt's information broadly substantiates what is here put down in connection with the identity of The Fatherless Boy and coincides with information obtained during this study concerning the early history of Cayuga moieties (see page 26).

In addition to differences in belief and ceremony among the various Iroquois tribes and reservations, some variations stand forth even in the ceremonial programs of the two Cayuga Long Houses still operating on the Six Nations Reserve itself—one at Lower Cayuga, the other at Sour Springs. The former perpetuates some rituals now discontinued by the latter, and there are other variances between the two as orthodox centers. Even in as important a matter as the relative seating position of the Wolf and Turtle moieties in the two active Cayuga Long Houses there is a reversal of order. Whereas in the Sour Springs Long House the Wolf moiety sits on

[1] Since the burning of the Mohawk Long House in Joseph Brant's time (1783-1807), according to tradition, the Mohawk conservatives have distributed themselves among the other Long House devotees. In 1927, about twenty families organized the adherents of their creed and started a Long House building on the upper end of the reserve, where for a number of years it stood unfinished for lack of funds. It has since been taken down.

the west side and the Turtle on the east side of the building, the position of the Wolf is on the east at Lower Cayuga and the Turtle is on the west. In the Lower Cayuga community, moreover, there are families having Delaware-Munsee-Mahican connections whose forebears were known to be agents in transferring some songs and elements of the Delaware-Munsee *genre* into the Cayuga complex. These observations merely give a glimpse of what may be discovered upon investigation of the wider religious horizons of the Six Nations. The significance of this is that in the new order of research independent studies of the distinct tribal groups are now being made by ethnologists. Dr. Fenton has sounded the marching orders for such undertakings.

The majority of the Cayuga Indians on the Six Nations Reserve are of an obstinately patriotic and religious temper. Among the seven or eight hundred members of the famous tribe, two Long Houses mentioned above are actively maintained. That at Sour Springs is still conspicuously free of influences of European social artifice, commercialism, and Christian sophistries. The Cayuga possess that quality which we know as the Indian heart. A delightful unsophistication redolent of an age-old atmosphere of dignified myth and "superstition" prevails, unfolding a coöperative health-preserving ideal framed in thanksgiving and rejoicing. The Long House Cayuga devotee has somehow fortified his inner spirit against most of the cheap ideas and untried innovations of an age of perplexities and hypocrisies in religious teaching alien to his tradition.

This condition, lamentable perhaps to missionaries and teachers employed in the vanguard of an overtense civilization, has indeed been a felicity to the ethnologist, no less than a guarantee to Cayuga national life. To the ethnologist it means an opportunity, one of no small consequence, to watch among American Indians the internal workings of a native religion which has not lost its vital force. One cannot believe, from what experience has shown among these people, that the rites of the Long House are destined to doom for a long time yet. It would be difficult—impossible statistically—to make an accurate estimate of the number of individuals in the Cayuga Nation who are bona fide Long House adherents. First, there is no enrollment system for the Long House members. Second, a number of them are bidenominational, participating in Long House rites and also attending occasionally or regularly, as the case may be, the Protestant churches on the reservation.

As may be surmised by the student who has essayed similar topics among other ethnic groups, any treatment of the superstitious mentality of a people like the Iroquois may, through unavoidable misunderstandings, nurture errors and shortcomings. In presenting the substance of material accumulated through the combined energies of my collaborators, I have avoided those ornate embellishments of theory and the delving into historical backgrounds so tempting at times, though one in particular has not escaped thought, namely, the derivation of Cayuga social and ceremonial institutions from some relatively advanced prehistoric cultures of the middle and lower Ohio and Mississippi valley regions.

The study as it stands is mainly something to build upon. It constitutes the results accomplished in the first stage of systematic investigation—the recording of observations and facts of Cayuga rites as practised by the Sour Springs group, without speculation upon their historical or comparative aspects. The speculative stage of treatment will succeed this stage and will, in time, produce results of similar study by others who are now investigating the Long House festivals of the Onondaga, the Seneca, and some of the Oneida and Mohawk in Canada, especially through the intensive investigation by Dr. Fenton of Seneca rituals in New York State.

Conciseness being an objective in the presentation of the material, as much of it as possible is arranged in tabulations and lists. These give the essential elements in the composition of the rites, the order of their celebration in the Long House routine, and the analysis of dances. Paragraphs of explanation follow the listings to furnish details and to add observations made on the spot. A great deal, of course, still remains to be said concerning implications of historical change and influences upon the performances from within and without Cayuga culture; but here the aim is to give the raw material.

It is expected, moreover, that the observant reader if interested in psychological problems of culture will find much in the following accounts of medicine society procedures that implies the principles of psychotherapy. The treatment of such a topic is left open for intensive examination.

In presenting the following study of Cayuga rituals it is most important to emphasize the fact that while the effects of mental influence in curing complaints are outstanding in prominence, they run parallel with a medical practice employing drugs, herbs and material substances, as well. Rituals of the medicine societies work in conjunction with medicinal agencies decided through diagnosis by native doctors and prescribed by them to sufferers. It would seem that in the thought-system of the Cayuga—as is usual with the Iroquois as a whole—that ritual curing runs parallel with ethno-pharmaceutics without implying a close interaction between the two; that is, the spiritual and therapeutic bodily processes operate side-by-side without mutual interference. One cannot, however, be blind to the difficulty presented in this view of interpretation, for native "doctors" hold their knowledge as professional property to an extent that resists disclosure. Since the present study does not include in its subject matter the use of medicines as such, the whole treatment of herbology is left open for approach by a botanical authority. The investigation of the practical folk-science of medicine of the Cayuga holds prospects to a degree sufficient to excite the enthusiastic attention of a specialist.

I feel obliged also to emphasize how fully it is realized that in treating any topic of Iroquois culture one can not assume to be a lone contributor. There are and have been many capable investigators, some of them silent and critical authorities, Indians themselves, others whose published observations and conclusions have to be considered in an undertaking of this character. Concerning the frequent instances where their testimony will be found to differ, even to contradict what is put down here, I may say that much of the sort has been anticipated, and should be understood by the ethnologist as a constant of deviation to be expected when dealing with topics in the uncanonized religious life of a native people continually undergoing change. Deskáheh, who ably conducts rites himself, may give data which deviate from good authority elsewhere and upon other occasions, but in such instances he is not wrong. What one sees, likewise, may differ from what others have seen, but it must stand as valid in exemplifying conduct and variations of conduct with definite ethnological value. I trust, therefore, that this attitude toward the building-up of knowledge in our common field of interest may explain the avoidance of discussion here of differences encountered in these pages and in the studies of other capable investigators: Morgan, Parkman, Hale, Cusick, Beauchamp, Hewitt, Converse,

Smith, Brinton, Orr, Boyle, Parker, Harrington, the Skinners, Goldenweiser, Waugh, Barbeau, Fenton, Olbrechts, and others, including the Jesuit scholars.

Our present state of knowledge of Iroquoian ceremonials owes much indeed to the prolonged and systematic research of Dr. Fenton. From his recent publications (1936, 1940, 1941a, 1941b, 1942), and reference to his Seneca manuscripts, as well as through the advantage of discussion on various points raised in the treatment of my material, I have come to an understanding of many things that would have remained unclear from Cayuga sources alone. Comparison with his Seneca and Onondaga studies has deepened the understanding of Cayuga backgrounds and provided suggestions for carrying out questioning and interpreting results.

Particular mention is due in concern of collaborator Alexander J. General, incumbent for life to the title and office of Deskáheh in the Council of Chiefs of the Six Nations. His untiring efforts and patience and his systematic, ceremonial mind made the study possible. Deskáheh whose personal name is Sohyówa, "Great Sky" (Pl. IB), is a devout Long House communicant and leader, well versed in the teachings of his forbears. Being thoroughly conversant with the English language in addition to several of the Iroquoian languages besides Cayuga, he was indispensable in carrying out research on the reserve. He was ever genial and willing to coöperate, in the same thoughtful manner in which he serves as a chief and leader. The Cayuga word transcriptions and equivalents are from his dictation.

The Cayuga are serious-minded enough in their worship to cherish a spirit of reserve in religious affairs. Some restrictions are enforced upon the liberties of aliens attending the rites, even though they are admitted as guests and partakers of the ceremonials in the Long House. Such restrictions applied to me. The leaders requested that no notes or photographs be made during attendance at the sessions, which made it necessary each evening to rehearse and annotate the procedures of the day under the supervision of Deskáheh.

Acknowledgment is also made of the courtesy and aid of the other chiefs and leaders of the Sour Springs Long House group mentioned by name in the list of ceremonial officers (see page 183).

The singers of the Long House are also due particular thanks. They made possible the recording of most of the songs and rituals of the ceremonies by repeating them for us after the Midwinter

Festivals were over in 1933 and in 1936. In 1933 the recording was done on dictaphone cylinders, forty in number. In 1936 composition recording disks were used; these totaled thirty ten-inch disks and twenty-nine eight-inch disks. The entire collection, then, comprises ninety-nine cylinders and disks, the latter used on both sides. The collection represents a repertoire of about one hundred songs, all Cayuga in origin except for a few of Tutelo derivation which are adapted by singers in Cayuga rites, either for group or individual performance, and a smaller number of Seneca, Tuscarora, and Delaware origin, possessing a similar status. Practically all these songs function, or may function upon occasion, in the devotionals and socials of the Sour Springs Long House group. Dr. George Herzog, of Indiana University, is transcribing these songs, and his transcriptions and notes are to form the substance of another monograph.

The apparatus used in making the recordings is an electrically operated machine which was economically assembled and handled during our field work by my son, Frank Staniford Speck, through funds supplied by the later grants of the Faculty Research Council of the University of Pennsylvania, acknowledged above.

I wish also to acknowledge my son's constant service in the field as assistant in noting and observing ceremonies, as well as his photographic work and sketches. Mr. Herbert Wheeler and Mrs. Louise B. Speck also kindly contributed some of the sketches.

I am indebted to Mr. Samuel W. Pennypacker II, Mr. Herman Walters, and Mr. Robert Riggs, of Philadelphia, for their interest in preserving specimens obtained for illustrating my study and for other incentives provided. A debt of gratitude is also due Mr. Merle H. Deardorff, of Warren, Pennsylvania, and Mr. Charles E. Congdon, of Salamanca, New York, through whose familiarity with Seneca ceremonies in New York State I obtained a fuller understanding of the breadth of Iroquois concepts.

For invaluable technical aid in the organization of topics and final revision of the manuscript I am deeply indebted to Miss Morelza Morrow.

The part played by Mr. William C. Morrow calls for more than passing mention. His long experience and intimacy of contact with native tribes of both Americas has taken tangible form in establishing the Morrow Research Fund which provided in large measure the means for publication of this book.

The specimens illustrated in plates and figures throughout the monograph are in the collections of the Cranbrook Institute of Science, Bloomfield Hills, Michigan; the Denver Art Museum, Denver, Colorado; the Peabody Museum, Salem, Massachusetts; the Museum of the American Indian, Heye Foundation, New York; the Public Museum and Art Gallery, Reading, Pennsylvania; and in the private collections of Mr. Robert Riggs and Mr. John J. Newton, of Spartanburg, South Carolina. They were obtained during the period of field investigation among the Cayuga as type objects for the purpose of illustrating the study.

The bibliography at the end of the text contains all the works here referred to. Whenever more than one work of an author is listed, reference in the text is made by the insertion, in parenthesis, of the date of the publication cited at that point.

Philadelphia, 1948   F. G. S.

PHONETIC NOTE

Since Cayuga has not been reduced to a standardized system of representing sounds by symbols, the method of recording terms in the study to follow has been to render pronunciations as given by Deskáheh. Many of the terms employed, however, have been checked by referring them to other informants.

Native forms are reproduced mainly in accordance with the suggestions for use of consonant and vowel characters in "Phonetic Transcription of Indian Languages" (*Report of the Committee of the American Anthropological Association*, Smithsonian Collections, 1909).[1] The use of symbols has also been adopted where feasible to accord with the system employed by Fenton for purposes of uniformity in recording Iroquois forms.[2] In particular the following should be noted in pronouncing Cayuga terms.

In Cayuga the labials (*p,b,m*) are absent, as is *l*. A weakly trilled *r* is present, occasionally following the stop *t* (or *d*) and sibilant *c* (English *sh*) producing *tr,cr* combined in one utterance. The consonants *k* and *g*, and *t* and *d*, though often difficult to distinguish, have been written separately as they were heard. There is a series of palatalized consonants, *ny-, dy-, ky-* (sometimes varying with *ni·y-, di·y-, ki·y-*). Parasitic, or whispered, consonants, and even syllables, occur at times and are written small and raised above the line, as ^hw,cra· *c* equals English *sh*. The glottal stop is shown by a raised comma'. Semi-vowels, *h,w,y* may combine, thus *hw-, hy-*.

Vowel signs to be noted are: *a,ā,α* (Greek alpha), *e, ε* (Greek epsilon), *ᵊ* (inverted *e*), *o, u, i,* which may be explained in the order given as equivalent to *a* as in English *father*, *ā* the same but pronounced lower and farther back in the mouth, *α* as *u* in English *but, e* as in French *été*, *ε* as *e* in English *met*, *ᵊ* as *e* in English *market*, *o* as in English *note*, *u* as *oo* in English *moon*, *i* as in French *fini*. Lengthening of vowels is shown by a raised period, · (*a·, i·*). Nasalized vowels are marked with a hook beneath them (*ǫ, ą,* etc.). A short release of

---

[1] See also Franz Boas, listed in the Bibliography of this book.
[2] Fenton, 1941, p. 80.

the breath after vowels (aspiration) is shown by a reversed raised comma ' ($a^‘$, $o^‘$, $u^‘$, etc.), and the same indicates an aspirated consonant ($t^‘$, $s^‘$, $k^‘$, etc.).

Primary syllable accent is marked over the vowel,′ secondary accent, often with a discernible lower pitch of voice, by`.

PART ONE

RELIGIOUS FRAMEWORK OF CAYUGA CULTURE

I

THE SOUR SPRINGS LONG HOUSE

HISTORY

THE fact that there are two Long Houses among the Cayuga of the Six Nations Reserve has been noted, and some remarks are called for to account for the existence of two ceremonial centers among them less than ten miles apart. Tradition places the responsibility upon a certain chief named *Di·yoʻhyǫ́go*, "Heron," for leading a group of Cayuga northward from the main division, who were living sometime after the treaty of Fort Stanwix (1784) at Cayuga Flats on lower Grand River. He established his band at Tutelo Heights near the village of Brantford, and built a Long House there. In the same locality the Tutelo tribe had its Long House. Later the Cayuga Long House was moved to a location within the bounds of the present reservation on MacKenzie Creek, in the proximity of some springs possessing a sulphurous taste. The Long House of this band thence acquired its name Sour Springs, *kanųhwatrũʼtonatedji·stayą* "medicine spring where fire is." The people of the Sour Springs division are called *kanų́ hwatruhóno*, "Medicine Springs people." This band has maintained its separateness as a ceremonial unit, and the present Long House (Pl. IA) has been standing, it is said, on the site it now occupies, since about 1855. It is located about three-quarters of a mile from the location of the original Long House. It is constructed of the old squared logs (seven horizontally from ground to eaves) removed from the site of the old building just mentioned. The name *Di·yoʻhyǫ́go* in its associations, beyond the fact that it was borne by the traditional founder of the division, as "Heron," is the name of the leading sib (clan) of the Wolf moiety, and therefore, since the Heron clan holds this position, the holder of the name *Di·yoʻhyǫ́go* is the firekeeper (keeper of the wampum string, the symbol of the "fire," or Long House), the "cornerstone," so to speak, of the group.[1]

For their part, the people of the Sour Springs band refer to the Lower Cayuga as *Kani·dagohòno*, "Down-hill people," and the

---

[1] The name-title is now held by Norman General.

Lower Cayuga Long House is called by them *Kaní·dago tonátedjï·stayǫ*, "Down-hill where fire is."

Both Long Houses, as representing the Cayuga tribe in Canada on the Six Nations Reserve, are covered by the eponym *Nawęndówa*, "Large pipe subject to."

It would also seem relevant to mention here the tradition among the people that the Cayuga represent themselves as a tribe by the symbol of a "mound," *kadáa'gwę`nǫt*, literally "earth (*kadáʰ*) made into a lump (*gwęnǫt*)*." This symbolic elevation of ground, representing a powerful people, attracted other tribes or nations (*wadonhwédja'atrǫ`*) who desired asylum with the Cayuga, and they came freely, "trampling the brush down (*hǫwátcǫdatǫdàʿni*) as they pressed onward to reach it."

Since the main Iroquois towns ("castles") were usually situated on natural hilltops offering excellent means of fortification and protection, serving also as observation points, the significance of this metaphor must be left to our imagination. Whether it referred to an artificial or natural elevation is not implied in the use of the term given.

The foregoing expression refers allegorically to the Cayuga Nation and is voiced in the condolence ceremony. So we turn to Cayuga history to note the adoption of foreign nations into the League by the Cayuga—the Nanticoke (1753), part of the Delaware-Munsee (1763), and the Tutelo (1753)—events too well known in Six Nations history to require further treatment here.[2] There are, however, adoptions of still less-known bands of wandering Indians whose admission and incorporation into the Cayuga fold are recorded only in native memory and whose identity is as yet an unsolved question. Among these there is mention of one band called *Ųráʿtǫgᵃ*, "Mossy-back (turtle)," or "Subjects of the Green Moss," adopted at one time. Their identity and linguistic affinities are now unknown beyond the fact that the name refers to the supposed "clan" connections of the band. Another is referred to by a Mohawk name *Dehonáʿkarǫ-*

---

[2] These dates are open to question within a range of a few years; some were taken from the Six Nations Council Records in 1924 (Nanticoke and Delaware). The Tutelo adoption date is from Brodhead, *New York Colonial Documents* (Onondaga Conference, 1753, pp. 811-14). This source credits the Oneida with the adoption of the Nanticoke, while the Cayuga chiefs now claim having adopted them, and also retain a tradition that they received the Tuscarora (1715-20), who were, according to the treaty referred to above, likewise accepted by the Oneida. The sources are, to say the least, confusing, as Hewitt has also declared them to be.

waks, "Rattling wood or bark." The name denotes that the people were so poor as to appear when first seen wearing bark coverings on their legs instead of skin leggings.[3] They are recalled to have a council house near Middleport, on the Grand River. Coming in abject poverty they asked if they could stay and were permitted to do so by an act of the Six Nations' Council, which is said to have been in session at the time. By some few informants the name was associated with a division of the Tuscarora, whose descendants still form a small national group among the Six Nations as distinct from the main group of Tuscarora in New York. Recent (1946) sources among the Cayuga disclosed in the meantime by Deskáheh assign this name as a synonym for the composite tribal group known as Nanticoke, which now seem to be conclusive as to its application.

SYMBOLISM

The upheaval in Iroquois social and religious history occasioned by the mission and teachings of the Seneca revealer Handsome Lake at the end of the eighteenth century will have to be considered in all studies of ceremonies and beliefs. As important as they may be, however, they call for reserved final judgment based upon specific investigations among adherents to the Handsome Lake religion in the different Long House groups of the Six Nations on reservations in Ontario and New York. A. C. Parker's intensive treatment (1913) covers the prophet's creed as it affects Seneca belief and ritual.[4]

Since 1799, the date of Handsome Lake's mission, Cayuga ceremonies have been authorized to be performed in the daytime. It is most important to note that prior to this period they were night performances, in conformity with the habits of other tribes of eastern North America. When the rites of these tribes are viewed comparatively in regard to the distinction between day and night performance, due weight should be given to the influence of Handsome Lake in effecting this change. As is usual in Handsome Lake's pronouncements concerning religious rulings, reasons are produced. They are as follows: He divided the day and night into four spiritual modes. From sunrise until high noon is consecrated to the living people; from noon till sunset, to ghosts or the dead; from sunset to

[3] A variant literal translation of the term was given by the Mohawk grammarian C. A. Cooke (Oka, Lake of Two Mountains Iroquois), namely, "they shake their horns." Mr. Cooke, however, knew nothing of the identity of the people referred to.

[4] See also Fenton, 1936 and 1941.

midnight, to good spirits; after midnight, to evil spirits. Handsome
Lake, however, added an apostrophe explaining his reason for transferring the Long House performances from nighttime to daytime as
arising from the menace of drunkenness. His wisdom on this point is
vindicated by the success of his followers in controlling the vice at
their Long House ceremonies.

It should be understood that all the ceremonies discussed in this
study are when occasion arises carried out in the Long House, which
to the Cayuga ceremonialist is virtually a temple. And this brings us
to a subject of some importance for consideration in the future study
of religious concepts of the Indians of the East and Southeast (Delaware, Yuchi, Creek). In the latter cultures we find that the ceremonial grounds, whether in the open or enclosed, represent a deeply
significant allegory, a phase of the sky-world on earth within which
human beings are carrying on actions in ceremonial form, the coun-
terpart of those of the spirits above, the latter being invisibly present
during the performances accompanying their living kinsfolk. This is
brought out in my treatment (1931) of the Big House annual ceremony of the Delawares. With this conception in mind, the question
was deliberately put before informants whether the Long House
stood forth as a symbol of the universe or sky, and whether its form
and its divisions and the rites within were symbol-reproductions on
the earth of the sky realm, mirrored annually in the life of man
below. The suggestion, however, failed to elicit a definite corrobora-
tive response. Nevertheless, the earth-sky analogy seems implied *in
obscuro* in a series of allusions, which one might refer to with tongue
in cheek for the present but which might be applicable here to tie
up the Iroquois with southern groups. Further discussion and a myth
bearing on the star and sky associations of the ceremonies are given
in another place (see pp. 30–31). Associations with the moon, the
Pleiades, the "seven dancers in the sky," the night performances
before the change of time wrought by Handsome Lake, the statement of one of the worshipers that some believed the spirits above
were dancing with them in the ceremonies—all indicate something
that will no doubt be better interpreted when further studied. And
with the two doors and fires of the Long House, east and west, linked
with the functions and the formal seating of the sex moiety groupings and its cardinal orientation, we can again sense the vision of a
cosmic symbolism which, if not expressed by the ritualists at the

present day, is apparent in the Long House interior—an implicit correspondence to a pattern of the celestial universe so clearly brought out in the sacred Big House of the Delawares.[5]

The Long House itself is called *kanúses*, "long house," but it is ceremonially referred to as a "fire." The type of reference in such a case is illustrated by the designation for the Sour Springs Long House, "Medicine Spring Where Fire Is" (see p. 15). Each Long House is, furthermore, represented in the scheme of the League and in the periodic meetings of the Handsome Lake religious sect by a strand of wampum. The wampum symbol for the Sour Springs Long House is a bunch of two or three white strings about two feet in length. The people of a particular Long House are referred to collectively as *honátedjiˑstayǫ`*, "People of the Fire-place, or Hearth."

[5] The attitude of the Cayuga toward the Long House can scarcely be called a sacred one in the sense that we discern it among the Delawares, whose comparison with the Cayuga is constantly being borne in mind. Nevertheless, the Long House precincts are held in a definitely respected esteem.

II

COMPLEMENTARY DUAL FUNCTIONING OF THE MOIETIES AND SEX DIVISIONS IN CAYUGA CEREMONIAL-SOCIAL ORGANIZATION

BEFORE turning attention to the analysis and discussion of Cayuga ceremonies, we should acquaint ourselves with the importance of the two moieties (dual subdivisions of the tribe also designated phratries) and their functions in the social life of the group. The term moiety, in this instance, is used to designate social and ceremonial grouping rather than grouping based upon consanguineous relationship or exogamic ruling.

Among the Cayuga, both at the Sour Springs and the Lower Cayuga Long Houses, we find the moiety divisions bearing the names of "Wolf" and "Turtle."[1] The Wolf moiety is comprised of four sibs, Heron, Wolf, Plover, and Snipe; the Turtle moiety of six sibs, Big Bear, Ball,[2] Younger Bear, Suckling Bear, Deer, and Snapping Turtle. The sib, or clan, is called *gacyáde*, "people standing in single file." The names are given in their formal order, which is that followed in ceremonial recitations when the sibs are enumerated. The sib sequence just given has descending value, but it cannot be

[1] The Wolf and the Turtle as nomenclative designations of the dual divisions are such outstanding features of the Cayuga civil and ceremonial contour that I am at a loss to understand what Dr. Goldenweiser (1913) could have had in mind in making the observation given below. Relevant to the lack of animal phratry names among the Iroquois of the Six Nations, where he put to work his unquestioned talents in social research, he wrote:

"*The Phratry:*—Each of the five tribes of the confederacy is divided into clans which are grouped into two 'phratries.' *These dual divisions do not, among the Iroquois, have any names, nor is there any evidence of a former existence of such names.*" (Italics mine.)

Had the Cayuga been excluded from the above generalized statement it could be accepted, since the Seneca and Onondaga in Canada designate the moieties by group, not animal, names. How can we harmonize these conflictions of data? As the content of this study shows, there can be no doubt as to the existence of animal eponyms for the Cayuga moieties, or phratries. Fenton's statement concerning Seneca moieties coincides with Goldenweiser's summarization for the rest of the Iroquois moiety names. "Moieties function as ceremonial units in Seneca society. They dominate their component clans in the ceremonies. They are nameless; the name for the socially prominent clan is not employed for the moiety as it is among the Cayuga." (Fenton, 1936, 19.)

[2] Information holds that the "Ball clan" was identified in some way with a bird, possibly one related to the martins, but no further details are given.

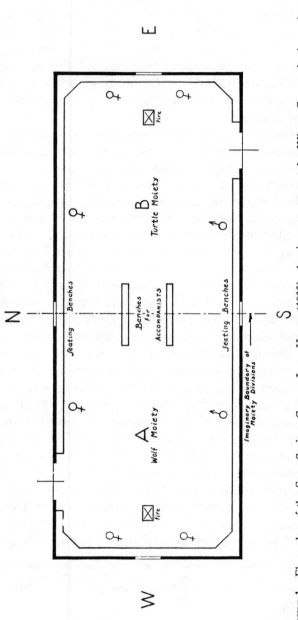

FIGURE 1.—Floor plan of the Sour Springs Cayuga Long House (1933), showing arrangement for Winter Ceremonies in seating of moieties and sexes.

A Wolf Moiety Side

Sibs { Heron / Wolf / Plover / Snipe

B Turtle Moiety Side

Sibs { Big Bear / Ball / Younger Bear / Suckling Bear / Deer / Snapping Turtle

NOTE: In the Summer Ceremonies and during certain days of the Winter Ceremonies the women (♀) of B moiety take places on the S side of A section, the men (♂) of A moiety change to N side of B section.

said in just what way those sibs mentioned first have prestige over the last mentioned. The English equivalent of the Cayuga vernacular expression for moiety is "division of the house," which refers to the seating of the participants in Long House activities (see Fig. 1).[3] In Cayuga the word is *t'odiˑnąswakwáˑtǫ*, literally, "dividing the house (Long House)," or *dé yąk'niˑdjèhǫt*, "sitting each side of the fire." Persons of the same sib are, however, "inside the house," which signifies close social relationship.[4]

Endeavors to obtain from the informants and councilors the reasons for the formation of the dual grouping proved futile, except to bring forth the tradition that the Cayuga had possessed the Wolf and Turtle moiety classification from the earliest times, even before the foundation of the League as an intersettlement principle, and that the idea had been carried over into the structure of the League as a social pattern adopted by all the tribal constituents. Rationalization is characteristic of Cayuga sages, wherefore emerges a *raison d'être* for the dual division in the assertion that two opposed yet related bodies are required by traditional ordinance for carrying out ceremonies; whence moieties equal necessities, and Cayuga creative genius scores another victory as the incubus of a great social vision! It was stated by Deskáheh as understood through tradition that in early times both the moieties and sibs were exogamous. The moieties are not so now, nor have they been in recent generations. At the present time the members of the sibs in Moiety *A* (Wolf) regard one another as "brothers and sisters" and call the people in Moiety *B* (Turtle) "cousins." Likewise, the Moiety *B* people are "brothers and sisters" to each other and call the members of the Wolf moiety "cousins." These terms are applied only ceremonially. In social address, on the other hand, the opposite moieties designate each other as "brothers," as Deskáheh explained.[5] When the Cayuga are assembled in *civil* council, the formal terms of address differ from those used on *ceremonial* occasions. The Mohawk, Onondaga, and Seneca are "brothers" to each other and "fathers" to the younger

[3] That the dual division also prevails in the council grouping of nations forming the League (Mohawk, Onondaga, Seneca, versus Cayuga, Oneida, Tuscarora) is too well known to require more than mention here. (See the cited works of Morgan, Hewitt, Parker, and Goldenweiser.)

[4] According to Deskáheh.

[5] Incidentally, it was Deskáheh's asserted opinion that the Onondaga and Seneca in Canada differ from the Cayuga in saying "cousin" when addressing a person of the "other side."

tribes, Oneida, Cayuga, and Tuscarora (See also Goldenweiser, *op. cit.*, 466). The Cayuga call the Oneida "elder brothers" and the Tuscarora "younger brothers." The Tutelo and Nanticoke are also called "younger brothers" by the Cayuga. And the Delaware are called "nephews," a junior relationship to which those adopted by the Six Nations now submit, as quite contrary to the tradition of the Delawares in Oklahoma, who insist on the prerogative of claiming to be "uncles" and "grandfathers" to all the eastern tribes, a distinction traceable to early documents mentioning the acknowledged seniority of the Delaware Nation.

When entering the Long House at Sour Springs, the members of the Wolf moiety go in by the west, or Wolf, door, and the members of the Turtle moiety enter by the east, or Turtle, door.[6] The males sit on the east side of the house and the females on the west side, following the formal seating arrangement in most Long House activities. The women of the Wolf moiety take their places opposite the Wolf men and the Turtle women opposite the Turtle men. On the morning of the fourth day of the Midwinter Festival the Turtle women sit on the west or Wolf "side." On the last day they return to their places opposite the men on the Turtle "side," as is required in the concluding rite of the Bowl Game (p. 141). There are two fires (stoves) in the Long House, one for each moiety, or "side." Throughout the ensuing chapters it will be noted that the performances of the two groups are reciprocal in most of the rites and in the ceremonial games. For example, if the Wolf side opens the Stirring Ashes Rite (p. 53) they stir the ashes of the fire on the Turtle side, and vice versa. Also, if a Turtle member requests for himself or his clientele the performance of the rites of a certain medicine society for the purpose of curing, it is referred to the members of that particular society in the Wolf moiety. It is they who perform for the benefit of their ceremonial "cousin," and vice versa (as for instance in False Face Society rites, p. 85). There is also rotation between the moieties in singing in the different rites.[7] The same rule holds in the recitation of prayers and in making addresses. Speakers in the Long House face the section occupied by the other moiety and direct their

---

[6] The orientation of the moieties at the Lower Cayuga Long House is, however, the reverse of the Sour Springs order; the Wolf side being on the east, the Turtle on the west. No explanation for the difference is as yet forthcoming from questioning among informants.

[7] As for instance in the Striking Stick Dance (p. 119) and the Skin Dance (p. 137).

remarks to it instead of to other members of their own side. One moiety furnishes a speaker to make the opening address of a day of ceremony and refers to him the duties of keeping the peoples' minds in attention; the other moiety speaker "closes up" the ceremony, alternating duties of sponsorship. In case of mourning we find the members of the opposite moiety taking charge of the funeral rites and condoling the members of the moiety to which the deceased belonged (see pp. 159–63).

It may be noted that the general rule of opposed seating of the moieties—the Wolf on the west and the Turtle on the east—is observed in gatherings for various purposes in the home as well as the Long House when assembly is for social or ritual performances. This dual arrangement is specifically stated, for instance, in the remarks upon the meetings of the Medicine Men's Society when convened in private homes for the purpose of curing with the doctor's masks.

The moieties function in the preparation of ceremonial foods and properties. They also contest in friendly antagonism as opposed groups or sides in such games-rites as Lacrosse (p. 117), the Pulling Rite ("Tug-of-war") (p. 124), Snow-Snake (p. 115), Bowl Game (p. 141), Football (p. 125), and the Moccasin Game (played only at a funeral "wake").

There is also a tendency for the ownership or custody of ceremonial property, such as paddles used in the Stirring Ashes Rite, instruments for accompaniment of singing and dancing, and the cook houses near the Wolf and Turtle moiety doors of the Long House, to reside in the moiety. In the case of the Stirring Ashes paddles, the animal emblems burned or drawn upon them represent the animals for which the moieties as well as the sibs are named. Sib and moiety representations undoubtedly appear in forms of art and personal decoration of which we shall know but little until the point has been definitely investigated. An example of no small significance is, however, found in a man's feather headdress of the "roach" or crest type obtained from Deskáheh in 1934. Upon a curved strip of wood as a base, a single erect eagle feather set upon a revolving swivel is flanked on each side by a row of five osprey feathers. Symbolism of the "clan" and moiety is intended; the erect eagle feather represents a chief (to wit, the wearer himself), the five osprey feathers at the sides are the five sibs "in a line" standing opposite each other grouped as moieties (see Fig. 2).

FIGURE 2.—Cayuga chief's headdress representing the chief by center plume and the chiefs of the moiety groupings by upright feathers on each side of the center plume.

Duality again presents itself in the sexual partition of ceremonial sponsorship. The winter ceremonies are sponsored by the men, especially the chiefs, while the women perform as sponsors during the summer ceremonies. At the conclusion of the Bowl Game on the last day of the Midwinter Festival, the chiefs formally transfer the duties of the presiding officers to the women, who take full charge of subsequent rites in the Long House until the conclusion of the ceremony in August at the maturity of corn, when they formally turn the official duties back to the chiefs. The ceremonial year is thus divided into periods of male and female control (see p. 34).

Without presenting an argument in detail, it would seem to be rational from our understanding of the moiety divisions here to propose that the Cayuga moiety organization may be defined in terms of religious rather than social (marriage, inheritance, or descent) function. We have it explained in convincing form that spiritual services between human beings themselves and between human beings and spirit-forces should be requested and performed reciprocally between the two "sides" or moieties. This expresses in general terms a tenet of the religious credo of the Cayuga in worship and in curing. And looking further, it appears prominently in Delaware teaching; evidently a functional element of general distribution in sections of eastern culture both Iroquoian and Algonkian. A word more: The principle of reciprocal or complementary service between inviduals and between moieties in religious intercession is based upon a native conviction that spiritual beings respond to supplication made by one in behalf of another, not heeding an individual's direct appeal for himself. Herein lies a distinct concept of the orthodox approach to spirits. The teaching is a literal altruism. Reciprocal or complementary performance, while it operates between individuals, finds in Cayuga its fullest development in complementary service between the moieties. Its varied phases are shown in rites to relieve illness, in condolence for the bereaved, in ceremonial games and pastimes. As a manifold cultural principle it is something to be stressed in social interpretations of the eastern Indian. Ethnologists so far have not been sufficiently aware of its existence.

Hewitt (1918) discusses the dualism running through all public assemblies of the Iroquois in the following manner. He does not trace it to factors arising from genic affinities or from common religious rites but to the dominant principles pervading life-conservation of life upon earth through the complementary functions of sex, the male and female principles, and performance of duties arising from the status of each sex as defined in Iroquois thinking. He also adds that among the people at present the reason for the persistent dual organization has been completely lost.

In another paper (1916) Hewitt cites his material as offering a suggestion for the explanation of dualism appearing as the basis of all public institutions of the Iroquois peoples. According to the text, "dualism arose merely from an alleged agreement between two Cayuga persons related to each other as Father and Son, or Mother and Daughter, to transact public affairs jointly from opposite sides of the Council Fire." Hewitt observes, however, that this account does not satisfactorily dispose of the reason for dualism among the peoples. He comments upon the explanation proposed previously by Miss Fletcher and himself, working independently some years ago, that the dualism is in brief a dramatization of the relation of male and female principles of nature in forms of governmental organization. The intent of those remarks is obvious to the ethnologist, and they are brought together here to show reason for regarding sex-functioning and group-complementation in social and ceremonial action as factors in Cayuga history.

Attributes of the moiety complex in Cayuga do not include increase rites, dietary restriction, killing taboos, color association, associations with the "above" or "below" concept, religious obligations, exogamy, kinship sentiments toward the eponymous Wolf or Turtle, descent theory, or group prestige.

Joking characteristics, however, exist within the moiety bonds, as several illustrations cited by Deskáheh indicate. The Wolf moiety people are "accused of being greasy and tricky"; the Turtle people as being "slow, homely, humpbacked, of sitting in the sun and liking it." "It is because he is a Turtle that he is that way" is a saying which explains the joking attitude of a Wolf member.

The moiety classification, moreover, as sustained in Cayuga social structure, is undoubtedly more fraught with historical values than R. L. Olson ascribes to it, and does not conform to the explanatory theory which he proposes for the Iroquoian peoples.

Iroquois data on moiety beliefs and performances, certainly those relating specifically to the Cayuga, will not pose as proving ground for any generalized "totemistic" theory. The practice may, on the other hand, prove to be a form of specialized development—an operating social device for the maintainance of coöperative relationship between man and the spirit forces, according to a pattern of "ceremonially courteous" dealing believed to have been imposed upon human beings by spiritual forces in the past. The next step is the superimposition of this method of coöperation upon the dealings of human groups among themselves. A question arises over the point of priority. Is the reciprocal practice one originating in man's social history, subsequently attributed by extension to the social sphere of spirit-forces? Or is it a "revealed" teaching, introduced in human relations through the influence of Dekanawidah's conception of reciprocal interplay in the spirit realm?

Pending final conclusions, until present investigations have yielded further results, it seems that elementary functions of the Cayuga moiety divisions, aside from what accretions may have gathered about them later, *have been to equilibrate society in social and ceremonial performances* and in interpersonal religious relationships. As phrased by Deskáheh, the principle of the moiety division is considered "more like a rule to go by."[8]

[8] See Chapter XIII, pages 138-40, 159, for mention of other duties of the moieties in each other's behalf.

III

CONTROLLING SPIRIT FORCES

SUCCESSION

THE Cayuga conception of the graded spirit forces that control the universe and their order of ascent from the youngest, or lowest, to the oldest, or highest, are given in Table I. I would not indulge in discussion of the history of change in Cayuga belief, except to point out that with the subtraction of Handsome Lake's teachings from the hierarchy we should have an ancient Iroquois system as the Cayuga preserved it. The succession given here is that followed in the prayer of invocation to the Great Spirit, which begins with mention of the youngest spirit, that is, the last in the order of creation, and advances to the oldest forces on earth; then comes to the "Controllers," the forces usually conceived as the "Four Winds," now identified with the "Four Angels"; and finally reaches mention of the "Creator."

The list is placed here to be referred to in the discussion of the ceremonies. It shows the spiritual forces in their order as they are invoked in the rites of the annual religious cycle.

The Upper Pantheon

The Upper Pantheon, including the Creator and the Four Angels, has undergone modification from the original because of the teachings of the revealer, Handsome Lake, at the close of the eighteenth century. The original Cayuga designation for the Supreme Being was *Hawéni·yu,* "Controller," but Handsome Lake was told by the angels to instruct the people to substitute the title *Sǫ́gweadi·sǫ,* "Creator of all," when calling upon the Deity in prayer or in thanksgiving. The reason was given, as a myth relates, that the Evil Spirit laid claim to being the "Controller" of the earth and its people and accordingly responded when the original term was used. The Creator (Great Spirit), through Handsome Lake, then condemned the original term and substituted the one which applies to Him alone.

Handsome Lake furthermore taught that after his death he would abide next to the Creator, and this accounts for his name being listed in this position in the tabulation.

TABLE 1

SUCCESSION OF SPIRIT FORCES

(Arranged in ascending order)

A
Upper Pantheon

Creator	Supreme Being	sǫgweadi·'so	"Our Maker," "Creator"
(Prophet Revealer)	(Handsome Lake)	skani·adaiу́u	"Handsome Lake"
Forces Controlling the Universe	"Four Angels," or Winds of the Four Quarters	géhnyǫgwédage dí·yǫkinyéniadǫ hadi·whi·ya kyǫ́nǫ	"Our Four Guardians Residing in Heaven"

B
Lower Pantheon

Spirit Forces Above the Earth	Sun	ędé'ka gá'kwa	"Day Sun"
	Moon	ǫkí·sot sǫhé'ka	"Grandparent Moon"
	Thunders	ǫkí·sot hegá'kwęs t'ɛné't'kwa hadi·wenótadyðs	"Grandparents from Sunset Coming, Sounding Their Voices"
	Stars	odjí·sǫdáwðnyų	"Stars"

C

Spirit Forces on Earth	Fire	odjí·sta	
	Water	nękano's	
	Food	dyąhé'kwe	"What we live on"
	Fruits	ohiacǫ́	All fruits (chiefly strawberries)
	Animals	katí·ni·yu	"Wild Creatures" (animals and fowl)
	Forest	otehadǫ́ni o'hundą́do	"Forest" "Brush"
	Fish	nený́wagu diyunadáwɛni a	"Under Stream Traveling Beneath"
	Medicine Plants	onó'kwatrà	"Medicine"
	Grass (includes ground-berries)*	awę̆''gra	"Grass"
	Earth	o'hwę́djage (or o'hwę́djate)	"On Earth"
Mankind	People	ǫ́gwe	"Humans"

* Includes also Tobacco, wiyą́'gwa', which is regarded as a "helper" but is not mentioned in the formal prayer on which this arrangement is based.

The concept of the Four Angels also needs some explanation, having been modified from the earlier belief of the Cayuga. The teaching brings out the understanding that the Four Angels are connected with the old concept of the Four Winds, the North, East, South, and West, controlling the universe. Handsome Lake was spiritually led and instructed by the angels and taught that the identity of the Fourth Angel was that of Christ. In the narration "The Fatherless Boy" (pp. 127–29), the identity of Christ is accounted for. Christ is accordingly called *Géhadòt'ha*, "The Fourth One," the other three being referred to collectively as given above.

Lower Pantheon

The Spirit Forces Above the Earth include the Sun, the Moon, the Stars, and the Thunders. The Thunders are conceived as the source responsible for changing the weather, bringing rain, snow, storms, clear days, and the like, which are in themselves not addressed directly, but only acknowledged and given thanks through the Thunders, who cause them. According to Cayuga belief, the Thunders are seven brothers, whom they call "Grandfathers." (For origin, see the Thunder Rite, p. 117.)

Spirit Forces on Earth

In prayer and in thanksgiving the Spirit Forces on Earth are addressed as they are listed, the arrangement being in the order of their so-called age and closeness to Earth. Thus we see that Fire and Water are the oldest spirit forces and were created before Food, Animals, Medicine, Forest, Fruits, and Grass. They all rest upon Mother Earth. The youngest creation is Grass, "so close to the ground where we start from," then Fruits such as berries which grow just above the Grass. Strawberries typify this group of growing things. The juice of the stawberry is a sacrament used in ceremonies; wherefore this plant does not belong exclusively to the level of the series of ground plants. Then comes the Brush, which is next in height above ground, and next the Forest, which overtops all. The Red Willow is the oldest of the Forest group, and the Maple assumes a venerable position amid the variety of trees, while the White Pine and Elm are outstanding as emblems of stability and are chosen to symbolize the League of the Iroquois.[1] Next in priority in the grouping of the spirits come Medicine Plants, in whose service we not only find vocal reference in address and thanksgiving, but societies of practitioners organized among those who have been blessed with cures by Medicinal Agencies. In the ceremonial program of the Cayuga, the Medicine Societies play a most significant role, as will be shown later.

Animal spirits follow in the order of mention in the prayer invocations and, like Medicines, are served by doctoring-societies who effect cures through their influence. The Cayuga observe a distinction between "wild animals" and domestic animals. The wild animals of the herbivorous group are those referred to in thanksgiving for their service in furnishing man with his nourishment. The Cayuga entertain a belief, common throughout northeastern North America, that the flesh of herbivorous animals only is fit for man to eat, because these eat plants having medicinal values and so provide food and medicine to human consumers at the same time. The flesh of carnivorous animals is apt to act as poison if eaten.

In the mention of Food, or "what we live on," which comes next in order, are included Corn, Beans, Squash, Wild Fruit from trees, and Nuts. This group rates high in the attitude of reverence and is treated to worship in some of the most important rites.

The oldest of the spirit forces on earth as viewed by the Cayuga are the elemental forces, Water and Fire.

Mankind

In a special category stands man, whose position in the universe is unique. The prayer of invocation includes thanks to the people by the people. This is explained as having the broad sense of gratitude for coöperation.

There are other spirit forces recognized as agencies for good, "helping the people," and evil on earth, such as Dwarfs and the False Faces. These forces are invoked by Medicine Societies of restricted membership and form an important factor in worship. They are not, however, mentioned in the formal invocation and are not given a definite place in the order of succession of the spirits.

---

[1] According to Deskáheh, some refer to the White Pine and others to the Elm as being the symbol of the League, with four white roots representing Peace, one reaching to the North, one to the East, another to the West, and another to the South. See Parker (1912), and especially Wallace (1946).

RELATIONSHIP TO PEOPLE ON EARTH

The spiritual relationship believed to exist between human beings and the forces of the Universe as just discussed, is outlined in the following list:

Corn ⎫	
Beans ⎬	Mother
Squash ⎭	
Earth	Mother
Sun	Elder Brother
Moon	Grandmother
Thunders ⎫	Grandfathers
Lightning ⎭	
False Faces	Grandfathers

Inquiry failed to disclose belief in other relationships with spiritual forces, although it was assumed that such might exist in reference to fire, water, tobacco, trees, winds, the tortoise, and stars.

IV

THE ANNUAL CEREMONIAL CYCLE

DUALISM as regards moieties has been thoroughly discussed in Chapter VI, and the division of the year into periods of control by each sex has been mentioned. It is to be pointed out further here that a functional dichotomy is linked with the division of control of the ceremonies between the two sexes as well as with the division between the two moieties. The winter series of rites, from November through February, which is sponsored by the chiefs representing the ceremonial officiation of males, functions as *thanksgiving* worship directed towards all spiritual entities. The other half of the ceremonial calendar, from March through August, is sponsored by the females, and the rites function principally as *supplicatory* and are addressed to the benevolent spiritual agencies for the maintenance of life and health and the food supply.

There is much to interpret here in the ceremonial dualism of the economic function of sex, of the seasonal periods, and of the psychological attitudes determined by these periods.

The following table constitutes a calendar of the ceremonial year and indicates the purpose for which each rite is performed:

TABLE 2

CALENDAR OF ANNUAL CEREMONIAL CYCLE OF THE CAYUGA

I. Midwinter Ceremony, or New Year's Festival, *cadɛkʷcra'hɛ kaihweyo'ni·*, "midyear ceremonial mark."
    Time: Five days after the January new moon (see page 49), during the period including the last week of January and the first two weeks of February.
    Duration: Eight days.
    Purpose: Thanksgiving addressed to all spiritual forces, especially to the Great Spirit, for the blessings of life, health, and sustenance and the privileges of social life. Curative performances are carried out by the medicine societies. This is the major recurrent ceremony, a synthesis, capitulating all the ritual units of the ceremonial system and marking the end of the ceremonial year past and the beginning of the new.

    Composition:

    Preliminary Day: Confession Rite (Confession of sins over wampum strings); Feather Dance

    1st day } Stirring Ashes Rites
    2nd day }

34

TABLE 2—*(Continued)*

3rd day ⎱ Medicine Societies' Dances (restricted and unrestricted), as re-
⎰ quested in behalf of persons who are ill, or those who have derived
⎱ benefit from rites of the respective societies and who desire them
4th day ⎰ again

5th day   Recess. (In the present Sour Springs program, the White Dog
Sacrifice is performed at this time in the regular order of rites
when the occasion arises; see note, p. 143.

6th day   Feather Dance

7th day   Burning Tobacco Rite
Skin Dance
Adǫ́wa (Individual Thanksgiving)
Naming Ceremony

8th day   Bowl Game* (Followed by the Forest Dance if the game is finished
on the morning of the eighth day.)
Forest Dance:
Feather Dance
Stirring Ashes Song
Informal False Face Dance
Skä'nye (Woman's Dance)

II.   Maple Sap Ceremony, *hanadréna wę́'daú'hɛs,* "gathering maple sap."
Time: When maple sap runs, at the end of March or early April (about Easter
time). The rites were performed formerly in the maple groves; now they
have been transferred to the Long House at the time the sap stops running;
about the second week in April
Duration: One day
Purpose: Thanksgiving for maple sap and syrup
Composition:
Feather Dance
False Face Society Dance. No curing is performed. False Face Societies
dance without wearing masks, and sing *djǫsi'tedí·has* song series
Bowl Game

III. Corn Planting Ceremony, *ɛgaųtǫ́wi·s ɛyit'i·ni·k'ówi djɑhé'kwa,* "to entertain
what we live on (grains and fruits)"
Time: Just before planting time, May 10 to 15
Duration: One day
Purpose: Appeal to Food Spirits (grains and fruits) in general (Table 1,
Group C)
Composition:
Feather Dance
Bowl Game
Woman's Song
Skänye (old type)
Corn Dance
Kadátrot (Round Dance)
Squash Dance

IV.   Corn Sprouting Rites (same Cayuga name as for III)
Time: When the corn plant shows above the ground, a week late in May
Duration: One day
Purpose: "To entertain our food-plants"

* The Bowl Game may be continued until the ninth day to finish securing a score
if necessary, excluding the Forest Ceremony.

TABLE 2—*(Continued)*

Composition:
>The last five rites of the Corn Planting Ceremony are repeated

V. Strawberry Ceremony, *ędwat'hi·yaúhek,* "gathering berries"
>Time: When strawberries ripen, in May
>Duration: One day
>Purpose: Thanksgiving for life and the privilege of reunion for ceremony
>Composition:
>>Feather Dance (Part I)
>>Intermission—During this period the leader speaks on the subject of Handsome Lake's Conversion, and strawberry juice is served to the participants
>>Feather Dance (Part II) concludes the program

VI. Sun Ceremony, *ędé'kwa gá'kwa,* "day sun"
>Time: When the sun begins to feel hot in the spring, late in May
>Duration: One day
>Purpose: Appeal to the sun for continuation of the blessing of heat
>Composition:
>>The *Adǫwa,* with the passing of the sun disk symbol (Pl X E, XII B) as each performer sings and prays

VII. Corn Ripening Ceremony (same Cayuga name as for III and IV)
>Time: When the corn is mature, in August
>Duration: One day
>Purpose: Same as IV, and thanksgiving for the crop
>Composition:
>>The same rites as the Corn Planting Ceremony

VIII. Raspberry Ceremony, same name as V.
>Time: When raspberries ripen, in August
>Duration: One day
>Purpose: Same as V
>Composition:
>>The same rites as the Strawberry Ceremony

IX. Thunder Ceremony, *ǫkí·sot hadi·wɛnótadyɛs ti·wɛnų'k'ta,* "grandfather-continues-sounding performing rite"
>Time: The dry season of midsummer, in August
>Duration: One day
>Purpose: Appeal to the Thunders to continue their warfare on the evil spirits of the underworld and to bring rain
>Composition:
>>Lacrosse (old type of game)
>>*Wasáse* Dance (war rite)

X. Harvest Ceremony, *gonát'ędi·'sat'o ɛgaųtǫwi·s,* "all being harvested will now sing"
>Time: The second Sunday in November
>Duration: One day
>Purpose: Thanksgiving for the crops
>Composition:
>>Feather Dance
>>*Skä'nye*
>>*Kadâtrot*
>>Corn or Bean Dance
>>Squash Dance
>>The dances are all sacred; no social dances are performed

The ceremonies do not always follow each other in the order shown in the foregoing tabulation; some of the rites may be omitted and other rites inserted in the program. In Appendix I will be found a listing of the Long House ceremonies performed by the Sour Springs Cayuga in 1933.

FUNCTIONAL GROUPING OF RITES AND DANCES

In addition to the calendrical organization of the rites and dances of the Cayuga, a grouping on the basis of function can also be outlined. The three principal groups include, respectively: rites addressed to the Creator, or Great Spirit, and to the Food Spirits; curative rites and dances of the Medicine Societies; and social dances having no medicinal function. These groupings are detailed in the accompanying table.

TABLE 3

FUNCTIONAL GROUPING OF RITES AND DANCES

Group I. Rites Addressed to the Dominant Spirit Forces

    A. Rites Addressed to the Creator, or Great Spirit

        Feather Dance ⎫
          Burning Tobacco Rite ⎪
        Adǫwa (Individual Thanksgiving) ⎬ The Four Sacred Rites
        Skin Dance ⎪
        Bowl Game ⎭
        Confession Rite
        Stirring Ashes Rite
        White Dog Sacrifice

    B. Rites Addressed to Food Spirits in the Spring

        Woman's Song
        Corn Dance
        Bean Dance
        Squash Dance

Group II. Rites Addressed to Spirit Forces on Earth—Curative Rites of the Medicine Societies

    A. Rites Restricted to Members of the Societies

        Bear Society Rite
        Otter Society Rite
        White Buffalo Society Dance
        Wooden False Face Society Rites
        Corn-Husk Mask Society Rite
          False Face Traveling Rite
        Medicine Men's Society and the Pig Mask Rite
        Dark Dance Society Rite
        Eagle Society Rite

    B. Rites Not Restricted to Members of Societies

        Snow-Snake Rite
        Chipmunk Rite

TABLE 3—*(Continued)*

Thunder Rite and Ball Game
War Dance, or *Wasáse*
Chicken Dance
Striking Stick Dance
Ghost Dance Rite
Dream Guessing Rite
Dreamer, or Fortune Teller, Rite
"Tug-of-War" Rite
Football Rite

Group III. Social Dances without Specific Medicinal Function

Fish Dance
Raccoon Dance
Skä'nye, or Woman's Dance
Duck Dance
Pigeon Dance
Naked Dance
Kadä'trot, or Round Dance
Clasping Hands Dance
Crocodile Dance
Delaware, or Skin-Beating, Dance
Chicken, or One Side Male, Dance
Drunken Dance (Seneca origin)
Garters Dance (Introduced 1931)
Sharpened Stake Dance*
Reversing Dance
Robin Dance
Shawnee Dance
Shivering Word Dance
Mouth-on Dance
Fishing Dance
Tormentor's Dance
Cherokee Dance (Introduced in 1938 from Oklahoma)

* Information on this social dance is incomplete, but it seems to be separate from the Striking Stick Dance (Group II, B).

V

CEREMONIAL OFFICIARIES, FOODS, INSTRUMENTS, AND COSTUMES

CEREMONIAL OFFICIARIES

ON EACH "side," or moiety, there are two groups, one composed of males, the other of females, the members of which perform in the capacity of ceremonial leaders and assistants. Each group has a leader, who is referred to as *honétcron*, "head" or "leading officer."[1] This office is permanent, and the men and women who have been accorded the honor of election are regarded as being possessed of the best characters; as one informant phrased it, "They are the purest people in the Long House." He also added that they are supposed to be strict adherents of the teachings of Handsome Lake, but pointed out the difficulties encountered daily by the head officers, as well as other participants in the Long House, in trying to live up to the high standards set for them in the "code" of Handsome Lake.[2] The number of assistants in the groups varies, and it was noted by the writer that there are more males than females. It is the duty of the head officers to appoint the speakers and to delegate authority to the other members of their respective groups who perform in certain ceremonial rôles. The officers and assistants have charge of the ceremonial equipment and attend to the preparation and the serving of food at Long House feasts. In the Midwinter rites observed in the Sour Springs Long House in 1933, it was noted that the chiefs who sponsored the ceremony conducted the programs through the head officers, who in turn instructed the assistants. In the case of a chief's performing in any rôle, he was not appointed directly by another chief but was informed by an officer or an assistant that his group desired him to address the people, to pray, or to lead in a certain rite. The formality of the procedure in Long House observance is most striking. The same formal attitude exists among the female officers and assistants. If a women or girl wishes to be treated by one of the Medicine Societies, she tells the head officer of the female

[1] The English-speaking Cayuga translate this term as equivalent to "deacon" and refer to the officers as such.
[2] Parker, A. C. (1913).

group of her moiety, who in turn tells the female leader on the opposite side, and she tells the male officer, who in turn notifies the master of ceremonies. If a child, male or female, is to be given a name in the ceremony, the leading female officer presents the child in the same way to the officers of the opposite moiety.[3]

In the formal seating in the Long House, the officers and assistants occupy the front benches, the men sitting with the chiefs. In the dances they have first place in the line. It was also observed that on the last day when the Great Bowl Game is played they are appointed among the first players.[4]

CEREMONIAL FOODS

Corn soup, corn and wheat breads, beef, and berry juice are the foods prescribed for consumption at Long House feasts. The informant referred to them as "foods that sustain us," also "the foods that we entertain," the latter having reference to the fact that certain ceremonies are performed in honor of food genii, especially of corn, to induce them to stay with the people (see Table 2, No. III). In ancient times venison was served at such feasts, but now since deer are not plentiful, beef is used as a substitute. The substitution of different foods for ceremonial feasts, with special reference to meat, is mentioned in the teachings of Handsome Lake, who is quoted as having said, "In time your ancient meat (deer) will become extinct and you will have to substitute some domesticated animal for your ceremonial food."[5]

In the Midwinter Festival, food is not distributed until the third day at the conclusion of the rites, when corn soup and bread are

[3] See Naming Ceremony in the *Adǫwa* (p. 135).

[4] See Bowl Game (p. 141).

[5] Substitution of properties as economic conditions have changed the surroundings of the people since the coming of Europeans has insured the continuance of Cayuga ritual. Conservative sentiment has not prevented the substitution of commercial goods for those given the people by the Creator, to wit, dry goods for leather, beef and hog meat for venison and bear meat, pig's head for bear's head in Medicine Society rites, peanuts for wild nuts, canned berry juice for wild berry juice at times in the Bear Society Rite, wheat bread for corn bread, pig hoofs for deer hoofs in making the ceremonial garter rattles, turkey feathers for eagle feathers, glass beads for wampum, china and tinware for pottery, to be mentioned in passing. The Long House has also become modernized, its iron stoves and stove pipes, lumber sides, floors, roof, and benches, doors and glass windows replacing the features of the old order. Externals do not count for so much where the old inner spirit rules! Indian tobacco is, however, punctiliously grown for ceremonial purposes and is used exclusively. An acculturation study is much needed here.

served to the members present. Berry juice is provided for those who are thirsty. It also represents a "sacramental" drink during the Skin Dance. On the fourth day, beef is added to the feast and is a part of the program every day thereafter until the festival is brought to a close. Sacred foods are prepared without salt. Certain male and female officers are appointed to take charge of the securing and preparation of the ceremonial foods. The men (called "arbiters" by the English-speaking Long House people) are supposed to go out and "hunt" for the meat. The informant explained this statement as follows: "In ancient times the men would go out and hunt deer to provide meat for the ceremony. Now there aren't any deer, so the men have to go out and 'hunt work' in order to secure funds with which to purchase the 350 pounds of beef required to feed the people during the ceremony." The men do odd jobs, and when they receive their pay they turn it over to the head assistant. The women prepare the various kinds of corn and wheat bread. There are biscuits of varying shapes and sizes, also bread in loaf form. The corn is cooked in twenty-gallon caldrons in the cookhouse, which is located just outside the door of the Long House, by the men of the Turtle and Wolf moieties, who also take charge of cooking the beef. After the beef is cooked it is shredded, pressed, and strained, so that all of the liquid is extracted. This work is done at night. In the morning certain women of the two divisions assist with the cooking and placing of meat and bread in baskets, preparatory to serving. When the caldrons of cooked corn are brought into the Long House, red beans are added from the containers brought in by the women of the Turtle and Wolf divisions who have cooked them at home. The corn and beans are mixed together and allowed to stand for an hour or two, or until the conclusion of the ceremony for that day. Those desiring corn soups[6] come prepared with a receptacle of some sort, usually a quart lard pail, which is placed near the fire at the west end of the Long House before the individual takes his usual seat prior to the beginning of the ceremony. When it is time for the feast to begin, one of the chiefs stirs the corn soup with the wooden stirring paddle (Pl. X C) and then with a dipper puts some in each pail. If

[6] The ceremonial corn soup of the Iroquois is the Indian dish known widely as "succotash." The dried corn is cracked and cooked to a thin consistency and to this are added the cooked red-kidney beans. On one occasion chicken was added to the mixture and it gave a palatable flavor. In the homes, pork is added to flavor the soup, but this ingredient seems to have been omitted in the ceremonial soup. It too is saltless.

there are those who have not brought a receptacle, a bowl or plate and a spoon are furnished by the officers in charge. Each person then goes forward from his seat and takes his own pail or bowl of soup. When the caldrons are nearly empty the officers take them to the men's side, one to the Wolf and one to the Turtle, and the men scoop out what is left with the short-handled ceremonial spoons which they carry in their pockets. The bread and meat are placed in large rectangular, shallow, ash-splint baskets, about 2½ feet long by 18 inches wide and 9 inches deep, made in the usual Iroquois manner in checker or diagonal weave. These baskets are passed to the audience by the officers and assistants. When an officer hands out bread or a handful of the shredded beef it is taboo to say "Thank you." The teaching says, "It is not the individual who is giving you the food but the Creator. It is also bad form to refuse a second helping. You must take what is offered you, and if you cannot consume it in the Long House you take it home."

Other foods, such as corn mush, pig's head, and certain ceremonial drinks, are mentioned in connection with the ceremonies of the various medicine societies (Chapter VII).

It might be noted as an incidental to the facts pertaining to provisioning of the Midwinter Ceremony that about 350 pounds of beef is the amount required (125 pounds for each of the days preceding the last day of the rites, which latter calls for 100 pounds). The amount of shelled corn is one-half bushel for each day.[7]

CEREMONIAL MUSICAL INSTRUMENTS

The series of musical instruments used in the Long House rituals includes a wide variety of rattles, but only one type of drum. In the following list, mention and short descriptions of all are given with reference to the rites calling for particular instruments. The illustrations are of specimens in use obtained for museums mentioned in the Introduction.

Large turtle rattle, *kani·á'te stáwędra*, "snapping-turtle rattle" (Pl. XIV A).

Complete shell and skin of a snapping-turtle, 12-14 inches long, with head and neck stretched and held by stick splints to form a handle. This rattle is usually beaten edgewise on a bench placed

[7] The food notes in the section above were prepared by G. Tantaquidgeon from field recordings made with Deskáheh.

midway between the fires in the Long House.[8] It is used formally in the Great Feather Dance and in the performances of the Wooden False Face Society, whose members also carry them attached by a string to their wrists.

Small turtle rattle, *kani·á'tɛ ni·gá' stawẹdrú·*, "snapping-turtle small rattle" (Pl. XIV B).

Similar to the preceding but made of a young snapping-turtle shell about 8-10 inches long. It is used in the Women's Song Rite (page 147).

Horn rattle, *wδnága·u stáwẹdra*, "horn rattle" (Pl. XV A).

Section of polished cow's horn with wooden disk ends and a 10-inch maple stick through the middle for a handle.[9] It is extensively used in Medicine Society and Social Dances.

Bark rattle, *k'hsná' stáwẹdra*, "inner-bark rattle" (Pl. XV B).

Made on the same principle as the preceding type, of a section of oak or elm bark. The horn rattle is said to be derived from it. It was formerly used in the Bear Society Rite (page 64). A variation in form has the bark cylinder about 8 inches long (Pl. XVI D). The perforated coconut shell rattle is a recent innovation.

Gourd or Squash rattle, *ohnyọsa stáwẹdra*, "squash rattle" (Pl. XV C, E).

A natural product, gourd (Lagenaria), squash, or pumpkin grown by the Indians, is used. It may be a curve-necked or long-necked variety dried with the seeds left inside for sounding, or one with the handle end cut off and a wooden handle inserted through the body and fastened by a cross-peg. Cherry pits are often substituted for the seeds to make the rattling sound sharper. This rattle is formally used in rites addressed to spirits of cultivated plants, and in the Corn-husk Mask Society.

Mud turtle rattle, *kanuwagáhe stáwẹdra*, "slanted-back-turtle rattle."

The small hand rattle of a Mud turtle (Chrysemys [sp?]) shell is remembered but is not now used in Cayuga ceremonies.

Wooden beater, *hwénga stáwẹdra*, "wood rattle."

[8] When singers sitting on the benches use rattles, in all instances they accompany the motion of the hand holding the instrument with emphatic tapping of the feet.

[9] The manner of holding and shaking the horn rattle undergoes some variation as the hands of the users become tired from continued exertion when conducting the longer chants. The rattle held in the right hand, while usually shaken free, may be struck against the upturned palm of the left (occasionally when the hand is resting on the left thigh) and also directly against the thigh, as the notion may prompt.

A flat slab of wood cut in the shape and size of a large turtle rattle is sometimes used as a substitute for the latter, to be beaten upon the bench in the Long House.

Striking sticks, *kanhyá'e*, "sticks."

Two rounded sticks of pine (about ⅝ by 12 inches) are referred to in tradition as time-beaters for dancing but are not now used by the Cayuga.[10]

Rasp, *kaksá gánye*, "stick rasp" (Pl. XV G).

One notched stick of oak about 2 feet long and a rubbing stick 1 foot long are used to produce a rasping sound accompaniment for a dance. The lower end of the rasp is placed on the floor. The notches number from ten to twenty-five. Their number has no assigned significance. One specimen has notches on both sides. The notches are on the broad side. This is used only in the Chipmunk Dance (page 116).

Water drum, *ganadjǫ́*, "covered pail" (Pl. XIV C).

This is the only drum used by the Cayuga. A small pail made of four fitted side-sections about 5-6 inches in diameter and 4-5 inches in height, slightly narrower at the top, is covered with a skin held taut by a cloth-wrapped wooden hoop. A similar binding hoop encircles the bottom. A small quantity of water is put inside. Originally the body of the drum was of two fitted sections of hardwood, bound with an iron hoop. The beater is a light tapper with knob end and hollowed place for the fingers between which it is held. Drumsticks are often elaborately carved.

Deer-hoof leg rattles (Pl. XIII A), *wudjïa nénda tcinhá'tra*, "hoof tied on the leg." Fifteen to twenty hoofs are attached as danglers by means of leather thongs to a leather band often ornamented with brass-headed tacks. Deer hoofs were formerly used, but pig hoofs are used as substitutes at present (Pl. XIII B). They are fastened like garters below the knee.

Box turtle rattle (Pl. XIV D).

The complete shell of the box turtle (*Terrapene carolina*), closed with leather thongs strung through holes, is known to have been used formerly as the small snapping turtle rattle (No. 2) now is; i.e., in the Woman's Song. A specimen thought to have been brought from New York State remained in the possession of

---

10 The Tutelo among the Six Nations, however, employ beating sticks in a specific ceremony: the Four Nights Songs or Adoption Ceremony. An account of this significant survival of Tutelo culture has been published (Speck, 1942).

Deskáheh and is now in the Cranbrook Institute of Science. One is said to be still in use among the Cayuga.

Flageolet, *odrénod'd'kwa,* "something to produce song" (Pl. XV F). (The five-holed cedar "flute" is known as an instrument of expression, but it is not employed in any ceremonies.)[11]

CEREMONIAL DRESS

Except in the Feather Dance there is no requirement that participants wear the traditional garb of Indians (feathers and paint). This does not apply, however, to the women, who may be seen in many of the dance rituals dressed in traditional fashion, in hair arrangement, silver ornaments, long figured-cotton tunic, ribboned or beaded skirt, and leggings.

The use of face paint is reserved in the Midwinter rites for the event of the Feather Dance. The men apply red blotches and spots to the cheeks, and the women also redden the cheeks more or less all over.[12] This is in accordance with the ruling that the people adopt the native garb for this part of the festivities, and especially that the men wear feathers in headbands or that they complete the national Iroquois costuming by wearing the feather-cluster headdress distinctive for this group. (For description of an especially significant form of man's headdress symbolizing the whole tribal body—the clans and the moieties—see page 25, Fig. 2.)

Masks, being actual images rather than part of the make-up of the participants, are treated in a separate section, together with the ceremonies which accompany their use.

[11] There being so few references to the flute in Iroquois tradition, I insert the following tale narrated by John Buck for those who may welcome it:

Legend of the Young Men Flute-Players

There were two young men, lifelong companions, who used to go frequently to a place in the woods to a fallen dead tree and sit there playing tunes on the wooden flute. They agreed that should one of them die the other would return to the place for ten days and play as they always had done. One became sick and died and the other carried out the promise. Every time he went to the log to play he was sure he could feel the presence of the other. On the tenth day after playing, he returned home and heard the voice of his dead friend call him to come with him. But he did not answer. The spirit never appeared again. If he had answered his dead friend would have been brought to life again, but he did not know it at the time. The songs which they played were handed down for a long time, but few know any of them now.

[12] Of particular interest, in view of other sources of evidence to point to knowledge in the eastern area of the use of stamping blocks in printing designs upon baskets and leather, is the testimony of several men of the Lower Cayuga Long House that carved potato stamps are employed to print face painting patterns upon the cheeks. The design is that of a curved semicircle enclosing a five-pointed star, about 2 inches in diameter, cut in high relief. Dipped in red ochre this device produces a regular pattern figure of the new moon and star appropriate to the Midwinter or New Year festival, at which occasion it is adopted as a symbol of the celestial ruling that determines the beginning of the rites as explained above.

PART TWO

THE MIDWINTER CEREMONY

VI

TIMING AND PREPARATORY RITES OF THE MIDWINTER CEREMONY

As ITS name indicates, the "mid-year ceremonial mark (division)," (p. 34) the Midwinter Ceremony, or so-called New Year's Festival, is the focal center of Cayuga religious observance. Its outstanding prominence is shown in the length of its celebration (eight days), in its highly sacerdotal character, and in its composite form. It stands as an integration of practically all the separate elements of ritual (medicine society rites, sacred and social dances, symbolical and sacrificial acts) which are known to the religious leaders of the group, and which appear either as independent performances or as grouped elements in the other periodic ceremonies of the Cayuga annual cycle. The Midwinter Ceremony corresponds to the Annual Ceremony of other cultural groups of eastern North America.

By reference to Table 2 it will be seen that, apart from possessing a distinctive ritual of opening and closing (the Stirring Ashes Rite), it requires the celebration of the four sacred rites—Feather Dance, Skin Dance, Thanksgiving Prayer (*Adǫwa*), and Bowl Game (Table 2 and Table 3, Group I, A)—and also that it provides occasion for the performance of the rites and dances of any and all of the fourteen medicine societies (3, Group II, A and B).

The rites of naming, choosing spiritual partners (comrades), dream guessing, burial, condolence (pp. 159–63), and social dances (3, Group III) may also be introduced, as was the case in the course of the Midwinter Ceremony of 1933.

The ensuing sections treat in detail this remarkable event as witnessed by the writer and as later analyzed by Deskáheh.

TIMING

The position of the Pleiades or Seven Stars, "group stars" (*ugényuá*), determines the date for the beginning of the Midwinter Ceremony. They must be directly overhead at sunset after the new moon first appears in January. Upon this observation, five days are counted, and the fifth day is the one when the Stirring Ashes Rite is begun. This brings the moon to about its first quarter. In 1933 the

49

day fell on January 30th; in 1934 it fell on February 18th. Both
Sour Springs and Lower Cayuga Midwinter Ceremonies are timed
by the same count and come simultaneously. The time determination
was founded by Handsome Lake. He ordained that it should begin
one month later than the white man's New Year.

Story of the Seven Stars

In the Bay of Quinte this happened. There were seven boys and one man,
a leader. He got the seven boys interested and they went to a certain knoll and
held a dance. Toward the last they told their parents they wished them to
make up food for the dance for the next day. Their parents did not believe in
it and were disgusted because they were always dancing. They did not, therefore, prepare food for them. So the leader told them to prepare to rise when
they danced and not to look down when they danced. So they began to dance
and began to rise. When their parents saw the boys rising they felt sorry and
came beneath and offered them food asking them to come back. There was
one young man (boy) who ignored the rule forbidding them to look down, and
he fell. The other six boys and the leader continued to rise, and that is how
the Seven Stars are in the sky. The one fell, and a "blood tree" grew where
he fell. Later on when warriors were on the warpath they went to that tree
and tapped it. If any blood flowed out it meant that they would not come
back alive.

This accounts for the Seven Stars being so important in determin-
ing the time of the Long House ceremonies. It has connection, too,
with the people dancing on earth. The five-day interval after the
observation of the Seven Stars has its bearing upon the women, for it
allows time for the women to have passed their menstrual period,
which, according to Cayuga belief, is supposed to begin with the new
moon. Women going through this period are not supposed to act in
any official capacity in the ceremonies, though they are not excluded
from attendance in the Long House.

The analogism between the earth and the sky disclosed in this
myth of the dancing spirits calls for short comment. Much more
knowledge of native conceptualization is needed. The timing of
the Midwinter Ceremonies with the zenith point of the Pleiades
brings to light deep-hidden associations. The people are believed to
be dancing on earth when the line of communication with the sky
realm is open directly above and while the sky spirits also are dancing.
From this point we may trace the earth-sky correspondence in the

performance of living beings and spirits—a conceptual starting point in the study of native religious philosophy in eastern North America (see page 18). The topic calls for close attention and sounds profound depths in the Indian philosophy of Nature. The student of comparisons will note that a version of the same tale is current among the Delaware-Munsee of the Six Nations Reserve. It may have a vague and indirect bearing upon the question of Cayuga time-reckoning for the ceremony, but the relationship is not clear enough to discuss.

Finally, I may emphasize the comment of Deskáheh that it is only the Midwinter Ceremony among the festivals of the yearly cycle which is timed in accordance with star or other luminary observations. Maturity stages of crops determine the others.

CONFESSION WITH WAMPUM

Preceding the Stirring Ashes Ceremony, which is performed the first two days of the Midwinter Festival, the preparatory rites are performed. A day is set aside for this purpose, at which time the people are afforded an opportunity to confess their sins and thus purify themselves for the performance of the sacred rites. A leader is chosen to read and explain to the people assembled in the Long House certain chapters of the teachings of Handsome Lake. The leader speaks until noon, at which time the Feather Dance is performed as a sign of rejoicing over the reading and explaining of the Great Spirit's word. After the noon period the explanation of the revelation of the Four Angels (see Tabulation I) through the teachings of Handsome Lake is continued. Following this a bunch of strings of white wampum is placed on one of the benches which is centrally located in the Long House between the two fires. Any man or woman present who wishes to confess his or her sins and to derive spiritual aid and blessings may go forward and take up the wampum strings, saying, "I repent this day for my sins and from this day I will do good the rest of my life." It is understood that all injuries done to one during the past years, all offenses and malice, should be forgotten. This act is not compulsory, but is expected of all who participate in the Midwinter Festival. The informant stated that the ceremonial songs should not be sung by one who is guilty of evil deeds and has not repented. Even though he is in earnest, if he has not confessed his sins and sought forgiveness in these

preparatory rites he will not derive any benefit from the performances of the sacred ceremonies. Upon the performance of this rite
those who are to participate in the Midwinter Festival are qualified
to take part in the exercises to which attention will next be given.

The Confession Rite has nothing to do with setting the time of
the Midwinter Ceremony. Until 1933 confession at Sour Springs
had not been observed before the winter rites since 1929, because
of the absence of a suitable speaker for the occasion. Its performance
is rather expensive, as it requires providing a feast for the public
during the four or five days when it is held. The chiefs and leaders
decide to hold confession when they observe the people straying
from the ways of right living. Confession is addressed to the Creator
(Great Spirit). During the confession, the confessor, while addressing the Creator, is intended to be heard by the person who has been
wronged. Secret sins (witchcraft) which may not be divulged in the
Long House, may be confessed by repentant sinners privately at
some remote place on an "old road" (*wahagáyu séntų*). This confession is also addressed directly to the Creator. Old roads are
chosen because of their remoteness from molestation during confession.

Discussion of the historical origin of confession in Long House
deism would be out of place here. I do not know of many historians
who would entertain the idea of its derivation from any source
other than Christianity. It has been supposed that it was one of
Handsome Lake's acquisitions through contact with missionaries.
A wider question is however opened, even in the specific case of the
Iroquois, through the analogy of a concept which pervades another
rite in the Long House category. The concept of cure resulting
from the guessing and confession of the dream source of the affliction is a factor in the Dream Guessing Rite, to be discussed in a
later section (see page 123).

Despite the suspicion of its Christian derivation, belief in the
rectifying power of confession seems to be a fundamental trait in
the group ritual pattern of the Iroquois, as well as of the inhabitants
of the Northern Plains, the Mackenzie, and Arctic areas, as pointed
out by Spier (1935, 8, footnote). More recently La Barre (1947)
has discussed its nearly Pan-American distribution with reference
to Asia (Kamchadal), adding to the list of citations and interpreting

ıt as a psychotherapeutic technique deeply rooted in North American social-religious thought.

THE STIRRING ASHES RITE

The Stirring Ashes Rite, *ganahawi·'*, marks the formal opening of the Midwinter Festival. The observance of this rite takes place

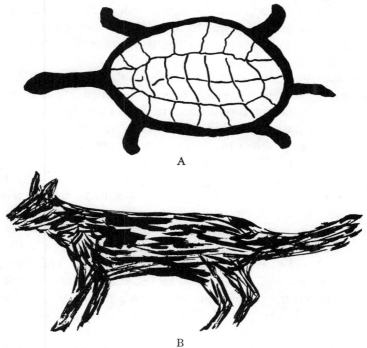

FIGURE 3.—Moiety emblems on Stirring Paddles used in Cayuga Stirring Ashes Rite. A—Turtle figure in blue (on the reverse side is the figure of a deer). B—Wolf figure in red (on the reverse side is a heron).

during the first two mornings,[1] and the public is invited. The officers have the two fires burning and ceremonial paddles in readiness early in the morning, as it has been decreed that the ceremonies should begin as soon as possible after sunrise. The head officer appoints two chiefs to take charge of this ceremony. These

[1] Under the old regime "as ordained by *Taɥ'hyawakǫ*" (Cayuga form of *Taronhiawakon*, the Mohawk name of the mythopoetic twin-creator), the rite was held at night. But Handsome Lake after 1800 changed the time of the celebration to the daytime. Formerly muskets were discharged by certain men outside the Long House during the rite of Stirring Ashes, but since about 1890 the custom has been discontinued among the Cayuga of the Sour Springs group.

men are referred to as "uncles," or "head chiefs." A speaker is appointed and he opens the ceremony by offering thanks to the Great Spirit and all the other Spiritual Forces. Following this, each of the two chiefs takes one of the ceremonial paddles[2] and goes to the east fire, then to the west fire. The two chiefs stir the ashes in the fires, alternating four times between the two fires. This symbolizes "stirring up (arousing) the people," or "to notify them that the ceremonies are about to begin." The two chiefs sit down. While walking slowly from one fire to another they were singing the Stirring Ashes Songs.

The speaker now arises and addresses the people, urging them to take part. He also speaks regarding the attitude one must have in offering thanks and supplication to the Great Spirit, even as to what to think during worship and what to say. When he has concluded, the officers select two men to distribute the paddles among those present, each participant receiving one. If a Turtle moiety man is first to perform, he gives the paddles to the first ten or twelve (the number of paddles is not specified) members of his moiety, who go out their own moiety door and return by the opposite door. They stand near the fire of the opposite moiety. The leader speaks and all stir the ashes. The leader sings, walks back to his own moiety fire, speaks, and stirs the ashes. The officer collects the paddles and places them in the corner, and the members of the group return to their places. Then a group of Wolf moiety people are given the paddles from their side and perform in the same manner. The officers divide the moieties into groups (of eight or ten) according to the number of persons present, and the stirring of ashes continues, accompanied by the singing, until all the small groups have performed. The speaker offers a prayer of Thanksgiving, which concludes the formal rites of the first day. It is important to note here that food is not distributed at the conclusion of the Stirring Ashes Rite on the first and second days.

On the second day, the two chiefs do not perform at the opening exercises, but the small groups continue to stir the ashes as on the previous day. When the rite has been performed by all present, the two chiefs stand up, go from fire to fire, and stir the ashes, thus signify-

2 The paddles are made of maple and are from 3 to 5 feet long. The officers take charge of the placing and handing out of the paddles, which are kept in the Long House. There are ten or twelve for each moiety. Figures of the "clan" animals and moiety animals are burned into the blades (Pl. X, D, and Fig. 3 A, B).

ing that the ceremony is being brought to a close. Then all of the officers take paddles and circle about the fire. One speaker and one singer have been selected to perform. The speaker *represents the Great Spirit* and he thanks the people for congregating to perform his (the Great Spirit's) ceremony.[3] When he and the assistant singer, who also represents the Great Spirit, start to sing, the officers stir the ashes. Then they move to the next fire and stir the ashes, and then return to the first, stirring the ashes at each fire twice. This performance is referred to as "lifting up the paddles," and concludes the ceremony for the second day.

[3] The idea of having a human interlocutor for the supreme deity has a number of interesting bearings. It denotes particularly the fixed concept of the purpose of the ceremony—opening direct communication with the high god.

VII

THE MEDICINE SOCIETIES

THE Medicine Societies of the Cayuga fall into two main groups, the restricted and the unrestricted societies, as shown in Table 3. Among the Cayuga they are not referred to as "Secret Societies," as among the Seneca for example.[1] It is said, however, that the Prophet, Handsome Lake, had a revelation in which he was commanded by the "Great Spirit" (Creator) to approve the Worship Rites (Group I A) but to tell the people that the medicine societies of ancient origin (Group II) which were involved with witchcraft agencies must disband after a final session of them all, in which a sacrifice of tobacco was to be burned. The members of the societies, as tradition states, agreed when approached by the chiefs with this command, and they held a meeting for the purpose of disbanding. But they neglected to burn tobacco in the fire at that meeting, and so the act of dissolving was not binding. The members of the societies met in secret for a while, but they soon resumed their activities in private homes and in the Long House—and the tabooed rites reinstated themselves.

The rites of the restricted societies are performed by *members only*, while in the unrestricted societies nonmembers may participate in the performance of the various rites. Since the Cayuga refer to the rites of all of the societies as "dances," it is noted in the descriptions of the "dances" that they may be performed in full or in part, that is, by *formal* and *informal* procedure. The formal procedure is carried out in private homes, while the informal procedure is in order for Long House or public performances. For example, if an individual should become ill and dream of a False Face, it is taken as a sign that the members of the False Face Society of the opposite moiety should be called in to perform for him. If he is cured he becomes a member of that society. If he is affected by the spirit of an animal such as the bear, the members of the Bear Society are called in. On such occasions, when the society performs in the

[1] Parker (1909). Comparison of the Seneca information given by Parker with the Cayuga details which follow shows interesting divergence between the forms of their societies. Dr. Fenton has more recently classified the societal structure of the Seneca.

home of the patient the rites of that particular society are performed in full. A person who has been cured by one of the societies must request the performance of its rites periodically to satisfy the spirit of the False Face or the animal invoked, in order to avert recurrent illness. The rites are performed for individuals requesting them by the members of the society of the opposite moiety. This is an important part of the program of the Midwinter Festival and takes place on the third and fourth days. The Cayuga refer to the performances as "partial" or "informal." Any person desirous of having the members of a certain society perform for him in the Long House on either of the two days which are set apart for the societies' "dances" may make his request through an assistant officer on his own "side of the house" (moiety), who in turn makes known the request to the leading officer of the opposite "side." The request is relayed to the presiding chief and thence to the speaker of the day, who makes the announcement to the people assembled. The requests apply to restricted and unrestricted society rites as well as to ceremonial games, such as Dice, Bowl, and Snow-Snake. If the ritual of a certain society calls for ceremonial foods or objects, the person requesting the "dance" provides the necessary furnishings. The Cayuga call this *ayǫndwanǫk^{cw}ta'^{c}nǫ*, which means, "passing their word," literally the observance of a specific society rite for the benefit of a member or nonmember. If the requests for "dances" cannot be fulfilled in the time allotted for their performance in the Long House sessions of the third and fourth days, the rite must be performed in private homes.

A word more as to the distinction between "restricted" and "unrestricted" societies. The former are those in which membership is extended only to those who have experienced cures from the performances. Thus the voluntary enlistment of beneficiaries perpetuates them. This observation applies to all of the more powerful societies listed in this group. Membership is, however, not obligatory in our sense of the term, the penalty for not joining being a moral one, namely, that the original complaint of the patient cured by the society is apt to return. His duty is to maintain the society by coöperation in behalf of others so afflicted. There is to be sure a slight element of secrecy in their festivals and rites, the members only participating. The "unrestricted" companies are those maintained by members qualifying for the first group but in which nonmembers may join at will, should they desire to contribute to the curing purpose of the rite by lending their presence. The "restricted" societies, furthermore, hold private meetings to which outsiders are not admitted, while the "unrestricted" do not.

The principles of curing through the performance of dances and songs may not have been made clear enough in the foregoing treatment. The following paragraph by Deskáheh is intended to explain:

> The society dances and songs are not regarded as the sole agencies of relief. But they are provided to act upon spiritual causes of ailment in conjunction with herb medicines which produce an effect upon the body. Only in rare cases are the rites of the societies called for or prescribed as cures without resort to other medicinal means. The underlying principles of pneumatism, as the use of the spiritual appeals through dances and song rituals may be denoted, are that the curing ceremonies, addressed to spirits who may be hindering the successful action of the medicines administered to the patient, should coax away the obstacle of the spirit's ill-will. They work on the idea that every time a native medical prescription (or for that matter one propounded by a white practitioner) fails to produce relief it is because of an obstacle in the guise of some spirit, animal, dwarf, ghost, or some other of the panphantasia standing in the way of the cure. The rites performed to effect the removal of the spiritual obstacle appeal to the unseen agency to cease, through the supplication of the people who attend the rites and who take part. The feast which is part of the event is in homage to the spirit. The Cayuga term denoting the curing rites is appropriate to this explanation, namely, ę`yǫndwanǫ'gwu'tʻ, "wish or request to go by," and may be understood from what has just been noted.

Expressed more simply, we may add that the procedure followed in calling for a dance-rite treatment, whether by one of the restricted or unrestricted societies or merely through the action of one of the games or social dances, is primarily the idea of a medicine man. When called upon to see if he can do something in a case where the medicine has been given and no beneficial results secured, he employs means known to him professionally to divine, often by dreams, what stands in the way of the cure. Then comes the suggestion that a certain dance, a feast, a game, or a society rite may secure the necessary spirit coöperation. He may, indeed, have recourse to repeated attempts and trials in order to reach the correct prognosis in the more obstinate cases.

As noted for some of the specific rites in separate treatment, it may be remembered in general that a medicine society dance is called for when a sufferer has had a vision of the spirit-patron of a society, such as the bear, otter, eagle, a dwarf, a false face of one of the various orders, or a ghost. And again, society rites must be repeated every now and again to satisfy the spirit-patrons and prevent return of maladies which they both cause and cure.

PSYCHIATRIC CAUSES OF SICKNESS

In the list below are named the specific maladies believed to be helped by the individual Medicine Society rites contained in Table 3. The grouping of the rites corresponds to that of the table. I have indicated in each case the symptoms of mental and physical disorders attributed to the spirit forces and the names of those persons asserted to have had their persecutions alleviated by the rites. The instances are provided from purely casual recollection on the part of Deskáheh and several helpers. No records have ever been kept; cases arise and are forgotten. Their bearing on the question of the frequency and character of neurotic disturbances in the Sour Springs Settlement will be appreciated by those concerned with data on psychopathic manifestations in any American Indian group.

Curative Rites Invoked for Specific Psychiatric Disorders with Examples of Cases

Group II A.

Bear Society Rite: relief from howling hysteria and attacks of dementia in which the victim "crawls on the ground in the manner of a bear"—Will and Tama Porter, brother and sister (about 35 years ago); Ernest Davis (about 5 years ago).

Otter Society Rite: relief from nervous tremors and associated afflictions (not dementia)—Jim Miller (about 15 years ago).

White Buffalo Society Dance: relief from dementia, convulsions, bellowing hysteria—an Oneida woman (about 35 years ago). At the first diagnosis of this case a medicine man prescribed the Bear Society Rite, but the patient had a relapse during the performance. Another suggested the White Buffalo Society Dance. They tried it and it worked a cure.

Wooden False Face Society Rite: relief from hemorrhages of the nose, facial paralysis, mouth drawn to one side, dream persecution by visions, and annoyance by False Face spirits and frights in the bush—most recent cure, Augustus Hill's daughter (1 year ago). For further details and cases see section on False Face beliefs.

Corn-Husk Mask Society Rite: relief from afflicting dreams or hallucinations.

Medicine Men's (Big Rattle) Society Rite and the Pig Mask Rite: cures bodily injury, wounds, and incurable diseases and immunizes against the coming of sickness foretold by a dream or vision—Mrs. Chauncey Powless (15 years ago); Ernest Davis (15 years ago).

Little Water, or Dark Dance, Society Rite: relief from general sickness, called for when a person has a vision of the dwarf spirits—Melinda General (convulsions) (15 or 20 years ago); Mrs. F. Martin (2 years ago).

Eagle Society Dance Rite: relief from nervous debility (St. Vitus's dance)—Mary General (5 years ago).

Group II B.

Snow-Snake Game Rite: relief for sickness in general when suggested by the medicine man, specific for sores on legs—Mrs. Alex. General (some years ago).

Chipmunk Rite: relief in general when prescribed, specific for compulsion to steal and hide objects. No cases remembered at Sour Springs; a very rare dance.

Thunder's Dance and Ball Game: for relief when prescribed. No case remembered in recent years.

War Dance (*Wasā'se*): for relief when called for, not specific. No case remembered. Used here only to make ceremonial friendship for a child who is sick when the medicine man prescribes "need of a friend" to give relief.

Chicken Dance: for social benefit, not therapeutic except when a chicken is seen in a dream or vision as a premonition of sickness. No cases recalled.

Striking Stick Dance: for general health when seen in a dream or vision. No case recalled.

Ghost Dance Rite: relief from convulsions and weakness, from paralysis which is caused by ghosts seen in a dream or vision, and for general recovery in obstinate sickness—Sadie Hill's daughter (Mohawk) (2 years ago), when only a feast was given to the members. Social dances of Group III are usually performed with this rite.

Dream Guessing Rite: relief from dream persecution by mask spirits—Hannah General (about 4 years ago); Mrs. Barbara Porter (1 year ago).

Dream Fortune Teller Rite: diagnosis for relief in prescribing any of the rites and dances. Services, more or less in secret, in constant and general demand in both the Long House and Christian communities.

Tug-of-War Rite: relief from nervous afflictions, trembling, griping. No cases at Sour Springs recalled recently.

Football Game Rite: for relief and health when suggested by the medicine man or in a dream or vision. Frequently called for in mild cases of illness.

Group III.

Fish Dance: social, not for curing.

Raccoon Dance: social, not for curing. Nevertheless, Charley Davis dreamed of it some years ago and has requested it performed for his benefit frequently since then.

Woman's Dance (*Skä`nye*): for benefit when called for as a source of relief by man or woman through dream suggestion.

Duck Dance: social, not usually for curing. Yet it is called for by one woman at Sour Springs year after year to satisfy her consciousness of need for the help it affords her.

Pigeon Dance: social, not requested for curing within memory.

Naked Dance: social, not for curing.

Kadä`trot, or Round Dance: social and very popular. Sometimes called for and given informally as a substitute for the Corn-Husk Mask Rite.

Clasping Hands Dance: social. Sometimes called for through instigation in a dream, and repeated periodically to avoid relapse into old or former complaints.

Crocodile Dance: social. No cases recalled for curing purposes.

Delaware or Skin-Beating Dance: social pastime only, and very rarely performed at Sour Springs.

Chicken or One Side Male Dance: social only.

Drunken Dance: social, though only rarely indulged in.

Garters Dance: purely social.

Sharpened Stake Dance: purely social.

Reversing Dance: purely social.

Robin Dance: purely social.

Shawnee Dance: purely social.

Shivering Word Dance: purely social.

Mouth-on Dance: purely social.

Fishing Dance: purely social.

Tormentor's Dance: purely social.

Cayuga medicine cults are noteworthily loose so far as esoteric teachings are concerned. The historical traditions and symbols of the various cults have not become standardized among members. Testing on this point shows that not all the associates of the societies —even of the most important ones, such as the Wooden False Face, Corn-Husk Mask, and Medicine Men's Societies—actually know the origin legends, or if they are informed they do not possess the same explanatory legend. The dissemination of the ritual teachings among the members seems to be by participation in the rites and by imitation. Hence the theoretical associations and the myth of history of the symbol concerned with the society to which a person belongs are left to chance instruction or to casual questions and answers, or, as in the case of some who were questioned, they amount to nothing at all. The ritualistic training of members, then, is decidedly informal. It is not the possession of secret and sacred knowledge which consolidates the members but the objective purpose, a real one, of effecting results in the community along lines of curing and healing. Viewed from the inside, the cults are loosely conceived, but from the outside they are semi-secret and exclusive. Definitely realistic in purpose, conventional in practice, and idealistic in conception!

It is natural that the reader should desire to see a sample program of the series of curing rites actually performed in the Long House on some one occasion. For presentation here the third day of the Sour Springs Midwinter Ceremony, as performed on January 31, 1936, has been selected. The thirty-three rituals and dances, all requested by supplicants,[2] came in the following order, beginning at eleven o'clock in the morning and lasting until about five in the evening.

Sample Program of Curing Rites

Opening address by George Bumberry, of the Wolf moiety, who referred to the Turtle moiety the duty of directing the minds of the people to the "rites and obligations" which were to take place. Alexander General (Deskáheh, the collaborator on this study) responded for the Turtle moiety and accepted the duty.

Bowl Game, in behalf of Jerry Aaron's wife.

Fish Dance, for the same supplicator.

Bear Society Dance, in behalf of two small boys.

Bowl Game, for Mrs. Katy Cook (Jerry Aaron's sister).

Football Game Rite (*Dyu`grɛhɛwí''t*ɔ, "Bringing forth snow"), played outside on the game field in the snow, for Mrs. Mackenzie Miller.

Bear Society Dance, in the Long House while the Football Game went on outside, for the same person.

---

[2] Having been requested by the officers of the Long House not to make notes during the course of the services, I was not able to recall the identity of all those whose request numbers were performed. Where no names are mentioned in the list, the lack is due to this circumstance.

Informal False Face Society Dance (without masks), in behalf of a young woman.

Buffalo Dance, for Mrs. Katy Cook.

Fish Dance, beneficiary not identified.

Eagle Dance (abbreviated form), for Mrs. Chauncey Garlow's niece (Mohawk descent).

Football Game, for the same beneficiary.

Informal False Face Society Dance, beneficiary not identified.

False Face Society Dance, for two young women, nieces of Mrs. Garlow (Mohawk descent).

Skä'nye, for unidentified woman.

Announcement of rites to take place on the sixth day (the rites of the Creator: the Feather Dance, the Skin Dance, the *Adǫwa*, and the Bowl Game), by Jacob Isaacs, of the Turtle moiety.

Otter Society Rite (Little Water), for Connie Smoke.

Football Game Rite, for Connie Smoke.

Bear Dance Society Rite, informal phase, beneficiary not identified.

Buffalo Dance, beneficiary not identified.

False Face Society Dance, for Chief Chauncey Garlow's adopted daughter (Mohawk).

Corn-Husk Mask Society Dance, for a child.

Informal False Face Society Dance, beneficiary not identified.

False Face Society Dance (Wolf moiety, ten maskers), for Chief Chauncey Garlow and wife (Mohawk).

Skä'nye, for family of Timothy General's wife.

False Face Society Dance (Turtle moiety, four maskers), beneficiary not identified.

Corn-Husk Mask Dance (Wolf moiety, two maskers), for an unidentified man.

Fish Dance, for Norman General's family.

Clasping Hands Dance (eighty-one dancers in two parallel lines), for Norman General's family.

Stirring Ashes Song, devotional requested by John Davis (Mohawk).

Dream Guessing Rite, for Mrs. Barbara Porter. (She dreamed of Husk Face Spirit and the dream was quickly guessed by David Jacobs.)

Closing Address, by Jacob Isaacs, of the Turtle moiety.

VIII

THE RESTRICTED MEDICINE SOCIETIES
AND THEIR RITES

THE ANIMAL SOCIETIES

THE following remarks will briefly introduce a few general features characterizing this series of curative performances. The Bear, the Otter, and the White Buffalo (as well as the Pig) Medicine Societies of the Cayuga were organized to appease the spirits of those powerful monsters which are said to have held sway on earth in ancient times. These animals were so powerful that their spirits have subsequently affected certain individuals as a form of retaliatory punishment for man's neglect of consideration of them, frequently causing insanity, in some cases to a degree productive of violence. Minor derangement is also attributed to these same causes. In such cases the victim of the attack is placed under observation, and his or her behavior interpreted to indicate what animal spirit is causing the lamentable condition. If it is thought to be the spirit of the bear, the sufferer imitates that animal in voice and actions; if the white buffalo, he bellows continually and wallows around on the floor in paroxysms. If it is difficult for a doctor when consulted for diagnosis to determine the cause of the victim's illness, a number of different societies may be called upon to perform for his benefit until the right one is found. When a society is called in, the person requesting treatment, or the members of his family, must provide the ceremonial foods and tobacco offering as required by the society. Finally if and when a person is cured he automatically becomes an associate, or member, of the society that cured him, and he should call for that particular society dance to be repeated for him in the Long House at least once a year to insure against recurrence of the ailment.

The Bear Society Rite

The rite is called *nyagwékya*, "bear dance." This is one of the societies which was condemned by Handsome Lake. The members sing and dance contraclockwise around the patient, using the short shuffle-step in single file to the accompaniment of the water drum and horn rattle. In former times it is said that the bark rattle was used.[1] The patient is seated on a bench, and on either side is an attendant holding a cup and a small pail which contains berry juice. Each member takes a drink of the berry juice and gives a drink to the patient, or vice versa; then the members take more of the berry juice in their mouths and spray it on the head of the patient. Herb tea is also used, because the bear likes herbs. In the Bear Society Rite observed in the Sour Springs Long House in February, 1933, peanuts were distributed among the patients and members participating in the dance, because the bear also likes nuts. The persons treated in this society rite must not wash off the berry juice and herb tea. The dance continues until all of the members have had an opportunity to blow the medicine on the patients. When performed in private usually only one person is treated, but when performed in the Long House the individuals who have requested the performance of this rite are treated collectively.

The Otter or Fish Eating Society Rite

The name of this society is *djutí·drǫ*, "otter." The individual who is afflicted by the spirit of the otter is thought to become nervous and cannot control himself. When members of the Otter Society are called upon to perform in such a case a feast of fish chowder and bread must be prepared for them by the patient. Members of the society arrange the food on the floor, and a single bucket of water is brought in. It should be noted here that running water that has been dipped up by a motion in the direction of the current is used. All present partake of the food as an offering to appease the spirit of the otter. Singing and dancing are absent in this rite. When the people have finished eating, each member having been provided with a corn-husk water splasher made by tying a handful of husks in the middle to form a whisk (Fig. 4), dips it in the water, and sprinkles the patient. The members also splash each other on the head and shoulders. This is said to symbolize sprinkling the otter to satisfy it. When a person is cured he, as usual with the other societies, becomes a member. The informant stated that the mem-

---

[1] This is evidently the folded hickory bark or the cylindrical elm bark rattle (Pl. XV D, No. 4, p. 43). John Buck (72 years old, 1936) has always seen the horn rattle used at Six Nations. (See Dodge, 1949.)

bers of the Otter Society are rarely called upon to perform in the Long House.

In 1944 an opportunity was given to observe the ordinances of the Otter Society during the Midwinter Ceremony at the Sour Springs Long House. The ritual was enacted to afford satisfaction to the spiritual tutelaries of the society, namely, the fish and otter and their living representatives, in order to avert illness that might come upon the people through neglect of the attentions paid them by the festival observances. The ritual procedure of the company

FIGURE 4.—Corn-husk sprinkler (Cayuga, Six Nations, Ontario) for anointing members of Otter Society doctoring cult, known as Djutiꞏ drǫ, "Otter." The sprinkler is used in the Long House ritual at Sour Springs (February 20, 1945) during midwinter ceremonies. Members of the society, mostly women, partook of feast of fish on north side of Long House while other dances were in progress. From a pail of water they sprinkled each other while feasting. It was done with apparent levity and humor. The Otter Society cures complaints caused by spirits of otters, fish and other water dwellers. The sprinklers were cast outside the Long House after the ritual.

was carried on while one of the other Medicine Societies was performing in the center of the Long House. Ten associates of the Otter Society took part, all females but one (Levi Baptiste). They assembled in a group near the center of the north side of the house. A pail of water had been placed on a bench in front of the bank of seats. Besides this provision about a dozen of the water sprinklers had been fashioned of dried corn husks ten inches in length tied together in the middle with a cord (Fig. 4). With no observed preꞏ liminaries the members of the group dipped the sprinklers into the water pail and began splashing each other with the water over their heads and shoulders. Considerable dodging and hilarity prevailed among them, especially when sousing the one man (Levi) of their company. After about five minutes the sprinkling ended and the members mingled with the rest of the assemblage. No invocation or dancing was observed. It was apparently only a rite of general placation of the spirits of the fish and otters. Later the corn-husk sprinklers were found thrown on a heap of brush and refuse near the cook house outside, and the specimen shown in the illustration was taken.

Later, when personally questioned about the matter, Levi Baptiste narrated a recent experience in which he had cured a child of an ailment, using his power as a doctor of the society. He implied, in his odd way, that this was the reason for the concerted "baptismal" attack upon him by the women of his society.

The child in question had developed St. Vitus's dance. Three white doctors had given up the case. Since the child was of part Indian descent on the mother's side, the parents decided to try an Indian doctor. Levi was sought out and consulted. His first question was to ask the father if he had been fishing. "Yes," said he, "a couple of months previous I did go fishing." "What did you do with the fish you caught?" asked Levi. "Threw it on the ground," answered the father. "Is that where fish belong?" asked Levi. "No!" said the father. "What did the fish do?" asked Levi. "It flopped on the ground, struggled then died," said the father. "Now you see, that's what you did wrong. You made the fish offended and so the fish made your daughter shake." Levi prayed and went through the curing service of the Otter Society. He repeated it three days and the child got well. Levi explained that the child, having part Indian lineage, was amenable to punishment by animal spirit agencies for disrespect, and likewise was susceptible to cure through the means provided by offended animals through her Indian descent, no matter how small the degree of Indian consanguinity might be. It was the aboriginal inheritance that influenced both cause and cure.

The White Buffalo Society Rite

This society is referred to as *dyaguna'ʻgaʉt*, literally, "(the society of) those who have horns," meaning the buffalo.[2] A person who is believed affected by the spirit of the White Buffalo bellows continually and wallows around on the floor. He cannot eat and becomes very weak. For this rite corn-meal mush is prepared and is eaten by the members of the society between dances. When the performance is in private the bowl of corn-meal mush is placed in the center of the room and the men and women dance around facing the mush. The water drum and horn rattle are used by the two singers and the leader singer on the bench. At a certain part of the dance the dancers face outward. They make motions imitating the buffalo bull, using his horns, bellowing, and pushing one another aside. At the conclusion of the dance each member dips his hand in the mush and licks it off. Then the dance is resumed. The patient is given herb tea to drink by the members, who blow some of the medicine on the patient's head. This dance is performed at least once a year to satisfy the spirit of the White Buffalo. When the ceremony is performed in the Long House the mush and the herb drinks are passed around to the dancers while in line. They usually sing seven or eight songs.

THE WOODEN FALSE FACE SOCIETY

In the series of Iroquois Medicine Societies the Mask Rite has been more widely discussed than any other by writers on Iroquois social and religious customs. Much attention has been given this engrossing topic by early as well as contemporary writers. Departing from the generalizing method of treatment followed by Iroquoian students from Jesuit times through to those of Morgan, Beauchamp, and Brinton, Fenton (1937) approached the study of medicine societies by devoting specific attention to the Seneca.

Study of the ritual of the False Face Societies of the Cayuga, whose members perform with as much fervor now as they evidently did in early times, emphasizes belief in the powerful spiritual force which works through the mask, affecting the wearer's entire being. A most striking observation made in connection with this influence was the masked dancers' immunity to burns from handling hot

---

[2] The confusion of the terms for sheep and "those who have horns" has led to the mistaken popular designation "sheep dance" for this rite among some of the people on the reserve, notably the Mohawk, in whose language the synonym applies. Among those participating who are thus misled, the cry of *ba* + is occasionally uttered as though in imitation of sheep, as was the case observed in the Midwinter Ceremony of 1936.

coals, a veritable fire ordeal understressed by most investigators in the field of modern Iroquois ceremonies. This will be discussed under a separate heading (p. 91).

The origin of the Wooden False Face Society, called *ǫki·sot hanatui·*, "grandfather *hanatui·*," dates back in legend to the period of the creation of the world under rule of the mythical beings. The version given by Deskáheh is the traditional origin, recited as part of a lecture given occasionally by the leader of the society to the members. Deskáheh is an officer of a False Face Society of the Turtle moiety in the Sour Springs Long House. It is of some ethnological significance to note that, while this version of the tale of the mask society origin is supposed to be doctrinal among its members, there are those among them who respond with another and quite different tale when questioned on the point. The traditional version is given hereafter along with examples of the other belief, showing what has been referred to in the introductory discussion, namely, the variability of traits not only within Iroquois groups at large, but among the smaller tribal units. Even Cayuga institutions cannot be confined to fixed outlines.

Stories of Origin

The Great Spirit was looking over his creations. The False Face said to the Great Spirit, "What are you looking at?" The Great Spirit answered, "I am looking at what I have created." They had a dispute as to who was the stronger, each one declaring that he had created all things. The evil spirit was influencing the False Face in making him try to overcome the Great Spirit, so they decided to test their power. The False Face was given first chance to prove that he was the stronger. He had a hickory tree for his cane and he made a great noise and rattled.[3] The Great Spirit said to him, "If you can move that rocky mountain then I will agree that you created all things." Then the False Face caused the earth and trees to shake, but the mountain did not move. The Great Spirit said, "Now you turn around and face in the opposite direction and I will tell you when to look." So the False Face did as the Great Spirit had told him, and while he was facing in the opposite direction the Great Spirit made the mountain move close behind the False Face. The Great Spirit told the False Face to turn around, and as he suddenly did so he struck his nose and mouth against the mountain, making them crooked. This made the False Face admit that the Great Spirit was stronger and that he had created all things. The False Face begged the Great

[3] Referring to the large turtle rattle carried by False Face performers (Pl. XIV, A).

Spirit to spare his life that he might live to help his grandchildren by alleviating diseases. He asked to control the whirlwind that brings disease to mankind.[4] And he asked to leave men the songs appropriate to his services. The Great Spirit granted his wish, but the False Face ever after had a crooked nose and mouth.

A variant version of the origin of the False Face Society was obtained from William John, of the Wolf "side" (moiety), who is an active member of the Cayuga Long House at Sour Springs. Inasmuch as Deskáheh did not know this origin tale, he declared his belief that it was learned from the members of some Iroquois mask society other than the Cayuga. The tale told by John is as follows:

There was once a chief's daughter who was set adrift in a canoe in the Niagara River, as a sacrifice to a spirit causing disease, and went over the falls. It happened that she was not killed and that after a long time she returned to her people. She had been living with some little people in the caves under the falls. This chief's daughter gave birth to a male child. When he was old enough to play with other children, his people noticed that he was very powerful. If he started to quarrel with one of his playmates and touched him, the child would fall dead instantly. So his people would not allow him to play with the other children because of his great power. This boy carved a lot of small False Face images. They were all different: some red, some black, some crooked-mouthed, some laughing, some with big noses. He said, "These are my people who live under the falls." He also made rattles of the shell of the Snapping Turtle, because there were large turtles where his people lived. The turtle is very powerful. The rattle is used to frighten away disease. It is said to be the noise of the Thunders.

The boy then left powers to those to whom he gave the images to cure disease with the aid of the masks as "medicine." Some of his relatives living under the falls have black skins, some red, with long flowing hair and gleaming eyes, whence the variations in mask representations are accounted for. The mask society thus formed functioned and grew.

Another member of the False Face company in which Deskáheh officiates gave the same origin myth in substance. This man, an active devotee, was Jerry Aaron, of the Turtle sib. He did not know the orthodox origin tale!

[4] The Cayuga belief is that the whirlwind is a spirit walking around and if it touches one it causes paralysis.

The individual False Face spirit character portrayed in the legend is not so easy to fit into the idea of the plurality of the succeeding False Face beings which seem to have developed from the original concept, unless we regard the original individual "being" as the collective representation of his tribal progeny. The concept of the mask-being consequently finds its expression in rites both in individual and in multiple form.

Another version[5] of the tale, which possesses the guise of authority, since it is supposed to be recited by the leader before the meeting of the society, is the following:

When Our Creator (*Sǫgwea͡ ii·'sǫ*) was looking over the newly-made world he was glad to see that everything had come just right. So as he was walking along he met the False Face, and asked him, "Where did you come from?" The False Face replied, "I made the world." "No, I don't think so. I think I made the world," said Our Creator. He said to the False Face, "We will try out to test who has greater power, I or you, and see who can make that great mountain move over toward us. If you can move it toward us, you have power also." So the False Face and Our Creator turned. The False Face took the first turn. The False Face shook his rattle and said to the mountain, "Come toward us." The mountain moved toward them about half way. Then the False Face said, "Now let me see." Then Our Creator said, "Now let me try." Then they turned again for awhile, then Our Creator said to the mountain, "Come move toward us." Then they turned to see how far the mountain had moved. As they turned, the False Face's nose scraped against the great mountain, that is why the False Face's nose is crooked. So Our Creator said to the False Face, "It would be better if you went away from here because there are people going to be born and live here." So the False Face replied asking if there was any possible chance for him to remain here. He made a promise that he would help the people and take them as his grandchildren.

The story of how the different colors occurred among the masks is this. The masks were all red before Our Creator first met them. The reason why the black ones are around now is because when False Face met Our Creator he got so excited that he turned black. When the others saw the black one they got excited too, some turning black, some remaining their natural color.

WOODEN MASK TYPES, TREATMENT, BELIEFS CONCERNING THEM

The masking complex is a living force in the minds of the Long House people; individual experiences are always adding to or

[5] Written and translated by Mrs. John L. Buck upon the occasion of the False Face Society Dance at Lower Cayuga Long House in February, 1936.

modifying the fundamental principles. There is indeed still much
to be done with the topic. The following observations refer to
masks of the Wooden False Face Society and do not cover all the
types of masks known and used as representing individual spirit
forces.

The False Faces, *gagǫsa,* are reverenced as mediums of spiritual
force and are referred to as *ǫki·sot,* "grandfathers." In speaking of
the False Faces and the power which they bestow upon their
wearers, Deskáheh explains, "It is not the object, not the False
Face itself, that we worship, but the unseen power behind it. The
False Faces represent the same power as the medicines that grow
on the earth. They are our medicine." In the succession of spirit
forces (see Table I C) they represent a power of the Forest group,
living among the trees of the forest—apparitions confronting man
at times when overtaken in the forest.

The mask representations of the spirits are made of the wood
of the forest: maple, white pine, basswood, and poplar. In making
a False Face the features are first carved upon a living tree, then
cut free. During the process, prayer is addressed to the evolving
mask and to the spirit force it represents, and tobacco is burned
before it. The particular kind of spirit reveals itself to the maker
when he has burned tobacco and prayed, and started to carve its
features. It is then painted and the long horse-hair arranged on it.
Tradition says that before horses were known to the Iroquois,
plaited corn-husks were used for hair, as some specimens still show.
Variations in the treatment of the hair occur, such as braiding and
the turning upward of the hair to form a cowlick or bristling mane,
but no symbolical meaning is attached to these modifications so far
as information goes at present.[6]

The red face or "laughing mask," as it is called, is generally
interpreted as the original type, but after the Great Spirit put the
"Grandfather" False Face to shame by making his nose and mouth
crooked he was no longer happy. This accounts for the large proportion of red as well as black masks with crooked noses and mouths
and wry expressions. The cause of some of the mythical False Faces
becoming black has already been noted (see p. 71). The red masks
are properly the "great ones"; representations of the spirit opposed

------

[6] See Fenton (1941) for details of mask carving of the Seneca which apply to the
Iroquois in general.

to the Great Spirit in the origin legend. Through the smiling mien he is portrayed as the self-satisfied spirit-entity expecting to demonstrate his power against his contestor. In the crooked-featured forms the False Face is portrayed as the chagrined arch-fiend. Often expressions seen on red and black masks denote the various moods experienced between the extreme states of emotion. The mask company has a leader, chief-like, whose mask is usually a large old one with extra long hair, exaggerated visage, and the conventional symbols of greater age. He typifies, in brief, a "grandfather" of his people, the Iroquois. A word more pertaining to the black visages: They are partners with the red in religious esteem, and "both go where they are called, together."

The sacred objects represented in these plates were purchased by me after they had performed their last services on the night of Friday, March 20th, 1936, at the Seneca Long House, by *yo'ré'yogá'we*, John L. Buck, with an injunction to perform the following rite in their presence. The rite, which has several interesting features peculiar to the occasion, is as follows. Needless to add, I enacted them faithfully according to instructions, to wit:

While I was away I dreamt that you were to burn some of the tobacco as an offering. In my dream I saw the Big Red Mask (one of those sent), and this is what he said: To give some tobacco to you to burn and to say, "Now I have you in my hand (burn some tobacco). Now you are here, my Grandfather (burn some more tobacco). So have your mind here and guide me so that we may work together from now on (burn more tobacco)." Then tell him (the Mask) what you are going to use him for and ask him to stay and be content there. As you talk along put some tobacco in the fire. I got this through my dream so please do this for me as I burned some tobacco offering before I sent them.[7]

On going to Hy-joong-kwas' house for the mask, I soon learned this was no common matter of bargain and delivery. He and the mask had been in communion too long to be separated in any every day business way. Having stirred up the fire in the stove, he left the interpreter and myself while he went into an adjoining room. In a little while we could hear the peculiar "Hoh-o-o-o, ho-o-o!" and shortly afterwards Hy-joong-kwas returned wearing the mask and still muttering, or rather, perhaps, uttering, the whole of the extremely limited False Face vocabulary until he reached the stove. Here he hung the mask by its head fastenings over the back of a chair and proceeded

---

[7] With the above may be compared an interesting and graphic description of an Onondaga rite, closely similar, observed by Dr. David Boyle (pp. 28-29).

to make up a small parcel of home-grown tobacco in a scrap of blue cotton print, and tied it with white thread over the brow of the mask, having first dropped a pinch of tobacco into some coals he had raked out in front of the stove.

After affectionately stroking the long hair which forms the wig, he replaced the mask on the back of the chair, whence he had removed it for the purpose of tying on the little parcel of tobacco. He then leaned forward, looking almost reverently at the mask, and speaking in a low tone to it, said: "My friend, (dropping a little tobacco among the coals) you are now going to leave me for the first time, and I am burning this tobacco to keep you calm and well pleased. (More tobacco.) You and I have been together for a very long time. We have always been good friends. (Tobacco.) I have been good to you, and you have been good to me. You have cured a great many people, and we will not forget you. (Tobacco.) You may still do good where you are going, and I hope Ah-i-wah-ka-noh-nis will use you well. (Tobacco.) I have put a little tobacco on your head that you may always have some when you want it. (Tobacco.)

"We shall not be very far apart, and we will often think of you, and will often burn some tobacco for you."

On concluding his touching little address he threw all that was left of his handful of tobacco into the fire, took the mask from the back of the chair, and, after once more stroking its hair, handed it to me with a request that I would rub its face with oil once or twice a year, as it had been used to such attention ever since he owned it, and would be pleased to be remembered in this way!

Amid the company of the False Face Spirits there seems to have been a special grouping of four of them having a definite and close association with the wind. These are the Four Brothers. They were represented in the mask series by four images known also as the Mystery Masks, two of them black and two red, in the recent ceremony on the Six Nations reserve, when they were brought into use and the specimens obtained to illustrate this study (see Plate VI). This old practice of having the Four Brothers associated with the wind personifies a belief which again may be best expressed in the words of Mrs. John L. Buck, Jr., since it has not been an active performance in the Sour Springs settlement for many years. It still holds sway, however, among the Seneca and Lower Cayuga Long House people. The Four Brothers, as we learn, take part in the convocations of the False Face Society, representing a special function—the power behind the winds.

These masks, therefore, have the power of the wind. If there is a windstorm approaching they [sic] can use them. Then they have to burn Indian tobacco for an offering in a basket made for the purpose. They say that the windstorm will pass above the reserve without harm if we perform the rite for this purpose. In the days of old they always made these masks, but nowadays we do not have them much. This spring is the first time we had it for a long time (about eight years).

The wearers of the four masks went and got ready separately from the rest of the company. These performers are those who do not take their masks off when they are going from house to house in the curing rites. The wearers come from a near-by bush. When the others are ready at the Long House they all join together and go on their mission. These masked men are not supposed to be known until everything is over at the Long House.

When they come back the Four Brother masks are the ones who give the members of the False Face Society a feast when they return.

These masks came from the wind. As the story runs, when they were first seen there was a small whirlwind and all of a sudden these spirits were seen traveling through the air with the wind. So it was first anciently witnessed.

Of the four specimens illustrated, all but one (red) have the long streaming horse-tail hair. Whether the Four Brothers are always represented by masks of the same form as those shown (being used in April, 1936), I have not been able to ascertain.

As has been stated, the observances connected with these four spirits and their masked representatives are not now carried out at the Sour Springs center. Deskáheh, when questioned about them, expressed the opinion that they originated from Delaware belief and were incorporated into that of the Lower Cayuga, Seneca, and Onondaga. We have, however, no prospects of tracing the four masked representations of the winds back to Delaware practice through the sources now known. Deskáheh reminds us in this connection that the "only agency of control over the winds is the power of the Four Angels, as quoted in the teachings of Handsome Lake. And there never was any representation in the form of masks made of the Four Angels." Therefore it remains an open question, and a significant one which can hardly be settled from Sour Springs authority, how to determine the probable original identity of the Four Wind Brothers with the Four Angels. (See Table 1, page 30.)

Another primary type besides the all-red and all-black masks, is the mask that is red on the right side of the face and black on the left side of the face—the mask of the Whirlwind Spirit (Pl. V, C, D). In only one specimen seen are the colors reversed.[8] This spirit genius is not ordinarily present among the companies of the False Face societies, though there is no objection to its inclusion in the society rites if worn by a member who produces it. The "Whirlwind Mask," *owadā''sɛ gagǫ́saʻ*, is a concrete symbol of the Whirlwind Spirit mentioned in one version of the origin myth (p. 69) and is in a degree equivalent to his power. The Whirlwind Mask is used by the devout to turn aside an approaching thunderstorm or tornado, being hung up in the first tree (basswood or hickory are specified) near the house facing the storm, or even thrown in the teeth of the storm to split the storm cloud asunder. The associated reasoning is, I think, clear enough. A smaller size of this mask is not intended to be worn, being intended to be hung up to avert the storm. It is from four to six inches in length. John Buck added that the coloring half black and half red (*tʻodyatʻkā́wɛ*, "half each side") symbolized east (red) and west (black), or the willingness on the part of the spirit at the bidding of man "to go either way from the middle of the sky (universe) where he resides in the middle of the path." Whirlwind Masks are of two sizes, one a little too small to wear comfortably, the other large enough for a man. They usually do not have horse tail for hair nor does the wearer require the snapping turtle rattle. The Whirlwind Mask, according to another legend, to be given now, arises out of an isolated event, one not connected with the orthodox tale of transformation of the False Faces.

Story of the Whirlwind Mask

How it was first seen. It was in the great forest. A man was walking along and heard a rattle. He looked up and saw the False Face looking around from behind the tree, and the man's nose started to bleed and he was killed by it. Another man later saw the same thing; when he got home he hired a medicine man to have his fortune told. In his fortune he was told to get this certain mask to cure him, also to offer it tobacco.

He looked for this mask. He could not find one. Then he dreamed that he was to get a certain man to make one for him. He got one made, so that's how the black and red mask was first made.

Later, a woman dreamed that a great storm was coming and that the only one way for them to escape it would be that the red and black mask was to be hung out on the first hickory tree they came to, and also Indian tobacco

---

[8] Collection of Mr. Robert Riggs, Philadelphia, Pa.

was to be offered. They were told to make a little fire and burn the offering of tobacco. Later were made the three different sizes, a Whirlwind Mask, a special kind for each purpose.[9]

Another dictation is given by old John Buck.

He goes fast, like the wind. When in the woods you hear him whistle (like the wind) and look around, he keeps out of sight on the opposite or far side of a tree, like a flicker. The Whirlwind Spirit is dangerous and does a lot of damage. The thunder and lightning try to strike him down but he is too fast. Whenever he stirs abroad a big storm and whirlwind follow.

Finally, we note that the Whirlwind Spirit may be employed, through the mediation of a medicine man who owns the mask, to do harm by raising a wind (a great evil one or a little one) by offering it a tobacco sacrifice and asking, "and it will happen."

In another category of mask types determined by color is the white or "messenger" mask (*hag'ǫsagɛ'da*), whose function, also derived from the event of the transformation of the mask-beings by the Great Spirit, was and is to serve as messenger of the False Face company. He precedes the errant company to "see if the people are ready," and gives them warning that the others are coming. He also can be invoked to notify the False Faces that they are wanted; "they know when they see him coming that he has something to say." Serving as messenger, the white mask is symbolized as being younger than the red and black masks, whence its shorter hair, or absence of hair. Its station is correspondingly not so high. The white mask may be of natural unpainted wood or it may be painted white. There seems also to be gradation in construction of the messenger mask toward the Corn-Husk Masks, which function it is also to be observed, as messengers or forerunners to the red and black "grandfathers." Accordingly, the white wooden False Face may be seen in some instances with a corn-husk border or "hair" fringe; technically, part Wooden False Face and part Corn-Husk Mask.[10]

[9] Narrated by the late James Davis to his grandson, John L. Buck, Jr.

[10] Harrington (1909) describes an identical mask, obtained from the Onondaga of the Six Nations as "*Ow'ɛⁿ'ga gajī'sa'*, 'wooden bushy-head' which, although made of wood, belongs to the Husk-face Society and is classed as a *gajī'sa'*. In appearance its connection with the Husk-faces is shown only by its encircling fringe of shredded husk representing hair. It differs however from the common wooden mask, or *ha'do'wo'*, in that it is carved to represent a normal human face, not distorted and hideous, while the painting is confined generally to a round spot of red on each cheek. It is considered more powerful than the ordinary Husk-face."

In his capacity of messenger for the great ones in their pere-
grinations of mercy, the White Messenger appears first in the home
or in the Long House where the red and the black ones are to come
and perform.

The designing and decorating of the masks is left largely to
individual taste; all, however, fall within the traditional pattern.
The Cayuga believe that the False Face images are very powerful
and must be treated with respect, lest the power which they represent be turned against those who do not observe the rules regarding
their care. First of all, when a new mask is made it should be consecrated to the service of mankind by being put in the hot coals
and ashes of a Long House fire. At this time one of the ceremonial
leaders throws tobacco on the fire and offers a prayer to the Creator
and the spirit-forces on earth, imploring their blessing on the mask,
that it may be of service as an agent of the great power which it
represents. Then a tiny cloth bag of tobacco is kept tied to the hair
near the forehead of the mask as a sacrifice offering to keep the
spirit satisfied. It is customary for the owners of the False Faces to
renew the tobacco periodically and to give the faces occasionally a
rubbing with sunflower oil and grease, the anointment symbolizing
"feeding."

It is taboo to ridicule or strike at a masked dancer who is performing either in the Long House or a private home. One may
laugh if he is amused by the False Faces, but never in ridicule. So
much for general features.

One of the regulations governing the treatment of masks, more
strictly observed formerly than now, was to anoint them at times
with oil of sunflower seed mixed with animal grease.[11] A formal
anointment ceremony is held in the fall on the occasion of one of the
Long House festivals. The members of the False Face Society
assemble at a certain place, then start with their masks on a journey
from house to house among the Long House families. At each home
they purge the premises of lurking disease spirits (animal and
witch), passing their rattles over the house furniture, and scattering
ashes as media of purification. After the house-visiting they start
toward the Long House, halting at the "edge of the woods" to
await the drawing near of a party coming from the Long House.

[11] This rite has not been celebrated at Sour Springs within the memory of
Deskáheh (at least 40 years).

provided with a supply of the oil to "feed" the masks. At the same time a burnt tobacco sacrifice is made to the masks, and the offerings of native tobacco in the form of little bags of the weed tied to the foreheads of the masks are renewed to afford satisfaction to them. Occasionally the successive offerings are left on the masks, which accounts for the presence of several small bags containing tobacco being attached to them. After the oil anointment at the wood's edge the Masks rest, and then come into the Long House to conclude the rite with a dance. This is a form of the False Face traveling rite (see p. 93).

The sunflower seed oil is prepared by crushing the seeds in a small hardwood mortar with a pestle of wood, made precisely in the form of the regular corn-mortar and pestle, the mortar being 4½ inches in height and 3½ in diameter, the pestle 9 inches in length (Fig. 5).

Another convention of mask symbolism is the featuring of age by the carving of a vertical row of projections in the center of the forehead extending from

FIGURE 5.—Cayuga mortar and pestle for crushing sunflower seeds to make oil for anointment of wooden masks.

the bridge of the nose to the hair line. This appears in profile as a row of notches on a frontal crest, each of which, as some Cayuga averred, designates a five-year period in the age of the particular mask spirit at the time of his transformation with all the other False Faces, as narrated in the versions of the origin myth previously referred to (pp. 69, 71).[12] The age notches, as observed on specimens used by the

[12] Seneca informants explained to Dr. Fenton (*op. cit.*, 231, illustration) that these spines are called "turtle's tail," from the spiny protuberances on the upper crest of the tail of the Snapping Turtle.

Cayuga, number from five to nine or ten, indicating, through some fabulous conception of estimating time, the respective ages of mythical spirits at some time ancient beyond count.

A survey of Cayuga wooden mask images of the False Face Society observed in use in the band, including those collected, permits of some general remarks on classification of types. Specimens are shown in Plates IV, V, VI, VII, and IX.

The wooden masks are of poplar, basswood, maple, and occasionally of white pine.

They are of four solid colors, red, black, red and black, and white. The red and black coloration, now made by commercial paints, was formerly of red vegetable dye (pokeberry stain for the red) and charcoal, the white originally simply that of the natural wood.

Hair is represented by strips of horsetail, or by tresses of braided corn husk with the ends left stringing. Occasionally the hair is braided into one or two pigtails hanging over the face; yet this is nothing more than a "matter of style" according to Deskáheh. The latter are stated by some to be the prototype of the hair feature, or to represent a type of spirit intermediate between the wooden and the corn-husk groups. Horsetails of three colors are used, black, gray and white, the different shades denoting ages of the masks as individual spirits.

The eyes are tin, copper, or brass plates inserted in the sockets, the metal representing eyeballs, sight being permitted through small punctured holes.[13]

Old age is represented by grooves and by projecting, inserted teeth of the moose (see Pl. VII, D), or teeth carved in the mouth.

The lips are generally funnel shaped or carved in exaggeration to symbolize "blowing."

Facial types are characterized by (a) crooked nose and mouth, (b) laughing, and (c) big (keel) nose. The modifications in features are almost without limit. They follow the free play of conception in designing and the handicraft of the carver, governed by the nature of the dream or vision which prompts the production.

[13] The insertion of metal plates for eyes of masks as early as 1687 is indicated by a reference in a letter to M. Cabart de Villermont by Rev. P. Thièrry Bechefor from Quebec, "2 pieces of a kettle, very neatly fitted to it, and pierced with a small hole in the center represented the eyes," *nota bene!* (Jesuit Relations, Vol. 63, 1667-87, 289). For the above notice I am indebted to Dr. Loren C. Eiseley.

The combinations of color, hair, and facial expression are not prescribed. Features of the mask images not included in these categories are assumed to be variations dictated by the fancy of individual image makers, and have no formal meanings. In some cases the unusual and grotesque features seen on the masks of the Cayuga are attributed to imitation of features observed on masks among the Seneca. In other cases they are direct importations from the Seneca and Onondaga who, the Sour Springs people say, create more varied and fanciful forms than they do.[14]

The formal requirements of the mask dancers when engaged in their rites are that the natural hair be covered, that old tattered clothes be worn, and that an untrimmed, rough hickory staff be carried in one hand and the large turtle-shell rattle (Pl. XIV A) in the other. For the head covering a deerskin falling down over the back and tied in front is traditional (Pl. XII A), while a potato sack over the back of the head suffices for the present. A "hunchback" padding is also occasionally added to the shoulders. Plate V A and B shows False Face Society members posing in their performance attire.

The Sour Springs Cayuga do not seem to possess so numerous a series of beliefs and observances in relation to masks as those of the Lower Cayuga Long House of the Seneca on the same reserve. Nor are so many varied types of mask spirits represented in their mask pantheon. I would not attempt to suggest a reason for this condition.

Some further notes on the functionings of images may be included with these observations. The members of the False Face Society may secure and possess small mask-images corresponding to the regular-sized masks. Therefore, they occur in the form of the red, the black, the half-red half-black, and the white and corn-husk masks. The miniatures average from 1½ to 3½ inches in length and often have the horsehair and occasionally the tin-plate eye and the head strings, as do the regular masks. While they serve specifically as mediums of cure for dream persecution by mask spirits and will be discussed in a subsequent chapter on the Dream Guessing Rite (page 122), there are associations between them and the False

[14] The Sour Springs Cayuga seem to lack certain developments, according to Deskáheh, recorded for the Seneca by Parker and Skinner. For instance, for a mask to sweat, or to have talked to its owner, or to have fallen down as an omen of death is not known among them.

FIGURE 6.—Miniature wooden masks used in Dream Guessing Rite.

Face Society images to be outlined at this time. In general, the small masks are kept as semisecret possessions by their owners who, upon occasion, furnish them with conciliatory feasts and also supply them with offerings of little bags of tobacco—again like the big masks. The keepers of the small mask-images expose them by hanging them on the wall in the room in the presence of the big masks when the wearers of the latter come to perform their society rites, as a sign to the leader of the False Face Society that the person being treated is also a member of some False Face company. We are told that occasionally the small images serve as substitutes for the regular masks. A small mask may furthermore be more or less permanently attached to the forehead or upper side of a large mask when the owner has received one in the Dream Guessing Rite. The small masks, indeed, seem to fit into a number of conditions in the masking complex, not by any means thoroughly understood as yet by us or by our informants.

One of their rather definite functions is to serve as mediums of witchcraft for their owners. It is specifically stated that persons who dream of certain of the known mask personages accept the visitation as a sign that the spirit so appearing is ready to lend its services to the dreamer for the purposes of magic, whether they be for good or evil. This circumstance depends upon the will of the individual. Current Cayuga opinion points out that it is generally malevolent; whence the maskette is considered as *ut'kǫ́*, "witch male." Some cases will illustrate. One man owned a pair of small masks, a black and a red one (Fig. 7), which he obtained after seeing them in a dream. He kept them under his sleeping pillow and effected his will, optionally good or evil, by their aid—pure witchcraft. Another dreamed of the presence of twin corn-husk mask spirits. He made a pair of masks of corn husk (5 inches in diameter), tied them together, and kept them concealed. They carried out his "wishes" whenever he invoked them and burned the tobacco offering with a prayer—wishes governing affairs of love, success in healing, or injuring a rival (Fig. 8). These are in the class of witchcraft masks. Another set, of three masks,[15] one red, one black, and one half black half red, were kept by Andrew Thomas to ward off a return of nose bleeding, by an attack of which he nearly died early in life after seeing a False

15 In the collection of S. W. Pennypacker II.

Face behind a tree. The three maskettes represent the three "original" types and were feasted and given a burnt offering of tobacco at different periods, the tobacco being burned in a tiny basket carved out of a peach pit and kept with the maskette.

The "witch" maskettes, it may be noted, are traditionally carved without the mouth openings cut through. The only reason so far

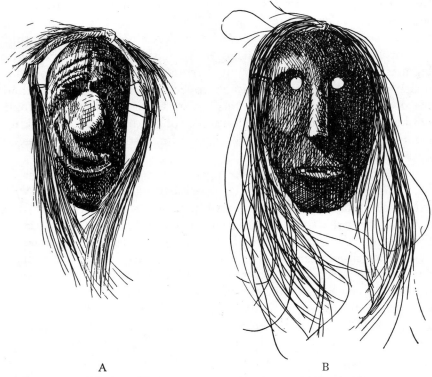

A   B

FIGURE 7.—Miniature Cayuga wooden masks used in Dream Guessing Rite. A Red. B Black.

vouchsafed for this negative constructional feature is the reason of traditional ruling—"that is the way they were always made."

A spirit form combining the miniature with the large mask—a manifestation of intensified evil—sometimes makes its appearance to the vision of a medicine man. This spirit form is characterized by the phenomenon of a small face appearing and disappearing in the hair of the large image, "evaporating on the tail itself (horsetail of the mask), here and there on the original masks in the olden days," to use the phraseology of John Buck. By evaporating he explained that it faded away at times before the sight when the mask was being used. The little mask tied to the hair is the symbol of this manifestation in the series of mask-images made and used by those who accept them. The specimen observed was a red, crooked-nosed, crooked-mouthed representation with wrinkles and long black mane. It came from the Lower Cayuga group. The little "evaporating"

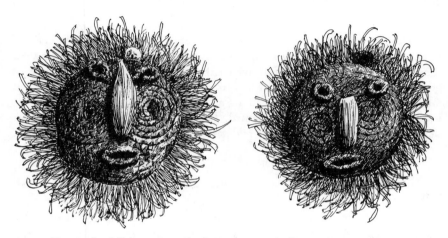

FIGURE 8.—Miniature corn-husk masks used in Dream Guessing Rite.

image (2½ in.) was also red. Its use is not reported in recent years among the Sour Springs people. A corresponding form occurs among the Onondaga of the Six Nations made of corn-husk and is discussed in an ensuing section of this chapter.[16]

Finally, in regard to those maskettes given to the patient as medicine when the spirit cause of dream persecutions has been guessed, we have specimens now available (Figs. 6, 7, 8, Pl. IX) to show the variations in feature, color, and composition which characterize them, as products of the handicraft of different spirit-impelled carvers.

[16] To the reader whose interest in phenomena of masks in native art expression may broaden into modern art, the following instance may be significant. As a cover design of *Vogue* (March 15, 1936) a color reproduction of a hydra-headed lady was painted by Tchelitchew, in which the artist has portrayed the face with two smaller faces on the left side peering from the subject's hair and neck. No comment on its symbolism, however, is given by the artist so we may only ponder the question of recurrence of similar expressions in two realms of art imagination.

Another medium through which destructive conjuring may effect its purpose by the use of the human face-image appears in a specimen brought to me in 1935 by a Mohawk of the reservation, who found it among the slabs of wood cut and sawed in the bush near the Lower Cayuga settlement. It is a crude outline of the human facial lineaments in natural size, cut with a knife into the bark of a living beech tree. The manner of functioning of this type of *ut'kǫ gagǫsa'*, "male-witch face image," as explained by old John Buck, was as follows:

If anyone carves a face on a tree and names it for the person he desires to harm, it will cause sickness to that person when he passes by and looks at it. The face is carved on a tree near where the intended victim is accustomed to go. Ordinarily no harm follows when looked at by others than the person it is intended for. Tobacco is offered in a fire as a sacrifice to the spirit within the image to "bewitch" the person named. It can, however, be induced to cause sickness to others if the conjuring malefactor urges it.

MASK CEREMONY FOR CURING IN HOMES

The False Face Societies perform only in case of serious illness. When other medicine has failed and the other societies have performed their rites for the sick person without success, then the False Faces are called in. The leading singer in such a case is a man of the opposite moiety from that of the person requesting the rite, while the assistant singer is of the same moiety. This is important. Sometimes when a person is ill he will dream of a False Face, a sign that if he calls on the members of that society to perform for him he will be cured. The performance of this rite is restricted to members and may be performed at any time of day or night to suit the convenience of the person who is being treated. Besides the mask, the garb of the dancers is for the most part made up of burlap bags or any ragged garments which they can obtain. Each dancer carries a large rattle made from the shell of a snapping turtle and some carry staffs of untrimmed hickory branches. Sometimes they are announced in the patient's home by the appearance of the Corn-husk Maskers (p. 93), who are referred to as "the forerunners of the Grand-fathers" (Wooden False Faces). The False Face dancers rub and hit the side of the house near the door with their rattles and make weird noises before entering. The sounds are nasal, like horses whinnying, and are said to be in imitation of the utterances which the "Grandfather" made when the Great Spirit made the mountain move close to him (p. 71). These noises are their sole utterances. They do not talk, but employ gestures. Upon entering they dance around and place the patient on a bench in the center of the room. The leader throws tobacco in the fireplace and gives a small amount to each member. They continue to sing and dance to the accompaniment of the large rattles which make a terrific noise. Some of the dancers go to the fire and scoop up the hot coals in their hands and rub the ashes on the patient's head. They also blow on the patient's head and neck. After the one or two singers have completed three or four songs, the mask-performers go outside, departing in a sortie of stamping and grunting. Then they re-enter and feed the patient with "False Face mush," which is made of parched corn meal to which has been added maple sugar and berries. The dancers also partake of this feast, which has been prepared by the members of the family of the person for whom they have performed. After this they depart, and when the person recovers from his illness he is then a *de facto* member of the society. Thereafter he must dance with the other members of the society when occasion arises, and he must also request the performance of the rites of the society at least once a year, usually at the time of the Midwinter Festival, when the societies' dances are performed in the Long House, to prevent the recurrence of illness. The foregoing is regarded as the formal procedure carried out only in private homes.

CEREMONY OF MASK SOCIETIES IN THE LONG HOUSE

In the public performance (*hanatui·'*) in the Long House, the burning of tobacco is omitted. In the informal observance of the rites of the False Face, the dancers do not wear masks and the members of the societies from the two groups, Wolf and Turtle, dance collectively. At the Midwinter Festival of the Sour Springs Cayuga Long House in February, 1933, was witnessed, among other ancient rites, the formal and informal ceremonies of the False Face societies. As has been previously outlined under Society Dances (pp. 54–59), these rites are performed in behalf of individuals who are ill, or prophylactically for those who have been cured formerly. The Society performs upon the request of the petitioners, presented

through an intermediary of the opposite moiety. The persons who
are to be treated are seated on a bench between the fires in the Long
House, behind the singer for the rite. The singer must be a False
Face Society member, but he wears no mask at the time. After a few
tense moments (during which all share a feeling of awe) there is
a scuffling outside the door, and as it is flung wide open the Husk
Mask dancers rush in. These little people (at the time of this
occasion, four boys ranging from eight to twelve years), wearing
masks woven out of corn-husks (Plts. VI B, and VIII) and long
trailing garments resembling female attire, precede the "Grandfathers" (False Faces). They too, form a separate society, which
functions in curing sickness in general. They perform in private
homes in the same way that the False Faces do except that they do
not carry rattles or staffs but mush-stirring paddles. The Husk Mask
Faces dance around and perform antics, much to the amusement of
the people. At this time they jump up above the heads of the patients
on the bench, blowing loudly upon their heads. This is the curing
act. They jump up and down behind the backs of the women patients
and blow upon their heads, making hissing sounds while grasping
the patients' heads in both hands and leaning over their backs. These
gestures and postures, imitative of the traditional False Face Beings,
have been misunderstood by some observers, which has caused the
False Face Rite to be described without reason as obscenely profane.

Then there are weird signals outside, and loud pounding on the
side of the Long House and on the door. The "Grandfathers," the
Wooden False Faces, have arrived and make a most dramatic entrance. Wearing the masks and tattered garb, the dancers, eight in
number, jump and fall in and some roll over and over on the floor,
making whinnying noises as they spring to their feet and dance
around the patients who are seated on the bench. The singer sits on
the bench singing the songs to the accompaniment of the turtle rattle,
while the mask dancers move about making all sorts of gestures,
completely under the spell of the mask-spirit. Meanwhile, as they
go back and forth from fire to fire, they plunge their hands into the
live coals and rub their hands together, and then take out ashes from
the fire and rub them on the heads of the patients. (See Fire Ordeal
in Mask Rite, p. 91.) They also blow on the patients. The dancers
and patients are given False Face mush, which has been furnished
by the members of the family of the persons who have requested

treatment by the Society. After this the dancers depart, while those for whom they performed take their places in the audience.

The informal or "partial performance" of the rite is called *djǫsi·dadi·'hǫs*. The members of the societies in both the Wolf and Turtle moieties dance collectively, do not wear masks, and sing twelve songs. If a member of the Wolf moiety requests the rite of the False Face Society, the members of the False Face Societies in the Turtle moiety lead the dance to the accompaniment of singing and rattling by Turtle moiety men, and the Wolf moiety people join them and vice versa. The mush is not served at this rehearsal.

The following instances are offered as being typical of the manner in which the members testify to the benefits of the Society.

Once a man struck at a False Face dancer when he came close to him in the Long House and danced in front of him. He said that the False Face dance was "nonsense." Soon he became ill and his people called in the False Face Society. They performed for the man and he was cured. Now he is a member of that society.

Another man (Lawrence Davis), a Mohawk associated with the Sour Springs Cayuga, who did not believe in the False Faces, had a son who was sick. He had been in the hospital in Brantford, and other doctors had failed to relieve the severe pains in his back. He was taken home after having been pronounced incurable. He could be comfortable only when resting against the bed with his knees on the floor. Finally the boy asked his father to get an Indian doctor. The father thought it would be of no use if medical doctors had failed. The son asked a second time for his father to send for an Indian doctor. The father consented. So the False Face Society was called in. They rubbed ashes on the boy and performed their dance, praying that the Great Spirit heal him so that he could "go on the road again." Then they left. Shortly after the dancers had left, the boy asked his father to hand him his shoes. His father told him that he could not walk. The boy said that the pain had stopped, and so his father got his shoes and the boy put them on and got up and walked around the room a little. The next morning he asked for his shoes and put them on and walked around the room. In a few days he went out of doors, and in a week he was "walking on the road again." (Both father and son devoutly attended the Long House in the Winter Ceremony, February, 1933.)

Another informant, Seymour Jamieson, tells of a False Face

Dance which he held in a private home to cure a baby who had a running ear. The dancers came in and rubbed ashes on the baby and its mother, because the baby was nursing. They had a feast after they had performed the ceremony. Jamieson also stated that when he was a small boy his grandmother became ill and the False Faces were called in. His family prepared a feast which included a pig's head. His parents would not allow him to be present at the ceremony because they were afraid that he would ridicule the False Faces; so he was sent to a neighbor's house to spend the night.

Another testimony is contained in the following tale, narrated by Wm. John.

How False Faces Make Themselves Known to Humans

"This is a true case, because it happened to my brother when he was a little boy. One time he went with mother and another woman to pick huckle-berries. The women were picking berries down in a swampy place and my brother was playing around. After awhile they heard him crying and calling to them. They went to where he was and he was on the ground in a weakened condition and his nose was bleeding. They knew that he had seen a false face. He had been playing in a clearing near a great pine tree that had been struck by lightning. When he could tell what he had seen he said that a false face had been looking at him from behind the tree, first one side, then the other. The women led the boy home and called in the False Face dancers. They came and put ashes on him and performed their ceremony and his nose didn't bleed again. After that he had to call for a False Face Dance every year.

"There is one event that happened in the year 1853 (!). The red mask was seen in the forest on our reserve near the Cayuga Long House. A man really saw a masked man whose hand and rattle was all in one, by which is meant that the red-masked man's arm was a rattle where his hand should have been.

"Another story. A man was walking along when he heard a rattle. He stopped and looked around. He saw the red-masked man look around from a basswood tree. His nose also bled but was cured when he called in the red mask of the False Face Society." (Contributed by Mrs. John L. Buck.)

The recurrence of nose-bleeding as an affliction caused by the Mask Spirits is an outcome of the encounter between the mythical False Face and the Creator, in the course of which the former had his nose and mouth distorted, as we have already learned.

A still broader vista of historical relationship between masking performances of tribes in the Eastern area lies behind what has just been discussed concerning Cayuga mask symbolism.

The wooden mask as a Forest Spirit associated with game animals seems prominent in Delaware teaching and to a certain degree in Cayuga. In the Cayuga it is brought out in the Mask Dance garb of Jerry Aaron, Deer sib (clan) of the Turtle moiety, whose outfit includes, in addition to the mask, an entire deerskin tanned and worn in the manner of the deerskin hunting decoy. The head of the animal covers the head of the wearer, the ears in place, the eye holes sewed up, and a short cow horn fastened on each side below the ears. Thus the deerskin serves as a head and back covering for the Mask Dancer. Questioning revealed that this garb is traditional, though Aaron did not directly associate his wearing of the horned deerskin with the Mask Spirit beyond referring to the understanding in general that the Mask Spirit is associated with the forest and its life. Aaron is shown in Plate V, B posed in the Mask Society garb referred to. The upturned horns of the deerskin decoy denote the chief, or leader, of the False Face Society. The moose teeth protruding from the mouth of the mask denote the age of the "Grandfather" (mask), as do the white wrinkles on the forehead of the mask. It would be interesting, in further research on the subject of Mask associations among the Iroquois, to trace deeper connections here between the Mask Spirit and Game Animal control, particularly as focused upon the deer as it is met with in Delaware belief.[17]

THE FIRE ORDEAL IN THE MASK RITE

An observation of striking importance in connection with the master power bestowed by the mask upon the individual who formally wears it now remains to be treated. I refer to the apparent immunity of the wearer to the effects of contact with coals of fire into which the members of the Wooden Mask Society frequently thrust their bare hands, simulating motions of washing them. This is done when they scoop up ashes from the fire-place in the Long House to rub on the heads of patients undergoing treatment. It means, in short, that among other "miraculous" powers invested in

[17] For suggestive remarks on the complex of masked shamanism in ethnographic perspective in the Northeast, also raising the question of Iroquois and Algonkian (Delaware) relationships in the comparison of their masked rituals, see Fenton, 1941 405, Harrington, 1921, 32-5, and Speck, 1931, 37, 137.

the wearer of the mask, such as ability to see with unusual clearness through the small eyeholes and the like, we have among the Cayuga what corresponds remotely to the "fire ordeal" referred to in several instances among North American tribes.[18] Especially conspicuous in this connection is the now classical account given by John Lederer in 1672. Referring to Santee (Catawba) priests in South Carolina, Lederer wrote,

"These miserable wretches are strangely infatuated with illness of the devil; it caused no small horror in me to see one of them wrythe his neck all on one side, foam at the mouth, stand barefoot upon burning coal for near one hour, and then recovering his senses, leap out of the fire without hurt or sign of any." (Lederer, pp. 17-18)

It would seem that this feature of the mask performances has been neglected by most authorities except Fenton,[19] who have recorded observations on the mask rites of the Iroquois, although it is frequently marveled at in the Jesuit narratives! The following observations, then, covering performance of the mask rite in 1933 at the Sour Springs Long House in connection with the Midwinter Festival of the Cayuga, will fix this trait as a present-day ceremonial. It should be given due weight. On the day that the Mask Society performed, the members plunged their hands in the glowing embers which lay several inches deep just back of the hearth. The performer first observed was less than fifteen feet away at the fire-place of the Turtle side of the house. He made no effort to avoid being burned; in fact, he seemed in his excitement to be unaware of the danger incurred. Several of the Indians sitting on the benches uttered exclamations when it happened. The ensuing evening when an oppor-

[18] For the Central Algonkian and the Plains Indians the references are abundant, as will be seen by referring to.Dr. Michelson's collection of sources (Michelson, 1932, pp. 13-14).

[19] In a synopsis of the characteristics of Iroquois masked medicine societies he calls attention to Champlain's account of the Huron Oki, or medicine man of 1616 who, although not always masked, handled hot coals and blew ashes on his patient and to his own observations of the Society of Faces among the Seneca of Allegany Reservation juggling hot stones or hot ashes while curing the patient and suffering no injury from plunging bare hands into the fire, and concludes by quoting a graphic account and reproducing a painting by a Seneca of the Tonawanda band who describes and portrays the mask wearer rubbing hot ashes between his palms and scooping up live coals, his hands protected from the burning embers by the power of the mask (Fenton, 1941, pp. 413, 421, 425, 428, and Pl. 25). The handling of live embers and hot ashes by the Iroquois doctor has also been noted by others (Keppler, 1941, p. 27).

tunity came to bring up the matter for discussion, William John, who was one of the masked company at the time, declared that the occurrence was a common thing, and that they neither knew nor cared whether they seized coals, and that they were never burned. Deskáheh, as well as other members, endorsed the observation, adding that they did not hesitate to pick up the live coals and rub them around as though washing the hands with them.[20]

"THE TRAVELING RITE" OF THE WOODEN FALSE FACE AND CORN-HUSK MASK SOCIETIES

The combined performance of the rites of these two societies is called ǫkiˑ'sot tanadáweniye, "Grandfathers traveling," and takes place about the first of May, or "as soon as the ground dries up," according to Cayuga informants. The purpose of this ceremony, which lasts one day, is to thank the "Grandfathers" (False Faces) for blessings received and to ask that they continue to bless their grandchildren by curing their ills and driving away the evil spirits that cause illness. Formerly it was customary in the Sour Springs Settlement for the members of the societies to go from house to house, the members of the Husk Mask Society preceding the False Faces ("Grandfathers"). The Husk Mask performers went ahead and notified the members of the household that the "Grandfathers" were coming. When the latter arrived, they went into all the rooms, making peculiar whinnying noises and beating on the sides of the house with their great turtle shell rattles. This was to cleanse the house so that the members of the family would be immune to disease. The leader invokes the spirit of the False Face and throws some tobacco into the fire. Then they depart, going to the Long House. The Husk Faces announce the arrival of the "Grandfathers," who enter singing the False Face marching song. This is followed

[20] In the winter of 1946, Deskáheh in discussing the handling of embers, affirmed the account and referred to the episode in the origin legend of the False Face Society in which the Evil Spirit was overcome by the Great Spirit who proved his superior power as controller of the universe. The narrative recounts how the Evil Spirit in submitting to his rival asked to be permitted to remain on earth, saying "I want to introduce the tobacco offering ceremony in memory of both of us to help my grandchildren (mankind)." The Great Spirit granted his request to give power to the members of the Wooden False Face Society to drive away disease and to handle hot coals and ashes without injury by reason of the "unseen power" resident in the face images.

by the False Face Dance, after which everyone present gives some tobacco to the leader, who in turn gives a small handful to each dancer. The leader addresses the people, reciting the promise of the "Grandfather" to help his grandchildren, and asking that he continue to serve the people through his aids. When he has finished, six of the False Face songs are sung, after which they are changed to the informal or "unmasked" songs. Then the "Grandfathers" dance around and try to induce the members of the audience to join the dance. Nonmembers accepting this invitation confer a favor on the society by expressing through participation their desire to help the afflicted. In conclusion, the Husk Faces sing two or three songs of the Husk-Face Society Dance series.

The abandonment of the spring procession of the False Faces through the village has marked a change in the rite; the False Face societies now concentrate their healing and disease-scourging performance in a rite in the Long House. After gathering about 100 paces from the Long House they enter by the west door, all wearing their masks with the exception of the leader, who is barefaced. He carries a walking stick with a small face carved at the bend of the handle. (The specimen shown in Plate XI, D has been used in this capacity for some years.) The face on the cane shown in the illustration is stained yellow, with a lock of hair attached as a miniature of the regular-sized False Faces, and the entire stick is stained black. As they march in, the leader, striking time with his cane, sings until he reaches the fire in the Long House on the "female side," the east end, opposite where they entered.

In the curriculum of the performances of the False Face Society, the spring rite of exorcism figures conspicuously as part of the proceeding; visitation of the homes of families in the Long House community in full masked costume takes place. Both the Wooden False Face and the Corn-Husk Mask Societies function at this time. Assembling at the Long House they are conducted by their leaders from house to house, repeating their ritual in each. The Corn-Husk Mask Society members precede the Wooden False Face group going down the road and entering the homes first as their "messengers." The latter exorcise disease from the premises by taking wood-ashes from the home-fire, scattering the purifying ashes about, entering each room of the dwelling, rubbing the woodwork with their large snapping-turtle rattles and voicing their nasal whinnies. When the individual homes have been visited and spiritually disinfected by the masked companies they return to the Long House and the rite is over. The whole procession going and coming is accompanied with the songs appropriate to the False Face Societies and using the large turtle rattles.

It happens that the rule of visiting the individual houses of communicants is often replaced now among the Sour Springs Cayuga by the performance of the rite in the Long House. The False Face Society members, appropriately garbed and masked, assemble and march into the Long House led by an officer who is not masked but who carries the walking stick previously described (Plate XI, D). Some remarks on this substitution rite have just been given.

CORN-HUSK MASK SOCIETY

The functions and properties of this society have been referred to in several paragraphs in a preceding section (p. 88). The general character of the society seems to be symbolical of associations with the spirits of growing grains, corn, and corn foods. Men and women are members, some of them hardly more than children. They perform when called upon to cure sickness of almost any nature, practicing in the home of the patient at any time, wearing the corn-husk masks and burning tobacco. When appearing in the series of society dances in the Long House, the so-called informal dances, they join in with the Wooden False Face dancers without masks, and also in the Round Dance, Kadā'trot (Table 3, Group III). Acting in conjunction with the Wooden False Face Society as fore-runners or "messengers," they have been mentioned in several places as an auxiliary body to the "Grandfathers." As the saying explains, "they go ahead to notify and prepare the people for the coming of the great ones."[21]

[21] An exceptionally dramatic performance of the Corn-Husk Mask "spirits" as announcers is the one performed during the Midwinter Ceremony of the Canadian Seneca at Six Nations, on the evening of Feb. 1st, 1936, on the fourth day of the great annual ceremony, at the end of the curing society rites. While not forming a part of the Sour Springs Cayuga program, it seems too stirring to ignore in this connection and worthy of at least a footnote. The description is by Mrs. John L. Buck.

First a naked husk-mask knocked at the Long House door at the Turtle side. The person in mask was John Panever, naked except for breech cloth and husk-mask helmet. He delivered a note. The note said there was a man husk-mask named Corn-Pounder and a husk-mask named Black Corn who were coming: The speaker (Turtle moiety) added, saying to the people, to treat them well when they came. The messenger went away and did not come in. The man made a speech and told the people what the note said. Then the two husk-masks announced by the messenger came in, and

The following story of the Corn-Husk Mask Society is narrated by John Buck.

Origin Tale of Corn-Husk Mask Society and Songs

Some hunters of the Cayuga tribe anciently discovered the Husk-Mask spirit. There were once two hunters camping in a far-away place. One day as usual they went hunting in different directions. And as usual when leaving camp they threw a big chunk of wood on the fire to last all day. One of the hunters came back to camp before the other and was "staring at the coals to revive the fire" (sic!). He stood up suddenly, for he heard something rustling like leaves blown by the wind. But no tree was near and no wind there! The sound of rustling continued. Then he looked downhill and saw a peculiar person stooping down. The person was wearing a corn-husk mask covering his head and face. He was shaking the dry husks of the mask by a motion of the head, which made the rustling noise. The hunter asked the person what he was around there for. The husk-masked person answered, "I came here to get some corn bread and you have some here made with blueberries. I am very hungry and we love it. I would like to get some. Tomorrow go downhill and you will see a deer which I shall drive toward you." "Where did you come from?" asked the hunter. The Husk Mask answered, "We live down a valley. There lies our settlement." (The hunter complied with his desire and carried out his instructions. That is the story. So they adopted the corn-husk mask to satisfy that Being. It was through this hunter that the songs heard from the stranger dressed up in "corn tassels" were introduced among those to whom he taught them and who joined him in their celebration.)

---

these were the man and woman referred to. (The male wore a tightly fitting husk-mask with long drooping nose and no ruff or mane around the face. The female wore a large husk-mask with thick bushy border and black fur tufts for eyebrows and moustache. A spot of red paint was on each cheek.)

The message they had was that the planting of this year was to yield a good crop. Then they went out the Turtle moiety door, the same as they had come in. They had whispered the message to him and the officer-speaker told the people.

Then the Husk-Mask Society came in. There were twenty of them, young and old. They danced awhile around outside the stoves, the singer on the bench. The naked messenger was with them, last in line; the man next, the woman husk-mask third from last. There was a woman from each moiety who made a short speech, and then two women from the Turtle moiety, and two from the Bear moiety made speeches offering tobacco and corn bread which the Society maskers were to get in the spring when they came around again (about April after the frost is out of the ground).

The Wooden False Faces came in after the Husk-Masks went out. The False Faces danced awhile (about fifteen of them) around the benches. Then two women from the Turtle and two from the Bear moiety offered them Indian tobacco and mush which they would get in the spring when they came around again.

The False Faces and Husk-Masks will come together in the spring. First they will go from house to house to drive away disease before they go to the Long House. Then they will receive the offering of tobacco and mush they were promised.

Mrs. Buck adds: "The temperature on the evening of this ceremony was but a little above zero. The naked husk-mask messenger was abroad, back and forth on his mission, for about half an hour. The following day I sent inquiries to learn if the performer had suffered ill effects. His answer was that he had not even felt the cold particularly."

The words of one of the songs of the Corn-Husk Mask ritual refer to the event just described, and their meeting is made clear only to those who have heard the legend recited. The words are, "The position he was in when singing was stooping over." We can understand how the spirit becomes associated in the Cayuga mind not only with the maize but with the control of the deer.

The Husk-Mask performers frequently handle ashes and rub them upon the heads of those being treated for illness, accompanying the act with blowing on the head, as do the Wooden False Faces. Only men and boys wear the corn-husk masks in the Long House curing rites.

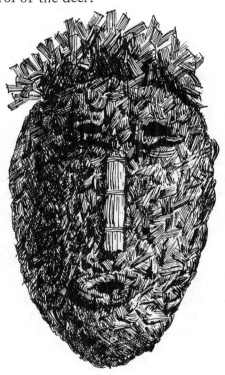

There are further notes to be added to the observations on corn-husk masks, showing that distinctions prevail in respect to their size and functions similar to those of the wooden masks. Besides the full-sized face mask, there is a middle-sized and a miniature-sized image. The middle-sized mask (6-7 inches) is that used in conjuring, and the smallest is used in the Dream-Guessing Rite (Fig. 9). They may

FIGURE 9.—Miniature corn-husk mask used in Dream Guessing Rite.

function as substitutes for the regular full-sized corn-husk masks, as do the miniature wooden images in relation to the regular wooden masks.

The corn-husk masks (*katci·'ʻsaʻ*, "husk woven") are of several types (Pl. VIII), as follows.

All are of braided and sewed corn-husk strips. The weaving permits a fringe of bristly ends to surround the face resembling a mane which distinguishes many of them. Similar tufts of fringed bristles form eyebrows and sometimes chin-whiskers. All are "pop-eyes" and have pointed, pursed mouths with small openings.

The main variations are, (a) with braided nose, (b) with single-piece stuffed nose (Pl. VIII, C); (c) with puffy cheeks (Pl. VIII, B); (d) with "medicine" drops, small packets of powdered herbs, attached to eyes, nose, lips (Pl. VIII A); and (e) the exceptional and striking "helmet" type, which has the braided netting continued around the rear to enclose the entire head (Pl. VIII D). There is no definite legend so far known to explain these variations in formal terms, except that the larger ones with manes are the "oldest," the "leaders."

Like the wooden images, all are provided with the little tobacco-sacrifice bags on the foreheads.

Like the wooden-mask wearers, those who perform in the Corn-Husk Mask Society cover the rear of the head with sacks or old cloth. They do not carry any rattle or staff but are provided with mush-stirring paddles from the kitchens, or sticks of wood, with which they strike upon the benches or floor of the Long House to make a din. The garb of these dancers is the long dress, often white, indicative of the female, although they are males, generally young boys and even children, as in the case of the ceremonies of 1933.

The foregoing remarks relate chiefly to the chorus masks of the Corn-Husk Mask Society. There are several types of solo corn-husk masks not associated with the rites of the society. They function only when brought out of the dark background of the spirit pantheon through apparitions appearing to persons, in which instances they become a source of affliction. For relief, the likeness of the spirit is produced in corn-husk false face form, a feast to the specific spirit-force is given, tobacco is burned for sacrifice, and songs are chanted. The two solo types given here, are specific. And there may, indeed, be others to be learned of as the secret life of the Long House groups is divulged.

The Flower Spirit is personified in the "smiling blossom" (*awahayóde*) mask.[22] Its appearance to an individual in a dream or vision is an omen that the spirit of the blossom desires a sacrifice of to-bacco and a feast. Then the dreamer borrows a corn-husk mask of the "smiling blossom" type or has one made if it is not available in the

[22] The plant in question is probably Burr Marigold, *Bidens* (sp.?), according to Dr. J. M. Fogg, University of Pennsylvania. That it is regarded by the Cayuga as a strong medicinal agency is important to note in its connection with the mask-spirit series.

settlement. A singer, the mask-wearer, and the patient are the masters-of-ceremony, and others are invited to participate in the sacrifice. It is not a stated society rite. The festival over, the mask is put away and kept by the sponsor to prevent a recurrence of the visitation. Several specimens have been obtained from the Lower Cayuga and the Seneca at Six Nations. No occasion has arisen among the Sour Springs Cayuga in recent years to call for the fulfillment of this rite, wherefore the source of this information has been the Lower Cayuga group. The Seneca also employ it. The corn-husk mask in question is not distinct from those of the regular Corn-Husk Society type, except in possessing the feature of a pink artificial "blossom" on the upper side portion of the face (left is specified, though one specimen obtained has several tissue paper flowers in black and red on the right side). The image may be smaller (7 inches in height) than a normal mask. In this case the maskette is not necessarily worn but may be hung up during the rite and preserved afterwards.

Another solo corn-husk mask-image of malevolent portent appearing to persons and requiring the propitiatory feast and mask construction is a *ut'kǫ́ katci·''sa*, "witch corn-husk," characterized by having a miniature corn-husk face-image fastened to its upper left side. It is defined as an evil spirit-force, which dissolves while being gazed at by the victim of its choice. Again we turn from the Sour Springs Cayuga, who seem to have been free in recent years from its baneful visitations, to the Onondaga for the data presented and for the specimens (Pl. VIII C). The Onondaga have preserved this representation more distinctly as an equivalent of the "smiling blossom" image just described. This specific type of image may also be made in the full size and in miniature, as the figures show.

The two latter images do not funcon in Long House ceremonies but only when called for in specific private rites.

Another force of the Corn-Husk spirit family which at times reveals itself to a medicine-man is the double spectre of the "twin-spirits," who lend their service to the fulfillment of purposes of witchcraft. They are represented by a pair of the middle-sized corn-husk masks, 5 inches in height, tied together, and made and kept in concealment by one who dreams of them and prays to them in working schemes of witchcraft.

Another spiritual agency of wish-accomplishment is the undressed corn-husk doll, a full-body figure of a person from 6 to 7 inches in length, made of folded and braided corn-husk. In certain specimens the head is formed of a dried apple. The hands and feet are left loose in long tangled shreds, whence one of its names, "loose feet." The spirit and its doll representative go by the name of *dĭ·ʹyǫ̆sĭ·dɛs*, "long foot," from the peculiarity of its physique. It is said that the doll represents a spirit who is friendly to children, granting their wishes in various forms of play: "Anything the child wishes for, the 'Long Foot' will bring," is the Cayuga nursery saying. Its services seem not to be employed in the machinations of the witch-conjuror or medicine man.

CLASSIFICATION OF WOODEN AND CORN-HUSK MASKS

The arrangement of mask forms in the accompanying table (4), based upon the handling of material as carried on in a museum, is an artificial one but unavoidable, since no fixed classification according to type exists in the minds of the people. Among them, the variations in color and structure arise through function. Function is determined by the dispositions of spirit entities who reveal themselves in visions. The differences in form are therefore inevitably vague. We may, nevertheless, indulge in the traditional diversion of the museum-trained ethnologist, as long as we take care that the features of native culture involved are not misconstrued. The table accordingly represents one attempt at schematic arrangement.

MEDICINE MEN'S SOCIETY AND THE "PIG" MASK

The Cayuga call the Medicine Men's Society *hanai·ʹtus*. The term is a very ancient one and Deskáheh could not translate it. Two other ancient terms were given as names for this society. It is said that *odjistauwę̆drowā́nɔs*, "big rattles," was a name applied to the society, because its members carried large pumpkin rattles when performing. The third term, *onaʿtci·nā́ʿkɛsǫ*,[23] "keeper of the bones of an animal," has reference to the bones of a mythical animal which had horns. The horns or bones of the creature were procured and kept by the members of the society and have been handed down as the secret property of the medicine men. This medicine is called *kanuʹda* and is believed to be very powerful. In case of a serious illness, when other practitioners have failed to effect a cure, treatment

---

[23] This term corresponds to the Mohawk for "doctors," whence the popular name for the society on the Six Nations Reserve, where Mohawk is the common language.

TABLE 4

MASK TYPES AND FUNCTIONS

	CHORAL MASKS (USED IN CURING—SOCIETY RITES)	SOLO (USED IN CURING, PROTECTION, WITCHCRAFT RITES)		
	LARGE, OR FACE SIZE	LARGE, OR FACE SIZE	SMALLER, NOT WORN	MINIATURE, KEPT AS CHARMS
Wood	Red (Original Spirit) crooked-nosed, crooked-mouthed laughing big-lipped black horsetail "hair"	Red (Dissolving Witch) crooked-nosed, crooked-mouthed, miniature red mask attached	Red, same as choral type, no mouth opening (goes with following as pair)	Same as choral types
	Black (Modified Spirit) crooked-nose, crooked-mouth laughing big-lipped black horsetail "hair" corn-husk "hair"		Black, same as choral type, no mouth opening	Same as choral types
	White (Messenger Spirit) corn-husk border "hair" black horsetail "hair"			Same as choral types
		Black-and-Red (Whirlwind Spirit)	Same	Same
	Four Brothers (Wind Spirits) company of four red and black forms	Black-and-White ("Pig" Spirit) Yellow, red-spotted (Small-pox Spirit)		
	(Leaders of each type, larger and wrinkled, often with gray horse-tail "hair")	Red, emaciated, deathhead (Fever Spirit)		
Corn-Husk	Plain (Corn Spirit) fringe, bristling border woven nose lump nose "medicine drops" on nose, eyes extra large, "leader" "helmet" type	Same with artificial flower ("Smiling Blossom" Spirit) Same with miniature attached (Dissolving Witch)	Pair of same (Twin Spirits) Same Same	Same as choral types
	Long-Nose (Messenger Spirit, male) Red-cheeked, fur moustache (female) (companion to preceding)	Same with artificial flower		

by the members of the Medicine Men's Society will restore the person to normal health. It was also a medicine for warriors in former times, and if a man were dangerously wounded, someone who had in his possession some of this medicine or a piece of the magic bone would treat the wounded man and he would recover. Formerly the rites were secret, and at the present time it is a decidedly restricted group society. It is difficult to find an individual who knows the method of procedure or one who will talk freely about the society. Before giving the notes on the treatment of a patient by the "doctors," I shall present the origin of the society as it was given by Deskáheh.

Origin of Hanai·'tus

Long ago before the existence of the League and before Hiawatha had made peace among the tribes, the Indians used to take scalps. The man who had the most scalps on a pole outside his house was regarded as a "king." There was at that time a good hunter who had never taken a scalp. He was a kind man, and when he had any meat or other food left from a meal he would take it into the woods and leave it as an offering. He would say, "I am leaving this to be consumed." One day he was overtaken by a party of invaders and scalped. They left him there in the woods, thinking he was dead. While he was in that state he had a vision in which he saw all the wild animals. They seemed to be having a meeting, and he could hear them talking. One of the animals said to the others, "Who will go after his scalp?" The raven said, "I will." But the other animals said that if the raven went he would consume the scalp. The hawk was the next to offer his services, and they let him go. The hawk flew off and finally he reached the settlement where the man's scalp was hanging on a pole. He secured the scalp and took it back to the place where the animals were holding their meeting. The hawk gave the scalp to the animals, and they put it on the man's head. Then they put all of the different kinds of herb medicines around him. They put more on one side of the man. Then the animals gave thanks for many days by singing songs. As the animals sat around singing, the man would often hear the leader say, "Watch out, he is coming back to life." The man felt that he was regaining consciousness. As soon as he moved, the animals knew that he had regained consciousness, and they all disappeared so that he would not see them. He was then able to turn over, and by so doing he covered the medicines that were under his body on that side. At last he was cured and able to return to the village where he told his people how the animals had cured him and revealed the medicine plants to him. That is how the medicines were given to the people.

Deskáheh said that at the present time certain men are the cus-
todians of the secret medicine. These men are members of the society
and are chosen because of their age and good characters. In case
a person is seriously ill and the other societies have failed to cure him,
or if he has met with an accident and something must be done immediately, the Medicine Men's Society is called upon to treat him.
Three men are appointed to go to the Medicine Men and tell them
about the person who is in need of treatment. The men take with
them as an offering three yards of white or light cloth and some
tobacco. Two of the Medicine Men, upon hearing of the case, will
leave immediately and go to the sick person. They administer some
of their secret medicine, and at the end of three days if the patient
does not show signs of improvement he is given a double dose of the
medicine. During the period of treatment the patient must not see nor
hear the voice of a stranger. Should a stranger (one outside of the
immediate family) enter the room the sick person would die. A
woman must be past middle age to care for persons being treated by
the Medicine Men. Only broth made from flour and water is given
to a person during the period of treatment. When the "doctors"
pronounce the patient out of danger and a decided improvement is
noticed in his condition, the secret medicine is not given any longer,
and the members of the Medicine Men's Society are called in to have
a feast and sing songs of praise to the Creator, the animals as healing
forces, and the Spirit of Medicine, the last or which they refer to as
"our grandmother." For the feast, white chickens are killed and
cooked; white beans are also cooked for the ceremony. First, the
songs referring to the spirit governing the medicinal plants are sung,
and then the songs for the various animal spirits are sung. The latter
are referred to as the "real songs of the society." There are three
types of songs. (See Appendix, Nos. 15 and 16 for the transcriptions
of those recorded.) A final song is chanted, and those present engage
in a dance with it. Then the feast is served. While this is a society
for men only, it is said that "in the beginning a woman was the
custodian of the large pumpkin rattles.

The Pig Mask is used by the members of this society. This type
of mask is old and rare. Since it dates back to the period of mythical
animals through its connection with the Medicine Men's Society, it
may be safe to assume that it is a representation of one of the animals
of that period and that in later times it became known as the "Pig

Mask."[24] The Cayuga regard the force residing in the Pig Mask to be extraordinarily powerful and attribute "miraculous" cures to the performances of the society when this mask is used by one of its members in an emergency which calls for it.

The following abstract of a tale narrated by Levi Baptiste (a Cayuga) in February, 1934, gives another version of the origin legend of the "bone medicine" and explains the function of Pig Mask.

Origin of the Hunter's Medicine and Use of the Pig Mask

There were two hunters (in mythical times) who, when they went hunting, took with them a man to prepare and carry their food while they were tracking and killing the game. They always secured an abundance of game because they had the hunter's power over the various animals as their medicine (which was known only to them). The hunting medicine consisted of the bones and parts of all the different animals. When they started out they spread out upon the ground pieces of the meat and other food provided for them by the extra man they took with them, and they scraped the bones they carried in their hunting medicine bundle. In this lay their success.

One day the man, who had on different occasions observed what the magical hunters did, said to his grandmother: "Prepare me a lunch. I think I can hunt." "You cannot hunt, you do not know how," said the grandmother. "Yes I can; fix me a lunch," replied the man. So she did it and he started off.

He went into the woods and cleared a space on the ground. He placed there bits of meat cut into chunks, as he had seen the hunters do, and sang the songs he learned from them. And the different animals came down from the air and gathered from the ground and began to eat of his feast. All the creatures came. Then when they had enough, the man started out and soon killed a deer. He took some more of the meat and spread another feast on the ground for the animals and they came and ate. Then he went home to his grandmother and gave her the deer to cook. "See," said he, "I have learned how to hunt." Thenceforth he became a successful hunter, because he followed the rules he had learned in providing a feast for all the creatures each time he went out. *This is how man learned how to hunt the animals.* A hunting medicine was prepared from the bones of different animals.

Finally one time he went hunting, and while he was preparing the usual

---

[24] The expression *hedǫhcyút'tadièskǫ'*, "in front that formerly was," referring to the pig's head, alluded to an extinct animal with a long snout: a long-nosed monster. Various conjectures may be made as to whether it was a bear or a mythical creature. Fenton has a similar idea of the prototype of the pig in Iroquois cultural history (Fenton, 1940, 230, fn. 27).

feasts for the animals of the air and the earth, a branch of a tree fell and struck him on the head. He fell down as though dead. When the animals came around and saw him lying there dead they were sorry for their friend and wanted to revive him. So they formed a circle around him. Each one then took a turn and danced around his body, singing his own song. And the man began to show signs of life by breathing, and soon he opened his eyes. Then the raven, when his turn came, went up to him and tried to pick out his eyes, croaking all the while.[25] Soon the hunter-man came to life, and the animals carried him back to his grandmother's house, and he recovered. So things went on.

Finally the hunter was taken sick and the animals learned of it. They came to where he was and danced around him again, all but several who were absent. This time, however, he did not recover. He passed away. But the hunting medicine he had got possession of was handed down to his descendants.[26] This is the origin of the Cayuga hunting medicine.

The hunter's medicine not only gives power to the hunter, as it did originally, but it causes the recovery of those who have been injured by violence, falls, accidents, or wounds. It is brought into use by those who form the society owning it and is administered to the injured when the society is called upon to effect cures in serious cases.

The members of the society perform over the patient by singing the songs of the different animals in a room or apartment where they are secreted with the patient. No outsider is permitted to be present. There are other restrictions, among which are the requirements that no meat be cooked in the house while the patient is there and that in the feast of corn-mush provided for the members of the Society after the ceremony at the side of the injured one, no salt be mixed with the corn meal. Furthermore, the room where the rite is performed is kept as dark as possible. Tobacco is burned as an offering to the animals. Should an outsider enter the place, tobacco must again be burned to purify him.

Of especial importance is the rite of *passing around among the members present a cooked pig's head*. The head is passed around in a trencher and is eaten with the teeth, no knife being used in securing a portion. When the member bites or tears off his share, *he croaks*

25 This is a well-known habit of the raven, a carrion eater, and became the habitual pattern.

26 It is said to be still in possession of members of the Medicine Men's Society among the Cayuga, who use it, as we shall see, to restore those who have been seriously injured.

like a raven, as did the raven at the original feast when the dead hunter was revived.

The rite of eating the pig head is the *fulfillment of the belief in the pig head mask as a curative medicine* for the restoration of the seriously injured. The pig-head mask is part of the "medicine" employed.

We may now note the result of questioning and observation among the Cayuga of the Grand River Reserve regarding the pig-head mask.

The pig-head mask is apt to be called into use at any time by friends of the victim of a serious accident. Therefore such a mask is kept constantly in readiness by some of the mask makers. It is highly valued. A number of cases are reputed where the power of the pig mask has saved the life of injured and hopelessly ill persons given up for dead by other doctors, white as well as Indian. The mask may appear in Long House rites worn by one of the dancers of the Wooden False Face Society.[27] It is not, however, necessarily worn on the face by any members of the Doctors Society when treating a patient.

A tradition comes from the Six Nations Seneca Long House group, evidently relayed from the Seneca at Cattaraugus, N. Y., that a long time ago this nation obtained knowledge of the rites of the Medicine Men's Society and some of the medicine itself from the Cherokee. Whatever the historical value of such an explanation of origin may be, it is to be noted that there is a tale among the Cherokee which accounts for the source of a magic cure-all from the scales and bones of a monster Stone Coat. The tale is a prominent explanatory myth in Cherokee, relating how the medicine songs and formulas emanated from the remains of the monster when he was burned sacrificially after his death at the hands of a party of magicians. Examination of the series of songs recorded from both groups, after transcriptions have been completed by Dr. Herzog, may provide a test for this claim in Seneca tradition.

Theory of the Origin of the "Pig" as a Medicine Power

The pig, known to the Iroquois only after the coming of Europeans, is thought by some to be derived from a prototype represent-

---

[27] Deskáheh once asserted that the pig mask was not supposed to enter the performances in the Long House; owing, inferably, to Handsome Lake's teaching.

ing a prehistoric mythical monster having long tusks and a long hard snout, small eyes, and a white face. What the original could be has not been definitely suggested. Some imagine it to have been a kind of bear, a monster, and from the myths of the people (notably the far northern Algonkian, the Delaware and the Munsee), this idea may be entertained as a possibility. The Medicine Men's Society is indeed thought to have originally passed a cooked bear's head around among its members when in session and the flesh was bitten from it with their teeth. Tradition at the present is, however, vague on the point (see p. 104 fn. 24). The secrecy of the Medicine Men's Society is a shield against too free disclosure of its mysteries and notions.[28] That surrounding the Pig Masks is such that some of the Cayuga chiefs, Deskáheh for instance, profess ignorance of their use and existence.

The two specimens represented in Plate VII (A,B), are of masks observed among the Cayuga in recent years. The material is maple and elm. In one mask the mane is of goat's hair, in another of horse tail (B); the third has a forehead tuft of curly wool (A). In all, the prevailing color is black on the upper parts, forehead, and eyes, and white elsewhere on the face and snout. Two have tin plates for the eyes. The third lacks the tin eyes, and has high prominent ears. Tusks, either of wood or actual tooth, are present in all. In one (Pl. VII, B) a noteworthy feature is a movable tongue protruding from the mouth, attached by a thong to the inner palate. They all have small bags of sacrifice tobacco attached to the top, and they are greased. The tobacco is renewed at times to "entertain" or feast them.

It was learned in 1939 from *Sadegą'hɛs* (Jeremiah Aaron) that in connection with the rites of the Medicine Men's Society several other types besides the Pig Mask are used. Whereas the latter rep-

---

[28] Aside from the information incorporated in these notes, which are drawn strictly from Cayuga sources, much light will undoubtedly be thrown upon the intricacies of the rite when comparative material from the other Iroquois has been assembled. To be checked up against the term given by Deskáheh (p. 104, fn. 24) is a term "Quisquis," or Hog, mentioned in generalized Iroquois folk lore as a "monster which gave the Onondagas great trouble, as did also the great bear, the horned water-serpent, the stone giants, and many other equally fabulous inventions" (J. V. H. Clark, Vol. 1, p. 43). See also H. R. Schoolcraft (p. 59) and W. M. Beauchamp (pp. 3-4). In these tales the "Big Quisquis" invaded the country, attacked the towns, pushed down houses, and was finally slain. These references were pointed out by Mr. Wm. Newell, University of Pennsylvania. The student of the still puzzling Medicine Men's Society and the Pig Mask Rite will find valuable data given by Mr. Joseph Keppler in a recent letter to Dr. Heye, on file in the Museum of the American Indian, Heye Foundation, N. Y.

resents the tutelary spirit appealed to for aid in serious cases of injury, two other masks of which *Sadegá'hεs* provided specimens (Pl. IV B and C), are representations of specific afflictions: fever (*odąkwá'*) and smallpox (*kunoskwáund*) or chicken pox. These masks had been used, he said, in treating some cases during the year past. In grievous cases of these maladies the specific masks mentioned are brought into service in the curing sessions of the doctor's company, the mask of the required form being worn by the leading doctor of the gathering during the curing ritual. The squash rattle previously described is used upon such an occasion. It was further stated that, like the Pig Mask, these images representing diseases were not used in Long House rituals of the False Face Society. Belonging in a different category, their use is restricted to performances of the Medicine Men's Society.

In conformity with the usual procedure of this group the members of the society seat themselves in the opposed moiety positions (Wolf on the west, Turtle on the east) at the home of the sufferer where the rites are carried out. The mask representations indicate the presence of the unseen trouble-causing spirits to which the administrations are directed. It should be noted that although this brief discussion treats the two images together, the two masks are employed separately in the Society feasts. They are collectively called *onókwatra' adédjąs kwun'hoktàn*, "medicine doctor for very sick."

The Fever Spirit Mask is 8 inches in length, with a small nose, an open mouth, and prominent white teeth. The base color is dark red, the eyeballs are tin plates painted light blue, and the eyebrows, moustache, and goatee are of skunk fur. The hair is white horse tail. The mask, as will be seen from the illustration, suggests the death-head; emaciated, flushed with fever, glassy, starey-eyed. In the words of its owner, it symbolizes the last stages of fever-emaciation (Pl. IV, C).

The Smallpox Mask is 12 inches in length, has "pop-eyes," a mouth pursed for blowing, and a long crooked nose. The base color is yellow, mottled with red spots. The forehead is furrowed and the eyelids red. The eyeballs, nose, and lips are painted black. Braided corn husks form the hair (Pl. IV, B). The symbolism was explained as follows: The yellowness of the skin is a sign of the sickness; the red spots, the pustules of the pox; the eyeballs are protruded with the sickness; the nose is crooked because "when people are so sick their noses turn out, and when they get well they become straight again"; the position of the mouth symbolizes the doctor's action when he blows the medicine from his mouth upon the skin of the patient. The corn-husk hair was explained as having no specific symbolical meaning; "it is just connected with the idea of the spirit governing the sickness."

The owner, *Sadegą'hɛs*, released these masks only after he had attached to their foreheads the necessary little sacrificial bags of native tobacco and addressed them, while casting a few pinches of the tobacco into the fire of the stove, with the usual prayer, admonishing them to go forth to their new locations and ownership without malice, stating that they would be respected, and begging them not to return to the Six Nations and not to inflict sickness anywhere.

The revelation of the two additional specific mask control-spirits, disclosed only after a number of years of supposed intimacy with the Medicine Men's Societies, came as something of a surprise to the recorder. It has been known that considerable secrecy shrouds the action of this important group of doctors. From the obscurity of the seemingly unapproachable background of their doings, it seems that information can only leak out from time to time. We may wonder, therefore, what other specific mask types, representing specific diseases, may still come to our attention. A brown mask pitted to represent probably smallpox is kept in the possession of Little Bear (George Green) a Cayuga-Mohawk on the reserve. It was thought, at the time of securing this information, to be more judicious not to press the informant for further discussion of the question. The doctrines of treatment are apparently flexible; anything that may arise in the shape of disease is treated through sculptured, symbolic representations in the form of masks, as pointed out to me by C. E. Schaeffer.

THE DARK DANCE, OR LITTLE WATER, SOCIETY[29]

The Dark Dance is called *diyút'sǫdàyɔgo*, "in the dark (ness)," and is performed in private homes to cure sickness in general in connection with medicine prescribed by a "doctor." Frequently the

[29] Among other Iroquois groups the Little Water Society is a separate order, as Dr. Fenton states regarding the Seneca. (Fenton, 1936, p. 17.) Deskáheh is, however, responsible for the statement that among the Cayuga it is merged with the Dark Dance Society.

treatment is for weakness and decline of strength. The performance
of the rite is restricted to members; persons who have been benefited
by the treatment. The speaker opens the meeting by announcing to
the members the reason for their visit to the home of the person
who has requested them to perform. He then takes a bowl of tobacco
and goes to the stove, throwing a little tobacco on the fire to "call
the attention" of the *djīgáhǫ*, "dwarfs, who are patrons of the
society." He makes known the desire of the patient for recovery and
the continuation of good health. A new clay pipe is filled, lighted,
and passed to the patient, to take one draw. He then passes it on (in
a clockwise direction) to the members, each one in turn smoking the
new pipe. The lights (lamps) are extinguished and the men start to
sing, the leader singing and drumming on the water-drum while his
assistant shakes a horn rattle. When one half of the song, consisting
of five verses, has been sung, the men's voices diminish and then
stop, and the women start before the men have ceased entirely and
finish alone, singing the second half. This half choral of males and
females alternating, in which the women "absorb" the song from the
men, is referred to in Cayuga by a definite term, *yéyanǫhǫdā`gǫ*,
"taking the song from." After this song, some of the female members dance. After a few songs have been sung there is an intermission
of ten minutes, during which period lights are again permitted in
the room and those who may care to smoke. When the period is up,
the same performance is repeated, followed by another intermission.
At the beginning of each intermission the house lamps are lighted
for a space of about ten minutes, and those who desire may smoke or
go outside for relief. At the end of the third intermission a special
verse of the sixty verses of the Dark Dance is sung. The concluding
movement comes when the women members dance in a circle (contraclockwise) to the final songs. The patient may be brought out into
the middle of the floor, where the performers dance around him
or her while singing six verses of the song. They all blow their
breath on the patient at intervals as they circle around in the short
shuffling step of the dance. When they have finished singing, the
speaker announces that there is food for the dancers. This symbolizes
the offering of food to the dwarfs.

It is an open question at present whether there is a connection
between the eating of the pig's head in this rite and in that of the
Medicine Man's Society in which the Pig Mask figures.

A pig's head has been previously boiled by the members of the patient's family. It is now brought forth on a large plate and passed around (clockwise) by the woman rite-leader: first to the head singer, then to the other men, and last to the women participants. As the head is held before each member he bites off a piece of the meat without using a knife, at the same time cawing like a crow two or three times or howling like a wolf, as he chooses. This enacts that part of the legend of the animals restoring the life of the scalped hunter (pages 102–5) in which the crow caws during the feast provided for the animal doctors, which legend is at the same time the origin tale of the Dark Dance Society. The usual corn soup or corn mush and the pig's head are the ceremonial foods required for such an occasion. Those present are expected to take some of the feast provender home with them in pails which they bring with them. The head of a pig has come to be used, it is said, as a substitute for that of a bear or deer, going back earlier than the memory of anyone now living.

THE EAGLE SOCIETY DANCE

Kanrugwa''e, "making a noise with a stick," is the term applied to this ceremony. It is performed for the purpose of curing sufferers who have been affected by the spirit of the eagle. A person dreams of an eagle and as a result becomes nervous or suffers from general debility. His case is difficult to diagnose. Then the members of the Eagle Society are called in. The performance, which is restricted to members, may take place in private homes at any time of day or night.

When performing for a patient in his home there appear certain differences in the mode of procedure from that of the performance in the Long House during public ceremonies. In the private administration of the rite an offering of tobacco is burned in the fireplace and a kettle of corn soup is provided by the family of the ailing one. When it is performed in the Long House, tobacco and corn soup are omitted. In the public performance anyone in the audience may get up and express his wish that the sick one be benefited by the performance; he may also offer a present. At the conclusion of this rite the gifts are divided among the dancers and singers.

There are a number of songs. The different singers know different ones, and according to the singers they may sing the ones they choose from their repertoire. At the last song each dancer lays down the feather stick and rattle and goes back empty-handed.

The Eagle Dance is one in which four dancers participate, accompanied by music furnished by two singers, a leader who employs the water drum, and an assistant who keeps time with a horn rattle. The four dancers crouch in a squatting position facing the musicians; they hold in one hand a horn rattle, in the other a feather wand to be described below. As the songs proceed they advance toward the musicians and retreat, keeping abreast and beating time with their rattles to the rhythm of the singers. Their posture imitates that of the eagle. In one of the advances, at the signal of a chief who stands near the singers with a staff or cane in hand and strikes on the floor, the dancer at one end lays down his feather wand before the singers. The same is done by each of the four at stated intervals, until the wands are all in a row. That ends the song. The wands are then taken up and given to the patient; these are "medicine." The patient, incidentally, is the maker of the wands for the rite in his or her behalf.

In the Long House procedure in 1933 the Eagle Dance was performed with the dancers holding rattles and depositing them before the singers instead of the feather wands. The chief, who stood near the singers, handed them the rattles in one of their squatting advances, giving them one at a time. In the performance of the rite, variations are noted as circumstances arise. At the finish of the song stanzas the dancers whooped on this occasion.

The feather wands are made of hardwood sticks tapered and smoothed, from 10 to 14 inches in length. Pendant from them at intervals of an inch or so from the outer end are six feathers. The feathers should be light colored and from a dignified bird. In the specimens (Pl. X, A, B) they are from the hawk (A) and the pheasant (B). Four wands are required for each time the rite is enacted. The attachment is interesting. The feathers are tied to grooves in the stick by thread passed up through the hollow of the quill and out a hole on one side, then held by a knot. Eagle feathers, while no longer obtainable, were originally used for the feather sticks. The story of how eagle feathers were obtained in olden times, as narrated by Jerry Aaron, describes a most particular process. The eagle hunter would smoke Indian tobacco and pray. Then he carried meat to the tallest dead tree in the district, and built himself a hiding place about a hundred feet distant, within range of his weapon. He hung the meat on a branch within sure range. Concealing himself he began to call the eagle by whistling, pausing between calls. At last an eagle sensed the meat and lighted on the highest branch of the tree, cautiously looking around for more than an hour. Then he dropped to a lower branch and did the same, until finally reaching the meat he began to eat, looking about for danger between bites. Sometimes the hunter would be a whole day in his blind before getting the bird within range.

When the bird fell the body was not touched until more than twenty-four hours had passed, because it was infested with dangerous "little bugs" which would cause death if they should get on anyone's body. After this the feathers could be taken. (Note a similar belief in Cherokee.)

Another aspect of motives in the rite of the Eagle Dance has been brought out since 1933 when Deskáheh gave the summary contained in this section. He has since devoted attention to the wider implications of the Eagle rites, at the suggestion of Dr. William Fenton when the latter was preparing a dissertation on the Eagle Dance in 1937. The following observations are fortunate in that they show a wider functional value of the rites as curative and protective means.

The dances used to be called *tcin'ke̓'da*, equivalent to "power to accomplish something" and synonymous with the designation for a bone (wishing-bone) taken from inside of the body or part of the skeleton of an animal, used for purposes of protection, in war, hunting, or witchcraft. If the spirit of an animal is neglected, it could act against some person in the family in whose possession the "wishing-bone" rests.[30] The "Bezoar stone" is denoted by the same term. It is believed to come from the stomach of ancient monsters, snakes, and similar creatures, as in the fables of the Old World. When used by its owner a feast was prepared and the object removed from its silk wrapping and scraped for dust particles to be mixed with medicine. It is generally understood that some of these magic objects still exist in the possession of native doctors, enabling them to practice miracu-

[30] Deskáheh compared this to the "wishing-bone" of an animal to which one prays to achieve success in fulfillment of a need or a wish. It is understood to be a bone which acquires some special magical relationship to the individual into whose possession it comes. Possession is kept in close secrecy by those who may have such fetishes, to avoid guilt and responsibility for misfortunes and sickness in the community. The sources of information are thus inevitably meager.

lous cures. The periodic feasting in behalf of this medicine is required to prevent the medicine "from feeding upon the family of its holders" to the detriment of their health. Investigation of the Bezoar stone legend among the Iroquois and the southeastern tribes invites attention as a topic of research. The idea involved is that of retribution for neglect, only to be averted by satisfying the spirit of the animal. The specific animal dance and ritual (Eagle Dance) is for release from the menace of punishment by the animal spirit. It is in effect an expiatory prayer.

That any persons now hold the fetish *tcin'kę'da* is not essential to the performance of the release rites.

IX

THE UNRESTRICTED SOCIETIES; CURING RITES AND DANCES

The Snow-Snake Rite

THE game, or rite, of Snow-Snake, *diyunanda'‘kwa,* "playing sticks" which is performed primarily for curing, is said to be of relatively recent origin. Years ago, the legend states, snakes used to bite people and cause sores on the lower portions of the leg. The skin would become spotted from poison and the victim would not know what to do. On one occasion an individual who was thus afflicted sought the counsel of a wise man, who suggested that snow-snake be played as a possible cure.

In performing this ceremony, several men are asked to choose two or three players on opposite sides. The players bring their snow-snakes into the home of the afflicted one. Tobacco is burned in the fire and a prayer directed to the snake spirits, asking them to keep away from the person. After that the leader addresses the patient and players and they go out to play the game. The players, it should be noted, are usually members of the opposite moiety from that of the afflicted person for whom they are playing. The contest may also be waged between players of opposite moieties. A person cured by the performance of this ceremony becomes a member of the society and should have it repeated yearly to avert the recurrence of the poison spots. Originally snow-snake was played at any time of the year, on grass in the summertime and on snow in winter, the sticks being first thrown on a trough made of bark. This gave the snow-snakes a good start, and at the end of the trough they would slide over the grass. The sticks of the early form of the game were long and thin, having a thick rounded head like a carrot, with a notch in the end for the forefinger of the thrower.

The number of scores to win is seven. While the game is going on, those of the members not engaged in the game and others present remain in the Long House and look on. When the game is over the winners are given a basket of cakes prepared by the patient. It makes no difference in the efficacy of the action as a cure which side wins. There is no divinatory feature in the winning or losing of the game by the team of the patient's moiety. Its significance lies in the rite alone, not the outcome, there being no stakes.

Aside from its origin, as a rite or as a pastime, the Snow-Snake game has developed into almost a national sport of the Iroquois, and it has witnessed a succession of changes, which have brought it from its original form to an elaborately modernized spectacle engaged in by different towns and reservations of the Six Nations. Its full treatment would therefore go beyond the scope of this study.

The Chipmunk Rite

The origin of the Chipmunk rite, *ngak'sagā`ni·i*, "rubbing the bowl," is as follows:

A mischievous boy was always robbing nests and disturbing animals. He knew where a chipmunk had stored away a supply of nuts, and he took them away and ate them. The boy became ill and no one knew what was wrong with him. After a while he had a vision in which the chipmunk was pursuing him because he had stolen his nuts. It was then decided that a rite must be performed to satisfy the chipmunk and remove the cause of illness in certain cases.

Participation in this rite is not restricted. It is thought to be beneficial for illness. Any number of strong men form a circle, and one man is appointed to stand in the center. Using the rasp (Pl. XV, G), he sings the Chipmunk rite song. At a point in the song (decided by himself) he attempts to break through the ring. If he escapes, the ceremony is ended; if he does not, he must repeat the performance. The rite is now rarely called for and performed.

The rasp which furnishes the rhythmic accompaniment is a piece of hickory, the one illustrated being 24 inches long and closely notched (twenty-four notches) on one side (on two sides in another specimen seen) in the mid-section. Its lower end is placed upon the floor, and with another stick 16 inches long the notches are scraped with a rhythmic motion as the song proceeds.[1] In Canadian Onondaga and Seneca specimens the notches are on the narrow edge.

---

[1] The rasp, or "notched rattle," as it has been termed by some writers, has a wide, interrupted distribution in North America, in the Southwest and in the Plateau area. Besides the Iroquois, the Choctaw is the only other group in eastern North America illustrated as possessing the rasp. The Choctaw source is an illustration in Catlin's collection of paintings showing a company of Choctaw warriors, engaged also in an Eagle Dance.

The Thunder Rite and Lacrosse, or Ball Game

The Cayuga say that there are Seven Thunders and refer to them as *ǫkỉ'‘sot hegá‘kwęs t‘ené‘t‘kwa hadi·wenótadyǝs,* "Grandparents from the sunset coming sounding their voices." It is said that originally there were six brothers in the sky (Thunders, or "Grandfathers") and the seventh one, who came from the earth, is accounted for in the following myth.

Long ago there were three brothers on earth who wished to find the land where the sun sets. They followed a trail toward the setting sun, and it happened that a lost spider had spun its web in their path. The men could not get through the web. Two of the brothers in their effort to get out became more and more entangled in the web, but the third one by some magic power managed to free himself. He found that he had reached the sky world. There he was met by the Six Thunders. They asked this man from earth if he would like to join them and work with them in the service of the Great Spirit and mankind. He agreed to be as one of them, but they told him that they would have to change his form. So they put him in a corn mortar and crushed him to pieces. Then he was taken out and molded into a different form. The Thunders then instructed him to be gentle; never to be too severe with the people. The Thunders have different sounds, and if you will listen you will notice that one sounds like two sticks striking together. That is the one from earth. It is the work of the Thunders to cleanse the earth by causing the winds and rain. Also, they must continue to wage war on the underground monsters and serpents so that they will not come above the ground to harm the people.

The Seven Thunders are mentioned in the thanksgiving prayers of the Long House ritual, but a special, one-day ceremony is performed in their honor during the middle of the summer. The purpose of the ceremony is to offer a direct appeal to the Thunders, or "Grandfathers," for the continuation of the service which they render mankind as agents of the Great Spirit. The principal part of this rite is a game of old-fashioned lacrosse, *gatci·'‘kwae,* "beating the mush," which is played between the old men and the young men. The players are not necessarily of opposite moieties, though sometimes this distinction is observed, seven players being chosen from each moiety. A speaker is appointed to address the players and the people who have gathered to witness the game and to participate in the ceremony.[2] The players are also taken to one side of the grounds and

---

[2] This game has also developed into a modern "sport," with rulings characterized by four distinct periods of change within the last century (Frank S. Speck, 1941).

given an *emetic*, medicine "to clean them out." A fire is built outside
the Long House, and the speaker prays to the Great Spirit and the
Seven Thunders. At a certain point in the prayer he throws a small
woven corn-husk basket (Pl. XI, B) containing tobacco into the fire,
as an offering to the Thunders. (The informant added, "The basket
is given to Grandfather [Thunder] to keep his tobacco in when he is
traveling around.") The speaker now addresses the players instruct-
ing them to play clean and fair and not to injure one another, and also
to be in good spirits while they are playing. The goal is seven paces
wide, and the goal posts "reach the sky," so the Cayuga say. The side
scoring seven points wins the game. It is of no significance which side
wins or whether there is betting on the outcome. When the game is
over the players begin to sing the Thunder, or War Dance, song, and
they dance going into the Long House. Any of the male spectators
who wish to do so may join in the dance.

Upon entering the Long House the singers change the song to
the *Wasáse*,[3] or "real war dance song," as the Cayuga refer to this
chant. When all the dancers have entered the Long House, those
who remained inside during the game rise and offer thanks, with
those who have just entered, to the spirit forces above the earth and
especially to the Thunders. Following this, tobacco and food (corn
mush) are distributed among the players. If anyone desires to derive
additional spiritual benefit from this ceremony, he brings to the Long
House a basket of gifts which are distributed among the players, as
in the Eagle Dance. The gifts are placed in charge of one of the
officers, who hands them to the chief appointed to speak on this
occasion. During the *Wasáse* Dance the speaker knocks on the floor
with his walking stick, at which signal the singing and dancing ceases.
He prays for the dancers and for the person who has supplied the
gifts. The dance is resumed and continued until the speaker gives a
second signal rap to stop. The procedure continues until every article
has been disposed of. This concludes the ceremony.

The War Dance or Wasáse

The *Wasáse* ("Osage"), or war dance, may be performed as a social dance or may be requested by individuals for curative purposes.
In connection with the Thunder Rite one may request its performance
to secure benefits of a purely spiritual nature. The water-drum and

[3] Term used by the Cayuga also to denote a tribe of Siouan linguistic stock. It
specifically refers to the Osage.

horn rattle are used to accompany the songs, of which it is estimated that there are about fifteen. The participants are all males. When the dance is performed for curing, those who request the dance come prepared with baskets of gifts, which are placed in charge of the speaker, who distributes them among the dancers at the proper time. The singers move the bench to the south side of the central floor space, and the dancers perform in the space between the two fires. At a certain part of the song the speaker knocks on the floor with his walking stick, as a signal to halt. He then speaks on behalf of the person who has requested the dance. When he finishes speaking the dance is resumed until he gives another signal, as before. He speaks again for the second person, and so on until all of the requests have been honored. At the conclusion of the rite the gifts are distributed among the dancers.

The Chicken Dance

The purpose of this dance, which is known as *dek'se't's·kéhā*, "chicken dance," is for curing sickness in general. It may be performed at any time upon request and occasionally as a social dance. The water-drum and horn rattles are used. There is a leading singer and as many more singers as desired, each using a horn rattle. The men sing and the women stand in a group near and around them. The step is the same as that of the Woman's Dance, a quick shuffle in time with the drum. After singing a number of verses, the men take women partners and continue the dance side by side with them. About the middle of the dance the men face their partners and continue in single file. This dance is now rarely performed. (In a rite in 1938, it was observed performed as a duet by two young girls during the intermission of a ritual.)

The Striking Stick Dance Rite

The Striking Stick Dance, *kanhya'°e*,[4] "stick beating," is one in which any who desire may join. Its purpose is to cure disease of

[4] In compliance with a memorandum added in 1938 by Deskáheh, the name of this dance should be *wa'ę'ac*, "Striking-pole." The correction is added according to instructions to him from William Isaacs, without changing the name originally given in the recording of data in 1933. The significance of the rite is changed by the second name, which is also the name of the historic "war dance" in which warriors are described as enlisting in a war party by striking a war-post. Further discussion of this point is not yet possible. Deskáheh learned from Jacob Isaacs, in 1937, that this dance originated from a Horse Dance. Its description coincides somewhat in its formation and movement with the Horse Dance of the Cherokee and Catawba.

almost any character, according to the condition of the individual requesting it. And it may be brought forth either in the home or in the Long House. It is now rarely called for. The musicians are a leading singer with the water-drum and an assistant with the horn rattle, seated on the bench. The mode of procedure is said to resemble that of the War Dance (*Wasáse*). Dancers of both sexes from opposite moieties line up in opposite formation, beating time with their feet. At certain intervals of the song, about the middle, they pass and change sides. This was one of the few dances not witnessed in 1933.

The Ghost Dance Rite

The *o'ki·'we*, "ghost," or "dead people" dance, is performed in the Long House to prevent and cure illness by satisfying the spirits of the dead; the anciently as well as recently deceased. According to the teachings of Handsome Lake, man has two spirits: one which the Cayuga call the "real," or "main," soul, which is eternal and goes to the Great Spirit; the other the "ghost spirit," which unless satisfied is apt to go about on earth disturbing people and causing illness.

In the dance the participants are women only, who move along slowly in circle formation (no specific steps) in single file, contra-clockwise. They hold their arms horizontally doubled outward, with hands closed in front of their chests. The leading singer with the water-drum and his assistant with the horn rattle sit on the bench and sing. The men sing the first half of the song, then stop, and the women finish it—"absorbing the song." When the dance is performed in a private home it consumes an entire night. In the annual Long House ceremonies, only a few verses are sung when the rite is requested. Occasion for Ghost Dance Rites arises when a person who is ill dreams of seeing dead people dancing. The afflicted one then calls for the members of the *o'ki·'we* company to come and dance for him. The approximately 100 songs of the series are chanted in the first treatment for a sufferer when the meeting takes place in a home. The following year when ceremonies are given in the Long House, the same person requests that a few stanzas be sung to satisfy the ghosts.

It is performed in winter or fall after the harvest is gathered or in the spring before planting time, lest cold weather or frost be brought about by the presence of the ghosts invoked by it.

Furthermore, it is the last dance to be performed in the night's series of rites—a dance of conclusion—when it forms part of a composite ceremony.

The second part of the dance is called *ganá'adjïˑt'ga'hǫ*, "taking the kettle out," or Kettle Dance, and constitutes a conclusion. While nothing is done in the dance in recent times to correspond to the action implied, it may have been the accompaniment in earlier times of the act of concluding the night's rites by removal of the feast kettle. Mr. Pennypacker was told that the kettle was carried formally around the center of the Long House by the fire-keepers.

The Ghost Dance rite shows similarities to the Dark Dance, which is also an invocation to spirits of the departed (see page 109).

This rite also forms an independent ceremony annually repeated in the Long House and continuing for an entire night, being concluded at daybreak. Upon such an occasion it is governed by women officials especially appointed. The formal order of seating is observed by the sexes, the women on the west or women's side, the men restricted to the east half of the building. The full complement of songs (100 or 102) is rehearsed, the chanting is divided into periods of three hours (continuous), followed by intermissions. The women, without restriction of number, do the dancing. During the intermission, for the space of about a half hour, social dances are introduced, the leaders announced by a "speaker" chosen for the occasion. Women are appointed to serve as fire-keepers. The concluding acts represent the participation of spirits of the deceased in the final dance, which is followed by a feast shared by all present. The final dance is climactic. The singers lead the group and all in attendance join the dancing circle. Food cakes are distributed and carried in the hands of the dancers held high. The leaders conduct the dancers thus out of the Long House and around it, holding the food up as an offer to the spirits. The company re-enters the Long House and becomes seated at the conclusion of the offering song. The speaker closes the ceremony with an address and offers thanks. The food prepared for the feast is then shared among those present. The speaker may in conclusion invite the assembly to enjoy a final social dance, with partners.

The singers, whose "mouths are open all the time," as the saying goes, are paid by the women hosts.

One of the important features of the rite is that tobacco is sacrificially burned to "call the spirits." This is a symbol of invitation to them to join the assemblage and share the feast. The presence of "strange persons" is known to have been sensed at various times by those in attendance. Living people are said not to be able to see them at other times. They are believed to invite their partners to depart with them, supposedly to the realm beyond. One narrative tells how a man had a vision revealing the presence of spirits during the dance and feast, thus giving the dance the name of Ghost Dance.

On the afternoon following the feast the company assembles to clean up the graveyard and burn the rubbish in respect for the departed.[5]

The Dream Guessing Rite

Another ritual procedure for the curing of mental disturbance and its attendant physical symptoms, which does not involve the action of the Societies, is described as follows.

The Dream Guessing Rite, *ságodiwenhā'gwus*, "her word (dream) taken off," is for one who has been harassed by a persistently recurring dream of evil portent or trouble. The victim of this disturbance, which is attributed causally to the Mask Image spirits, can divert its recurrence by asking for the Dream Guessing Rite to be given in the Long House during the course of the Midwinter Ceremony. The time for its introduction to the program of the ceremonies is on the third or fourth day during the Society Rites, not at other times.

Chiefs (generally of the opposite moiety, it is understood) are asked to exert their powers to guess the nature of the dream. The one to be treated renders only one answer, negative or affirmative, to each guess made by those in turn of the party which offers to effect the cure. The divination continues until the dream has been correctly guessed and the answer is affirmative. No hint or other suggestion is given to help the diviners. And on some occasions it is reported to have been drawn out to cover several sessions of the Long House

[5] In the section above I have incorporated the valuable notes on the Ghost Dance ceremony of the Sour Springs Cayuga obtained by Mr. Samuel W. Pennypacker in April, 1939, just prior to the annual repetition of the feast. Deskáheh was the source of his information.

days. At other times it has been done in three or four guesses. For the dream to be guessed is the cure!

It now requires that the one who gave the correct solution make a miniature mask, either of the wooden or the corn-husk type, to be delivered to the patient any time during the ceremonies. The donor chants a few words, wishing good fortune to the recipient when the "maskette" is handed over. This is the "medicine." The object is then kept in the home of the relieved dream-sufferer. One individual is remembered who had her little mask buried with her.

A small series of such Mask Image talismans, obtained from chiefs of the Sour Springs group, is shown in Plates VIII and IX, A. They are of wood and of corn-husk, the former from 1½ to 3 inches in length, the latter from 3 to 3½ inches. The small images are replicas of the large ones as to color design and features. They are not, however, furnished with the little bag of the tobacco sacrifice, as are the large masks. The specimens shown in Pl. IX are black and red, of the crooked nose, big nose, and laughing types. All are of wood except for C, which is a small shell 1 inch in length, with yarn for hair and D which is a corn-husk image. None is remembered to have been made of stone.

The small image made by the chief who has guessed the dream is presented in a formal manner to the person in whose behalf the rite is called, usually, as in 1936, on the day after the guessing, during which ritual there has been time to make or obtain one. In that year the presentation of the image was accompanied by the performance of the Feather Dance, as an appropriate sign of rejoicing, on the sixth day of the Midwinter Ceremony (Feb. 3rd), on which occasion it was a corn-husk miniature mask, given by Jacob Isaacs (Turtle Moiety) to Mrs. Barbara Porter (Wolf moiety). Occasionally, if the patient is a member of the Wooden False Face Society, the small image so received is kept as a "charm," tied to the hair near the forehead of a large mask.

The Dreamer, or Fortune Teller, Rite

Among the Cayuga there are certain men and women who are called "dreamers." They are privately called upon to diagnose cases which have baffled practitioners in the various societies. The male dreamer, or fortune teller, as he is sometimes called, is known as ha'dra'ut'a'; the female as hǫ'draut'a'. The term deyu'ki·'yǫ'wędjǫ'-

niā, "dream fortune teller," is applied to these men and women. In case of serious illness, some one takes a piece of the sick person's clothing, puts some tobacco in it, and wraps it up. He then goes to the dreamer and tells him of the person who is ill. The dreamer puts the small parcel under his pillow and that night he dreams. He has a secret medicine which he drinks before going to bed, and sometimes the medicine makes him sleep all night. The next morning the person seeking the advice for the sick one returns to the dreamer. The dreamer returns the article of clothing and keeps the tobacco. Then he tells what he has seen in his dream-vision. He tells whether or not it is a certain medicine that must be prepared and administered, or if one of the medicine societies should be called in. The dreamer sometimes sees in his dream-vision that the sick person needs a "ceremonial friend." He describes the person he has seen in the dream to the members of the family of the person who is ill, and they know who the person is from the dreamer's description. The making of friendship ceremonially is performed in the Long House during the performances of the Society Dances. The members of the society, to which the person belongs who is going to be the ceremonial friend, perform the rites of that particular society while the two "friends" are seated side by side on the bench in the center of the floor.

The "Tug-of-War," or Pulling, Rite

The ceremony called *t'adi·'nyac*, "they (both sides) grab the stick," has not been called for or performed at the Sour Springs Long House since about 1915. Like others of its kind in the category of curative rites, it is not performed for practice but is held in abeyance until the malady for which it was given as a cure makes its appearance in the community; or it is prescribed as a remedy by a medicine man or called for by a patient who becomes conscious of its need as a measure of relief. The ceremonial contest of pulling in opposite directions by members of the two moieties resembles the vulgar "tug-of-war" of Europeans, but only in its external aspects.

The rite is a cure for an urge to seize hold of something—manifestly a seizing compulsion. The psychotherapeutic treatment is the following performance.

When the "requester," or victim of the malady—usually a woman, according to Deskáheh—has called for the rite, it may be introduced during the procedures of the third day of the Winter

Ceremonies, in the sequence with other unrestricted curative society dances and songs. The "requester" provides a stick about 2 feet in length, which is given to two men, the ceremonial "directors," one chosen of each moiety as representatives of their groups. These men become first position players in the pulling contest between the moiety groups—another form of moiety functioning among the Cayuga.

These two men grasp the stick, facing each other in the middle of the Long House above a dividing line on the floor, which also represents the division boundary of the two moieties, each man on his own moiety side. They grasp the stick—hands alternating, one palm up the other palm down—with a firm hold. Eight men from each moiety have moreover been chosen by the moiety "directors" to form the team supporting their leaders. They range behind their leaders, each holding the one in front of him tightly by locking his hands over the other's chest, one arm over the left shoulder the other under the right arm. The nine moiety contestants on each side of the line are then ready for the signal to pull. The struggle is to pull their opponents over the line to their own side. Should the leader's grip on the stick give way, his side loses. There is no restraint upon mirth, nor are there wagers laid upon the outcome of the contest. And the efficacy of the cure is not affected by whether the patient's moiety wins or loses; thus it is not divinatory. The cure develops from the symbol of the pulling act. Generally the men form the opposing sides, but cases are recalled when the contestants were women against women, though it was not specified whether the decision of sex bore a relation to the sex of the patient requesting the rite.

The song is terminated in the record by cries of *anyo` sadε` sastǫ,* "pull harder," addressed to the contestants.[6]

The Football Rite

Another game which functions as a rite when called for by a patient as an adjunct to herbal medicine or suggested as an auxiliary to treatment prescribed by a medicine-man, is the football contest. It is called *wǫsǫt'was gatci·'kwai·,* "kicking game."

When requested or prescribed it is played on the third day of the

[6] The recording was made by Bill Buck, a son of the Tutelo chief John Buck, who has occasionally performed it at the Seneca Long House. It is included in the collection (see Speck, Speck, and Herzog) as it would be sung were it called for at Sour Springs, when someone who knows it would have to be called in.

Midwinter Ceremony, when the society dances are in order. Its purpose is, like the other curative rites, to coax the withdrawal of some unfriendly spirits who are standing in the way of the successful action of the medicine administered. There is no specific ailment toward which it is directed by analogy of magic.

The person who requests the game provides the ball, made of rags stuffed in a canvas covering, about 6 inches in diameter. The goals, each represented by two pieces of firewood stuck on end in the snow about 8 feet apart, are located about 150 feet distant from each other, north and south, in the open space for games on the north side of the Long House. There are five players on each side, chosen by name by the requester or by the speaker of the day, from the two moieties. The game is played for three points, the first side reaching three wins. There are no rules except that the players can use hands only to strike the ball to the ground; the rest is all kicking. One player stands guard at each goal on his own side. The person requesting the game tosses up the ball starting off each play, and also furnishes a portion of corn mush for the players; a symbol of feasting the spirits by proxy to satisfy them.

In the 1936 winter ceremonies the Football Game was given upon request three times in the afternoon[7] for different persons. In 1933 it was not called for once.

[7] While not so performed at Sour Springs, according to Deskáheh, a bystander at one of the contests said that it was sometimes played at night in other groups with a "fire ball"; one soaked in oil and ignited.

X

THE FOUR SACRED CEREMONIAL RITES

THE Feather Dance, the Skin Dance, the *Adǫwa,* and the Bowl Game, all four, are called the "Great Spirit's Ceremonies" or "Four Sacred Words."[1] These are carried out in the Long House after the performances of the Medicine Societies Dances, beginning with the Feather Dance, which takes place on the sixth day of the Midwinter Ceremony. The Cayuga maintain that the teacher sent them by the Great Spirit (Creator) was Christ, and offer the following evidence in support of their view. First, and most significant of all, is the belief in the virgin birth of the teacher; second, that he was sent by the Great Spirit to teach the people the "Sacred Words" (sacred rites); third, that he left them to go to another part of the world to teach the people; and last, that he returned to them in spirit to teach them the last of the Great Spirit's "words" and to tell them that the people where he had gone to teach his Father's "words" had not believed in him and had killed him, and that he was returning to his Father (Great Spirit). The Cayuga say that he became the "Fourth One," or the "Fourth Angel." (See Table I, Spirit Forces.) It is, nevertheless, highly possible that the origin of the group of the four sacred rites antedates Handsome Lake, as Dr. Fenton suggests, and that these four rites belong to the stock in trade of Iroquois ceremonialism which Handsome Lake preserved, since they are also mentioned in Hewitt's Iroquoian Cosmology.

The origin of the "Four Sacred Words" according to Cayuga tradition is given in the following story, which is entitled "The Fatherless Boy."

THE ORIGIN OF THE FOUR SACRED CEREMONIES

The Fatherless Boy

In the old days, in an Indian village, twelve male babies were born the same night. Eleven had fathers and one was fatherless. His mother was a pure (virgin) woman. When the mothers of the eleven infant boys who had fathers were able to be about, they wished to visit the mother of the fatherless boy.

[1] A. C. Parker (1913, Sections 30, 40) refers to "Four words devised in the heaven world and given to the people for the purpose of bringing happiness."

127

One day they took their sons and went to the home of the twelfth baby, all arriving there at the same time, as though having previously arranged the meeting. The eleven mothers took their sons to see the fatherless baby frequently and, strangely enough, all arrived at his home at the same time and never had it been previously planned. As the boys grew older they met often to play together. The fatherless boy had a nice place in which to play, and the other eleven boys were happy when in his company. One day when the mothers went out to look for their sons (now well-grown boys), they saw the eleven seated in a circle and the fatherless boy standing within the circle talking to them and teaching them. The boys listened in earnest. The fatherless boy said, "Now, I will teach you the opening Thanksgiving Ceremony of the Long House." He asked for a volunteer to practice the *Adǫwa* [Individual Thanksgiving songs addressed to the Great Spirit]. One boy said that he would try; so he got up and the fatherless boy taught him. He could perform as well as though he had been singing the *Adǫwa* for a long time. The next time they met together, their mothers found them dancing in a circle. The fatherless boy was singing and teaching them the Feather and Skin Dances. He asked for volunteers to learn the songs, and one of the boys said that he would try. He could sing them perfectly, and the fatherless boy told them that the songs that he had taught them were to accompany the Feather and Skin dances which he had taught them.

Now they were grown men. One day when they met at the usual place, the fatherless man told his eleven friends that he was going away to another country in the East to teach the people there. So he left them. There was a trail down a lane between tall pines, and so the eleven men watched the fatherless man disappear down the trail toward the east. They never saw him again. Some years later one of the eleven men, now old, began to think of the fatherless one and wondered what had become of him. He thought that he would visit the scene where they used to play. When he reached the spot he found the other ten men there. All had gathered at the same time, as in the days of their youth. As they looked down the lane they saw a figure approaching over the same trail. As he came nearer the eleven men recognized him as the fatherless one. He came close, but he would not shake hands with them. He said, "I cannot shake hands with you because I am a dead man." He said, "I have come to teach you the Bowl Game, which will be the last act of our gathering." [This is the last of the four sacred rites.] So he gave them the peach pits ["dice"] and a bowl and taught them how to play the game (Pl. XI, A). He said, "Where I was they killed me and I am going back home. Before I go to where I shall stay I had to come back here to teach you the great Bowl Game, which I forgot to do when I was here before." While they were playing the game, he disappeared.

Hewitt (1916) records that the Dekanawida tradition as told by Mohawk and Onondaga annalists to account for the founding of the League is largely repudiated by Cayuga statesmen now living, and identifies the Fatherless One with Dekanawida. And he declares that there seem to be grounds for their doctrine. Hewitt recorded a Cayuga version of the story in which the great statesman is anonymous. In this version Dekanawida is known by the descriptive title "The Fatherless." Hewitt goes on to say that the title was designed probably to emphasize a prophecy that he would be born of a virgin by "immaculate conception." According to the Cayuga, "The Fatherless" established among them a form of government the exact type of which he later founded among the Five Iroquois tribes inclusive of the Cayuga. It is stated that the Cayuga statesmen did not realize the suitability of that form of government to the affairs and welfare of all men, and so they limited its scope and benefits selfishly to their own people. "This made it necessary for 'The Fatherless' to return [from the sky] again to the mission of establishing the League among all the tribes."

THE FEATHER DANCE

On the sixth day of the Midwinter Ceremony, the Feather Dance, one of the four sacred rites (see origin in the tale of the Fatherless Boy, p. 128) is performed. It is known as *osto'wago'wa* or "Great Feather head-dress," signifying "bunched split feathers."[2] Split feathers denote peace. This rite should be performed as soon after sunrise as possible. Everyone is expected to take part, wearing Iroquois costume; ceremonial attire is urged for both men and women.[3] Feather head-dresses are worn by the men, constructed of various kinds of feathers arranged as in a bonnet, the true Iroquois pattern, forming a bunch and attached to a cap or framework of wood. Some choose "crane" (Great Blue Heron) feathers, because the Cayuga say, "The 'crane' is so often seen in a prayerful attitude —looking upward." Feathers of birds of prey, hawk and eagle, are more suited to the men of warrior age. Deer hoof leg-rattles are also

[2] Deskáheh states that *staus,* an ancient term, is in some way connected with the Feather Dance. He was unable to give a translation of the term but suggested that it probably had reference to the deer hoof leg-rattles worn by the male dancers.

[3] According to Deskáheh, it is stated in the teachings of Handsome Lake, "If there are men and women who do not have complete costumes to wear when performing the Great Spirit's ceremony, let them remove their hats as a sign of respect."

worn by the men (Pl. XIII, A). The direction of the dance is con-traclockwise.

Men wear face paint, usually two hoizontal red stripes on each cheek, or one red dot on each cheek. Some dip four fingers in red paint and draw them across the cheeks. The women do not paint.

No specific number is given for Feather Dance songs, though there are a large number. In the midwinter ceremony the leader sings as many of them as he knows. Two large turtle shell rattles (Pl. XIV, A) only are used to accompany the singing, which is led by the chief or leading singer and his assistant who sit on the center bench.

The leading dancers take their places in the single file dance formation, and as the singers proceed, other men and women join the line, walking about the singers on the bench, while four songs are chanted in slow time. At the end of the songs of introduction, the tempo changes to fast time, and the men dance very vigorously, making body and hand gestures, stooping and strutting as in the War Dance. The women do a fast shuffle step during certain parts of the songs. There is an intermission, during which time a speaker is appointed to quote certain passages from the Code of Handsome Lake. The dance is then resumed. The duration of each song set of the Feather Dance is about fifteen minutes, twelve to fifteen songs being sung. At the conclusion of the dance one song of the Corn Planting Rite is sung.

The association of the Feather Dance with the Great Spirit, or Creator, comes out in a teaching current among the Long House people that the Feather Dance is "His Own Society Dance." This is most interesting as indicating a conception of parallelism in the patterns of divine and human society forms. The people at large "living on earth," then, as members of "His Society" are under obligation to participate to further the health and well-being of all, through the power of their supreme patron. The Feather Dance, coming at the culmination of the days of the Medicine Societies' Dances, represents the beginning of the ceremonial climax of the Midwinter and other festivals, as may be noted in the table (Table 2, pp. 35–36) showing the annual cycle of rites. The meat and vegetable feast-foods distributed to all at the termination of the Feather Dance are the Great Spirit's universal gifts to members of "His Society," namely, "all the people." Note that in the distribution of the food an abundant portion is given to everyone present, that none is to refuse, and that it is not expected of the recipients that they say the usual *Niáwę*, "Thanks" (see section on Ceremonial Foods, p. 42).

THE ADÓWA (INDIVIDUAL THANKSGIVING)

Burning Tobacco Rite

The performance of this sacrificial rite, *cadεkᵂcráhę kayǫkǫ́twę*,' "mid-year tobacco put in fire," precedes the *Adówa* rite on the seventh day. It is sometimes referred to as *hadeyokǫ́twas*, "they are putting tobacco in the fire." The six leading officers (males), three from each side, form a semicircle in front of the fire on the Turtle side. The opening prayer is directed to the Spirit Forces above the earth, the Creator, the Four Angels, the Sun, the Moon, the Stars, and the Thunders. The prayer is repeated five times by the speaker, and every time the Creator's name is mentioned the speaker throws some tobacco in the fire and utters a single short whoop, the purpose of which is to attract the attention of the spirits. As noted in the Table of Spirit Forces (p. 30), tobacco, *wi·yą́'gwa*, is mentioned as a "helper" to aid the people in communicating with the Spirit Forces. At certain intervals the prayer cry *gwu'ye he* + "Now hear me," is uttered by the men on both sides, calling the attention of the Spirit Forces above the earth. When the first speaker is finished, the second speaker from the Wolf moiety continues the prayer chant, which is directed to the Creator and the Spirit Forces on earth. The procedure is the same as that followed with the first speaker.

In the Midwinter Ceremony of 1933 the rite was celebrated outdoors, near the Turtle moiety door and cookhouse, as is occasionally done.

A translation by Mrs. John L. Buck of the Cayuga Thanksgiving Prayer recited by James Crawford (of the Wolf moiety) during the Midwinter Ceremony on February 4, 1936, at the Lower Cayuga Long House is given below. The chanting was done while sacred tobacco was being burned in the fire of the cookhouse to carry the people's worship to the "Man Above" (the Creator). It is essentially the same chant recited upon the occasion of the Skin Dance and the Burning Tobacco Rite at the other Long Houses, variations occurring only according to the ability of the speaker, as Deskáheh affirms.

In addressing the Creator the speaker chanted as follows. In the chant the term *"thought"* means that the Creator brought it to pass by the power of his mind.

The Cayuga Thanksgiving Prayer

That everything is to happen again; the same things which had happened when they first heard about Handsome Lake's Code. And also he prayed that they were to see again all things that bear fruit and all the different grasses that grow, and during which he has made medicine out of it.

He [the Creator] also *thought* that it [medicine] would help the people at times whenever some people get sickness, also different herbs that grow in the bushes that he has made for the people on earth.

He *thought* that there would be a special tree that would be the great tree of the forests, and this tree is the maple tree, he *thought* that this certain tree would run sap.

All of the people pray and rejoice that they have drunk the only sap, those that are living on earth, and that he has left all the animals on earth. He *thought* that it would be a cause for thanks to the people on earth. There are bigger animals far away but only the small animals are around nearby now. That is the most of it nowadays.

Now we thank all that is on earth that the Man Above has given.

He *thought* he would make four companies. The first company is the Thunder of the west that guides the things on earth. And [he *thought*] that they would bring fresh water to the rivers, creeks, and the great lakes, also to all that he made grow on earth for the people, and whatever the people plant.

Now we people turn all our minds to those things and carry on our work that the Man Above has ordained and that their minds would be directed toward the Man Above, not to dwell upon how people on earth are lost and have strayed from him. [Addressing the Creator] Now you have heard us, the people, praying as above.

Now he *thought* that the sun would be our light, as we call our brother, he *thought* that he would give heat on earth also to look after what he had planted on earth, he thought it would be a great thing on earth until the end, and (the Sun) still is carrying on what he is ordained for.

Now we people turn all our minds together to praise him that has his mind on the Man Above; not to look upon how we people on earth have lost and strayed away from him as we have, that our minds would be turned to the Man Above.

He *thought* that there would be two moons, one we call our grandmother, and *thought* that she would also look after things on earth and *thought* that the people on earth would keep track of how she moved from month to month. And he *thought* that people could still be learning from her.

Now we turn all our minds together to thank her that she still carries on her work for what the Man Above has ordained her.

All her helpers, the stars, he *thought*, would look pretty. We turn our minds together that we thank all her helpers, that all their minds would be turned to the Man Above and not look upon us people how lost and strayed from him we are. Now you have heard us people talk. Still our prayer is toward you, the Four Angels. They are the beings who look after us, even in our minds. Now we turn all our minds thanking them that they still carry on their work for what he has ordained them for.

That our minds would be turned to the Man Above and not look upon us people on earth how lost and strayed away from him we are.

Now he has been on earth our Great Master [Handsome Lake], that he is the one who brought all the messages to the Indians which they are still carrying on.

That now as we put all our minds upon it, we thank him also, that now he has passed on to the happy Promised Land.

Now that the Man Above is still sending us his great offerings [blessings].

He (the Creator) still thinks that all the people should be forgiven for their sins because he wants to get all the souls back. He can get everyone if [they make it] possible. Now we turn all our minds together to praise and thank him that he is still sending us his great offerings.

The speaker of the day, in concluding, announces that the *Adówa* rite is about to be performed and urges the people present to take part in this sacred ceremony. A second speaker, representing the Great Spirit, appeals to the people on earth to take part in His (the Great Spirit's) ceremony.

The *Adówa* rite follows.

The *Adówa* proper is observed on the seventh day. The participants are here afforded an opportunity to express individual thanks to the Creator[4] by means of songs and phrased beatitudes recited while standing. There is no instrumental accompaniment. The first speaker, selected by the officers from one moiety stands up, prays and urges the people to express their faith by taking part in the *Adówa* rite. He also thanks the spirits who guide the people and begs that they be granted the privilege of attending another annual ceremony. The second speaker from the other moiety represents the Great Spirit, and his interlocution is a direct appeal to the people on earth to take part in the ceremony.

The *Adówa* chanting is opened with the thanksgiving chant;

4 See origin of rite in the tale The Fatherless Boy, p. 128.

which is known as the "Great Spirit's" *Adǫ́wa,* and which came to
the people as revealed by Handsome Lake; this is also known as his
Adǫ́wa. The officers have decided previously which moiety shall be
asked to provide a leader to chant this. The appointed chanter talks
before and between repetitions of the song, encouraging the chiefs
to do their part in coming forth to sing their thanksgiving prayers;
in one section of his address he encourages the warriors to do the
same. Finally, he announces that it is free for all to participate with
their chants. As discussed below, the male members of the Long
House gathering respond until all who are so moved have chanted
the *Adǫ́wa.* Then the "Great Spirit's," *ergo* Handsome Lake's,
chant is given again, to close this section of the ceremony.

Anyone who feels moved to do so may sing the *Adǫ́wa.*[5] According to the procedure, a man will begin to sing while seated and then
slowly rise. He will move very slowly, singing his thanks to the
"Great Spirit" for life and the many other blessings he has received,
especially for the privilege of attending another ceremony. Continuing in the same reverential attitude he halts, makes a few remarks
to show that he is in good faith, and then repeats his song. If a man
has a very close friend in the audience he may call him up to walk
with him. Some sing only a short *Adǫ́wa* and others perform much
longer. During the singing the men on both sides keep time by saying
"he'he'he'he'."

Usually men of middle age enact this rite. That the maturity of
the individual lends something to the performance is evident in the
attitude of the congregation. An illustration of this is afforded by
the words of the *Adǫ́wa* song of one of the performers,[6] which says
"I have now reached the age when I can sing my thanksgiving."
They may also be the compositions of the individuals who sing them.
A person may possess more than one of these songs, employing them
upon different occasions or on the same occasion, according to his own
wish. The songs frequently repeat a sentence denoting the spirit of
thanksgiving of the singer, as in the instance mentioned above. Another song betrays the singer's eloquent sentiments in the words, "I
love all the living people"; the same chanter had one which ran "I
am a Turtle, that's why I run so slowly" (Jeremiah Aaron). In an-

[5] The response is often generous; twenty-seven men and seven boys volunteered
at the Lower Cayuga Long House on February 4, 1936, and sixteen at Sour Springs
on February 6, 1933.

[6] Joseph Martin, a Cayuga-Mohawk.

other is repeated "Everybody is mean to me; the people living on earth." This burden has an origin story: Anciently an orphan boy once sang it thus and they took it up for society dance songs for some reason. But when it is used for Individual Thanksgiving the phrase is changed to "I am solicitous for everybody" (Richard Buck's version). Others consist of burdens of meaningless syllables.

The Naming Ceremony

At one period in the rite, names are given to children and to adults. This ceremony is called *ga'senahadiwado,* "name road it says." The person to receive a name is called to stand beside the speaker, who announces the names of the clans of the recipient's parents and the name that is to be given to him. The speaker continues his address by expressing the hope that the individual named will enjoy the blessings of a long and useful life in the service of the "Great Spirit." He or another officer then sings his *Adǫ́wa,* and the man just named walks with him. If a male baby is given a name he is carried by the man who sings the *Adǫ́wa* for him. Songs are not sung by females or for females. When a female is given a name she stands beside the speaker, and when he has finished his address she returns to her place.

In concluding the *Adǫ́wa* rite the speaker representing the "Great Spirit" again addresses the people, thanking them for taking part and urging them to continue to perform his, the Creator's (Great Spirit's) ceremony. The speaker then directs the minds of the people to the next ceremony (the Skin Dance) and urges them to be of one mind when they worship the "Great Spirit" by performing the sacred ceremonies.

Corn soup, meat, and bread are distributed by the assistants, and this concludes the program for the day.

The Sun Disk Rite

In the Sun Ceremony, an appeal to the sun and thanks for his beneficence of warmth and stimulation of plant growth are voiced by the man singing the *Adǫ́wa,* or individual thanksgiving song. The performer steps forth from his seat on one of the benches along the wall of the Long House and begins his personal thanksgiving chant.—the *Adǫ́wa* song. Every male worshipper possesses, or should possess, at least one *Adǫ́wa,* often several, to be chanted in the Long

House when individual prayer performance is in order, either voluntarily or when called for in the ceremonies. If a worshipper has several such songs he chooses the one he wishes to be given at any time, there being no order prescribed. In the case of younger men there is often some diffidence about chanting in the Long House. They think it more fitting to those of mature age. Again, there are cases in which the singing voice is weak and the prayer-giver lacks confidence. In such instances a man desiring to pray and give thanks yet feeling himself unable to chant asks an experienced chanter to perform for him as a proxy, the two marching in procession side by side.

Adǫwa chants are acquired and kept by individuals as personal worship-property. The method by which they are acquired is by imitation of other chanters, their songs being learned either by paying attention to them while they are being sung in the Long House rites or by practicing them over with the help of the singer from whom they are being acquired. No payment is made and no permission even is necessary when one adopts the *Adǫwa* of another. Their status is that of free property for anyone. They often pass, too, from a father to his son, as in the case of John Buck's family.

The rite of prayer and thanksgiving in singing the *Adǫwa* was, it is said, formerly not one of adoration, but one of boasting about war exploits. The personal chants were tinged with the warrior's spirit and were associated, according to certain evidences, with the counting of "coup" in the central regions. This point will however, require the analysis of a very large series of *Adǫwa* songs before relationship with counting "coup" can be traced. They express personal emotions and sentiments and are quite devoid of anything but altruism and veneration. The change in attitude is attributed to the influence of Handsome Lake, who permitted no warlike demonstrations to invade the Long House atmosphere. The spoken prayers uttered between the repetitions of the *Adǫwa* songs as the singer parades in the Long House are addressed to the Creator. And this is all that can be asserted from the material collected and the observations recorded up to the present.

The procedure followed by the performer of the *Adǫwa* rite is to chant the song while walking slowly forth toward the center of the floor, generally with his hands folded behind him, repeating it several times if he desires, until he has covered enough space to be in full view of the assembled company. Then he ceases his song to pray aloud and to express his thanks for blessings, general or specific, as they occur to his mind. His short prayer concluded, he resumes his chant, advancing while singing, to another spot, at which he pauses and prays again. The *Adǫ́wa* is impressive. There is no rule governing the number of repetitions of the chant or the distance around the floor to be covered; all is a matter of option with the performer. He traces his return to his seat in the same manner, alternately walking

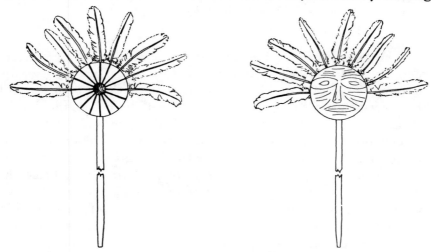

FIGURE 10.—Sour Springs Cayuga Sun Disk Wand used in the prayer in the Thunder Ceremony (front and rear views). Symbols of sun's rays and face. Length of staff, 25½ inches; diameter of disk, 5 inches; thickness of disk, ½ inch.

and singing, then standing and praying. The directions of movement are always contraclockwise.[7]

In the Sun Ceremony the *Adǫ́wa* is conducted with a specific feature—a symbolical staff held in the hand of the prayer-maker, representing the luminary toward which spiritual attention is directed. This is a symbol of the Sun—a hardwood (oak) disk 6 inches in diameter and ½ inch thick, bearing in red and yellow paint the simple lineaments of the human face, as shown in Plate X E. Another specimen has on the opposite side of the disk a red circle in the center with rays reaching to the margin (Pl. XII B). The disk in use at the Sour Springs Lone House is surrounded by a rim of 12 light

[7] In native thought a contraclockwise course corresponds to the course of the sun and moon.

gray and white feathers, those of a bird of prey only, inserted in holes, and is set upon a round staff 3 feet in length and ¾ inch in diameter. The Sun-disk is held in the right hand of the first worshipper to chant his *Adǫwa*, and is elevated while he chants and prays. Upon resuming his seat the singer passes the staff to the worshipper at his side and it is passed on around the Long House from east to west, and on again, in the direction of the sun's course. This singer uses it in the same way, should he desire to chant; if not, he passes it on to his neighbor. So it passes around the room.

THE SKIN DANCE

The Skin Dance[8] is the third of the Great Spirit's, or sacred, ceremonies and is performed on the seventh day. The term *gunehǫ́*, meaning "covered with skin" (referring to the head of leather of the water-drum, see p. 44), is applied to this rite. Before the time of Handsome Lake the purpose of the Skin Dance was to afford an opportunity for the war chiefs and warriors to recount their war records and to discuss raids and cruelties inflicted upon other tribes. Handsome Lake condemned this type of performance and told the people they must give up the mention of their exploits and the evil deeds of the past and speak only of the wonders of creation. The modified performance in the present program of events is for the purpose of general worship, in which the public may take part.

The leading singer and assistant singer are appointed by the officers in charge of the ceremony. They represent one of the moieties. There are idiomatic differences in the "prayer call" and in the wording of songs as given by the two moieties. The leader and his assistant take their places on the musician's bench and start to sing, accompanied by the water-drum and horn rattles. The number of Skin Dance[9] songs sung during the dance depends upon the ability of the leading singer. The leading dancer steps out near the bench and he is followed by other male and female officers, the females forming at the end of the line. They proceed around the singer's bench in a trotting step, the leading men making warriors' gestures,

---

8 See origin myth, p. 128.

9 At present Eli Jacobs, a young man of the Turtle moiety, is the only singer who knows the entire set of songs for this rite, which he estimates at forty-eight songs, and can give them in their proper sequence. He has sung this exceptional repertoire since he was about twelve years old; an unusual demonstration of ability. The entire set and dance require at least an hour to perform.

but not as vigorous as the movements made in the Feather Dance. At the beginning of each song the leading officer of the opposite moiety utters a shrill whoop, which is taken up by the chiefs of his moiety. At the conclusion of each song the dancers walk slowly until the singer starts another song, and then they resume the dance and continue as before. The line of dancers increases steadily until it is necessary to go around both fires. It was necessary to dance in double file in the dance observed in the Midwinter Festival in 1933, owing to the number in line (about 100).[10] At a certain point in the dance the songs are changed and a different type of Skin Dance songs are sung. The speaker who chanted the opening prayer in the Tobacco Burning Rite[11] steps to the north side of the singers' bench, and at the end of the song he calls out "*kwi·yā*" (if he belongs to the Turtle moiety) or *hyuwi·hi·yā* (if he represents the Wolf moiety), a signal meaning "stop," directed to the singers. The purpose of this cry is to attract the attention of the Great Spirit, so that he will know that his people are worshipping him by performing his ceremonies. The dancers walk slowly as the first speaker repeated the thanksgiving invocation, which is directed to the spirits above the earth.[12] The dance is resumed, and again the speaker ends the song by uttering the same signal or prayer cry. The dancers walk slowly and the prayer is repeated. This is done four times. When the first speaker has concluded his prayer, the second speaker[13] takes his place and repeats the prayer that is directed to the spirits on earth. The procedure is the same as in the first half. The duration of the Skin Dance is from thirty to sixty minutes, depending upon the number of repetitions of the prayer.

In the formal thanksgiving invocation referred to in the last paragraph, addressed to the spirits above the earth, the respective speakers from the Wolf and Turtle moieties chant in turn standing on opposite sides of the singers' benches during the Skin Dance Rite. The general wording of the chant follows that given by Parker (Code of Handsome Lake, 1913, pp. 95-100) for the Seneca at Cattaraugus. The order of reference to the spirit forces is, however, different in the Sour Springs ritual. Deskáheh gives it in the follow-

[10] On February 1, 1936, 80 were observed in line.

[11] See p. 131.

[12] Spiritual Forces; see pp. 30-31.

[13] The informant stated that in some Long Houses one speaker chants both sections of the prayer.

ing arrangement. The Wolf moiety speaker starts the Skin Dance chant with two or three lines which are taken up by the singers.

Wolf Moiety speaker:

Thanks to the people for coming to the ceremony, for "laying their minds together." A blessing is asked upon all that the Creator has done for them

Thanks to the Thunder.

Thanks to the Moon (female).

Thanks to the Sun (male).

Thanks to the Stars.

Thanks to the Four Angels (the Winds as regulators of the universe).

Turtle Moiety speaker:

Thanks to the people.

Thanks to the Earth (mother).

Thanks to what grows on the Earth (grass and strawberries).

Thanks to fruit-bearing bushes (raspberries and fruits higher above the ground than the preceding).

Thanks to the Forest (maple, fruit-bearing trees, and their kind).

Thanks to Medicines (herbs and their like).

Thanks to Wild Animals and Birds (from the small up to the large).

Thanks to all sources of food (in general).

Thanks to Water (streams, springs and large bodies of water).

Prayer that the people may live until the next ceremonial gathering.

Thanks to the singers; prayer that they may reach the next ceremonial period.

Thanks to the Creator.

It should be noted here also that these addresses may vary within the limits of the above pattern of worship, according to the ability of the speaker, the time, and the occasion.

At the conclusion of the Skin Dance the speaker "directs the minds of the people to the Great Bowl Game," the last of the sacred ceremonies, which is to be performed on the following morning. Four runners, two Wolf and two Turtle moiety men, are appointed to canvass the community to secure articles which are distributed among the members of the side winning the Bowl Game.

The territory is divided into two sections, one Wolf and one Turtle runner working in each section collecting from their respective moiety members. Articles of value, including wearing apparel which has not been discarded, are offered in this ceremony. Money is taboo. One must give something that he values, so that it comes as a sacrifice from the donor. The purpose of the giving feature in connection with the Bowl Game is to benefit the individual. The more one gives the greater his spiritual blessings. The stakes are paired, and if the Turtles win, every member of the Turtle side receives something of equal value with his own offering. The members of the losing side believe that their reward will be even greater in heaven; so they are glad to lose.

THE BOWL GAME

The fourth and last of the sacred rites taught the Iroquois by the Fatherless Boy (see origin myth, page 128) is referred to in Cayuga as *gayędowána*, "great game." This rite is formally performed in the Long House twice a year, at the Midwinter and the Thanksgiving festivals. It may also be given informally at any time in private homes for the purpose of healing.[14]

In the Midwinter Ceremony the Bowl Game Rite is enacted on the sixth day, as a form of worship addressed to the Creator. There are two players, representing opposite moieties. The game is played with six "dice" in a large bowl.[15] The dice are peach pits burned black on one side. The players kneel on a folded blanket on the floor and make the dice bounce and settle, white or dark side up, by vigorously jouncing the bowl, held in both hands, upon the folded blanket. The onlookers lean over their shoulders. The counters are 101 beans. The Bowl Game must be played until one of the two moieties wins all the counters. A ruling for starting the game when played in the Long House program is that the moiety which lost the last ceremo-

[14] In February, 1934, this rite was witnessed and noted as performed at the home of Timothy General, "Earth Splitter," officer of the Turtle moiety (see p. 183), at the request of his wife to aid in the cure of female ailment for which she was being treated. She had been helped earlier in life by the Bowl Game and was accustomed upon occasion to have it repeated for relief. Part of two days was required to finish the game-rite.

[15] The bowl now in use by the Cayuga of the Sour Springs Long House has historic associations in the tradition of the Long House group. It is a relic made over a century ago by a man named *Ska·ni·'sa'ti,* "Opposite side of the sand," and has been in use continuously in its formal capacity for over eighty years, it is claimed. It is a polished knurl bowl, 16 inches in diameter.

nial game shall have first throw. The rules and plays of the game are given later in this section.

If the game is not finished at noon, food is distributed to those present in conformity with the usual custom, namely, the bread and meat feast foods which have been provided each day since the Great Feather Dance on the sixth, and the continuation of the game is postponed until the following morning. Upon former occasions two, and even at times, three days have been required in which to finish the game.

Stakes, which, as will be seen, are really "sacrifices," are placed on the outcome of the Bowl Game. On the seventh day (that preceding the Bowl Game whenever its turn comes in the order of sequence) after the performances of the day in routine, several "runners" or collecting agents are appointed from each moiety by the officer of the day to go from house to house to gather the wagers offered by their moiety members. They make their rounds late in the afternoon and in the evening, bringing the wager-offerings to the Long House as soon as possible. The articles collected are paired off and tied together in packets of two of approximately equal value, one each of the paired articles from a person of the opposite moiety. On the morning of the day of the Bowl Game (the last day), it may be the eighth, the people convening at the Long House behold a pile of goods on the benches at the south side of the house in bundles of two articles, waiting to be distributed to the bettors of the winning moiety. The details are in the hands of the "collectors" who are aided by the memory and ownership-identity of the wagered goods.

There is a certain moral overtone and symbolism attached to the Bowl Game which should not be underrated in the scheme of native thought and teaching. The rite is a patent allegory of life and ethics. It is presented here in the phraseology of Deskáheh himself.

"Wagers are collected by moiety agents and held, to be given to the winning side. Wagers include any small articles of practical value. They must, nevertheless, be articles of some worth, constituting a gift as an act of sacrifice; clothing, best articles of apparel, and ornaments of value. Wampum is the first choice.

"As each article is given it is tied to something of equal value given from the opposite moiety (the Turtle or the Wolf). When the game is done, each person on the winning side receives back the article given with the similar article tied to it. It is, in a sense, an investment. The investment made, if the game goes right, will return interest plus itself. The same may be applied to life; one must give something to receive something, whereupon one goes to "heaven" provided that in the game of life he plays straight and right. If he does not play straight he will lose all.

"According to the code of Handsome Lake, the winner does not gain anything; the loser gains all the benefit, not because he lost, but through the act of sacrifice. This is the blessing he receives.

When one does bad and evil things he does good for the evil spirit. He then goes to the evil spirit's side. At the end he goes to the place of the evil spirit and receives the rewards of that place, punishment and discomfort.

When one does good he does good for the Great Spirit. He goes to his place and lives satisfied forever.

"One is expected to want to give sacrifices; to give to the poor and help the needy. When he lives his life he must live according to the codes and teachings; he must play straight and good or he will lose the game, his sacrifices and all rewards or 'interest.' It might be thought that when he loses he helps the evil spirit and to him goes his sacrifice, but this is not our idea of the game.

"The Great Spirit is said to have told the people (through his prophet, Handsome Lake) to play this Bowl Game in the Thanksgiving and Midwinter ceremonies to satisfy him. It is the Great Spirit's game. It makes him feel good to see his people play. Some say he wants his people to enjoy themselves when they worship.

"The game is sacred, for it is the Great Spirit's game. It represents life, to some extent. The sacrifice, the playing straight to win the reward, and the danger of losing—all teach the lesson of love, of sacrifice, and "good" with the fun of a wholesome game." [16]

If time permits, that is if the Bowl Game reaches a conclusion early enough in the afternoon and the wagers or "sacrifices" have been distributed to the winning moiety members, the Feather Dance is performed as a symbol of rejoicing and demonstration addressed to the Creator.

Counting System for Bowl Game*

The bowl is held by the upper rim in both hands and dropped forcibly on a folded blanket laid on the floor. A group surrounding

[16] Deskáheh, in writing the above, was manifestly impelled by a poilte urge to let go in answer to accusations of missionary zealots who harass the Six Nations deists, berating them as "pagans who profane the Sabbath by gambling for gain." His deposition should have a tempering effect upon those who refuse to see any virtue in non-Puritanical practices which may strangely involve an altruism deeper and more sincere than what they themselves profess.

* Notes made by Frank Staniford Speck, Feb. 4, 1936.

the players cheers its own moiety by cries of *he*+, *ca`*+, *hau*+. The six dice roll wildly in the bowl. If all six come to rest with the same side up the thrower wins five counts from the "pool." Five pits turned the same way counts one. A scoring throw entitles the player to another throw. Any other "turn-up" of the pits is non-scoring, and the player passes the bowl to his opponent. When five is scored by one player, either by a direct throw or by single scores, the opponent surrenders his place to another player, who is called, by his Indian name by the moiety leader, from the same moiety. The counters are white beans, kept in charge of the moiety supervisors. The game may be played for a count of 101 beans or, in a short form, for a count of fifteen beans. The players accumulate their bean counters from the pool, each opponent being allotted six to start his playing. When a "throw" is won, the player takes the number won from his opponent's allotment, and the latter retires from the contest when his six beans are taken. The beans won at each play are placed in a separate pile behind the six allotted to each player for his turn. When the "pool" is exhausted, each player takes counters from his opponent. To win, one side has to take all the beans. Since the game when once started has to be played to a finish, the long form may actually run from one to three days, depending upon the vagaries of fortune, as it vacillates from one side to the other.

To show that variations in the details of rites exist in the different Long Houses, it may be noted that at the Seneca ceremony each player has seven beans in his pile throughout the game. When one player is "thrown out" and a new one comes in, the opponent who stays in does not replenish his pile but plays on with what he has left.

There is an extremely elaborate system of counting score brought into use on certain occasions in the home-played Bowl Game, which as far as I can learn depends upon the ability of one among those present to operate it. The counting procedure requires a set of carved wooden sticks in pairs, which are representative of scores earned by each side. During the game as witnessed for curing at the home of Earth-Splitter, the counters were put in and taken out of a pail of sand by the score-keeper. Neither Deskáheh nor any other officer at the Sour Springs Long House is acquainted with the system sufficiently to explain its intricacies. On the occasion observed the counting was managed by Levi Baptiste, who has since left Canada and is accordingly not available for help at the time of this writing.

THE FOREST DANCE CEREMONY

A composite ceremony known as the Forest Dance, *dehadǫni* ("the forest"), which is addressed to the Creator and to the spirit forces of the forest, may succeed the Bowl Game on the same afternoon if time permits, i.e., should the latter terminate early enough. The ceremony consists of the following separate rites and dances.

(a) Feather Dance

(b) Stirring Ashes Song

(c) *djǫsiˑtadiˑhąs* (informal round dance of the False Face Society without masks)

(d) *skāˊnye* (old style; old songs)

These are given in detail under their headings in the course of the study.

Should the Bowl Game consume the entire afternoon of the eighth, or last, day, the Forest Dance Ceremony is celebrated on the afternoon of the seventh day following.

THE SACRIFICE OF THE WHITE DOG†

In ancient times the White Dog Sacrifice took place on the fifth day of the Midwinter Festival.‡ The Cayuga call it *hadiyadǫ́dwas*, "burning dog." A pure white dog is regarded as a sacred animal, and if one is born or appears in the village they believe that it has been sent them by the Creator. The dog is well treated by all and is kept in a family as a pet until the time set for it to be sacrificed. One of the officers sets the day and appoints a man to strangle the dog. It is the rule that the dog must die without shedding blood, according to Deskáheh. Yet John Buck says that at the Seneca Long House it may be bled while tied by the rope, its wind-pipe cut, and the body hung up head down. Still, we learn that the kill is done in secret by appointed attendants and no one else is a witness, Deskáheh has never seen the rite. On the day preceding the sacrificial rites, the slain dog is carried into the Long House and white wampum strings are placed on its body. Other offerings consisting of beads, ribbons, and other

† The Cayuga performed this rite about fifteen years prior to the time of writing and since that time they have not had a white dog. The informant said that they cannot perform the sacrifice until the Great Spirit sends them a pure white dog.

‡ In the original order of ceremonies, the Fifth Day marks a recess in the activities, but in the Thanksgiving Ceremony observed in the Sour Springs Cayuga Long House in February, 1933, the Feather Dance, the first of the Four Sacred Dances, was performed on the fifth day.

trinkets are brought in by the people and placed on the dog. Many people gather in the Long House and stay all night. A fire is built outside the Long House, and at sunrise the body of the dog with its decorations is brought out and put on the fire. Anyone who desires to do so may go around the fire singing his *Adǫ́wa*.

An officer is appointed to chant during the sacrifice, which is conducted by one of the two moieties. The songs as sung for the moieties are different, as will be observed in the versions recorded (Herzog), John Buck chanting. We have Onondaga songs for the Turtle and for the Wolf moieties.[17]

[17] The Onondaga at Six Nations celebrated this dignified rite in the winter of 1931-32, the Seneca in 1933. Buck officiated as chanter and would have been invited to act for the Sour Springs Long House had there been occasion.

XI

WORSHIP RITES ADDRESSED TO FOOD SPIRITS

THE following rites comprise a special group called for in the ceremonies of spring and autumn "to entertain" the grains and other crops under cultivation (Table 3, Group IB, 1-4, p. 37) during the growing time, and again to render thanks to them for their blessings in the fall at the time of maturity (see Table 2). They are not society rites, nor for curing, but are participated in by those whose sentiments prompt them to join; which should mean all those present so far as the dancing participation is concerned. They were approved by Handsome Lake.

THE WOMEN'S SONGS

The Women's Songs, ɛgaɥto'wi·s, are a series of important song rituals associated with the growth of life-supporting crops. They are performed in the Corn Planting, Corn Sprouting, and Corn Ripening Ceremonies (Table 2, pp. 35–36).

In this rite the women emerge from the background as ceremonial performers. They form in two lines, facing each other. The step is a single short sidewise alternate shuffle. At stated intervals the opposing rows change sides, passing to right and left. Each woman in the row is expected to chant a song. She accompanies her chant with the small Turtle Rattle[1] (Pl. XIV B) held in her right hand, the fingers point outward over the top of the shell. The drum is not used. When she has finished her song she passes the rattle on down the line to the next woman, who, if she does not desire to chant, passes it to the next. The rattle then is passed from hand to hand until it has been through the two rows of dancers. In the women's songs the stanzas sung by the women performers are alternated with a chorus of male singers' voices. In the Long House ceremonies a few songs of the series are occasionally requested and given. Women's songs from other tribes fitting into the ritual scheme of the Cayuga

---

[1] At the present time the rattle for this dance is the entire small Snapping-Turtle shell made with the neck handle in the fashion of the large turtle rattle of the False Face Society. We know however that the Box Tortoise shell hand rattle (Pl. XIV D) was formerly used as is shown by a specimen retained in the band.

are adopted into the series, as for instance an old Tuscarora example (Speck, Speck, and Herzog).

THE CORN DANCE

The Corn Dance, *onéhewęna* ("corn song"), is a single-file round dance resembling the *kadā'trot,* in which all take part. The instruments are the water-drum and the horn rattle, each in the hands of a singer seated upon the bench of the Long House. The dancers trot in close formation around the bench or the fire, contra-clockwise. The first group of songs are sung as the company stands around the fire, the second as the women circle the fire. There are no distinctive features. The animate elements of Corn and Beans are invoked and thanked, the words recurring in the first group of songs meaning "good corn."

THE SQUASH SONG DANCE

The *o'nyo'sa''węna,* "squash song," or *gatc'e't'qtātq`,* "shaking squash," takes its name from the squash or pumpkin rattle used exclusively in the rite. This dance is similar to the single file dances in which the men dance first contraclockwise, and then, at an interval about the middle of each canto, the women join and the men turn around their women partners. The two musicians use the water-drum and the horn rattle. The squash is the object of reverence. Anyone may participate.

XII

SOCIAL DANCES

INCLUDED in Group III, Table 3, page 37 (Specific Rites and Dances), are the fifteen dances which the Cayuga call Social Dances proper, from the sense in which they are largely viewed. These "dances" are unrestricted as respects participation and have no specifically formal medicine function allotted to them. They are, however, occasionally requested by individuals in the Long House festivals to satisfy a personal desire for relief from affliction. We find in this group some dances introduced among the Cayuga in the past and even in recent times, as is indicated by some of the names—steps and formations with appropriate songs brought into the Cayuga complex through outside contacts.

The direction taken by the dancers is contraclockwise, the line of advance going around the benches where the musicians sit at the center of the Long House. The water-drum and the horn rattle are the most frequently used instruments. No distinctive costume is worn in any of them.

Yells, in the form of short "yips," are usually given by the men at the ends of the verses or between them. These are not merely expressions of emotion; they are rather, invocations representing older symbols of invocation to the patrons of the rites or to the people present.

The Fish Dance

The term *kayówa* is the ancient name for the dance which goes by the modern name *wudjǫ́dawɛna*, "fish dance." This dance may be performed at any season of the year. The new generation has changed the name to Fish Dance and changed the songs, too, with no explanation for so doing. Deskáheh thinks the quick time of the modern version may be due to the acquired taste for speed and pep among the Indians. The water-drum and horn rattles are used to accompany the six singers who sing the twelve songs. The dancers circle both fires in pairs facing opposite, pounding their feet unusually hard, with toe and heel foot-alternating step among the

149

women especially.[1] On account of the noise of feet the singers regard this dance as a hard one to sing to, for it is difficult to make their voices heard. They usually show the effects of their efforts in the straining of their voices. The duration of the dance is about fifteen minutes.

There are two sets of songs, the old (*kayó wa*), or slow time and the new, or fast time. There are eight or ten songs in the "old" and the same number in the "new" series. The different Long Houses select and use certain songs as favorites.

The Raccoon Dance (*Sanugɛ́ha*)

The procedure, details, and duration of the Raccoon Dance are approximately the same as for the Fish Dance, except that each has its own series of songs. The men begin, single file, and the women choose partners dancing in between the men, two women together between the men chosen as partners, one going forward, the other backward, facing the men. Then at the change of song the women separate, one going behind one man while the other is ahead of her partner, backward. They return, at a change of the song, to their original position. There are two or more singers, and the instruments used are the drum and horn rattles. Several interesting expressions in the last two verses show something of the social purposes of this dance, namely, "Dance decently" and "She is looking at me with a smile."

The Woman's Dance (*Skā`nye*)

The word *Skā`nye* refers to the motion of the feet. There are two types of *skā`nye:* (a) that having the original sacred songs that have never been changed and which are connected with the sacred dance of the women, and (b) that referred to as the "new type," which is more or less social and to which new songs are being added continually. Music for the *skā`nye* is furnished by a leading male singer, who uses the water-drum, and usually more than two assistant singers, who handle the horn rattles. Four such assistants have been observed. Only women enter the dance line.

A most important note concerning the "old songs" is that they are attributed by the Cayuga to the Tutelo, as being part of the song ritual of the Four Nights Ceremony of this tribe. The original

[1] This is jokingly likened to the Charleston, which is indulged in by white people when they are present and take part.

Tutelo chants have been recorded and comparison can later be made.

The Woman's Dance does not have a regular place in the Mid-winter Ceremony or in other stated festivals, but is produced only when a request has been made for it. In the Midwinter Ceremony of 1933, it was danced on the second and third days upon request.

The women who take part in it move contraclockwise around the musicians seated on the bench in the center of the floor, the oldest women at the head of the line. The characteristic step is a quick toe-heel tap step, from which the dance derives its name. The women make gestures with their hands, alternately raised and lowered at the waist line, which symbolize "gathering corn."

The Duck Dance (Twętwęt ge'ha)

The Duck Dance is performed at Long House socials. It consists of one song which lasts about ten minutes accompanied by singers who do not dance but use the water-drum and horn rattles. The dancers proceed in double file, contraclockwise. Two male leaders start, then two women join, facing the men and coming toward them until they meet. Then the women dance backward, ahead of and facing the men, until a change in the song is signalled by the singer's rattle, when the women pass the men and go around until they meet them again. They repeat the movement described. Other men and women join in behind their respective groups. The dance has no definite function. At the terminations of stanzas the participants quack like ducks.

The Pigeon Dance (Tsa'k'owa'᾽kyā')

The Pigeon Dance has many songs and continues for about fifteen minutes. The dancers, two men and two women, proceed contraclockwise in double file, each headed by a singing leader carrying a horn rattle. The drum is not used.

The Naked Dance (Da᾽nist'dā`kyā)

The Naked Dance was introduced from the West. The water-drum and one or more horn rattles are used to accompany the singers. The women stand up while a certain number of verses are sung. The women stand before the singers. When the fast time begins, the women begin to dance contraclockwise, in two files, side by side, two facing forward and two backward. Then two men choose to dance as partners with two women dancing backward and they join in before them. The two women behind them keep going forward until two men decide to dance with these as partners, then they reverse and face them, back toward the other women. It is a double file dance. This may be performed upon any occasion when requested. There is nothing to indicate the name of the dance in the attire of the dancers, nor is there a reason given for the name.

The Round Dance (Kadā'trot)

The Round Dance may be performed in the Long House festivals or informally at social gatherings. The dancers proceed in single file, repeating in unison the syllables of the dance song after the leader. No musical instrument is used. The leader and the dancers in the line alternate in singing bars of the song, as the transcription shows. Different leaders have their own variations of this set of songs, gaining popularity as leaders by their musical skill and good voices.

The Clasping Hands Dance (Dehyǫdanént'sǫt'a)

The Clasping Hands Dance, a very old dance, was condemned by Handsome Lake but was modified by omitting the clasping of hands, in which manner it is now performed. The horn rattle is used by the leader, who strikes it on the palm of the right hand. At the beginning, a group of men dancers form an oblique line, on the Turtle moiety side, and at a certain point in the song proceed in single file, contraclockwise. The time is very slow, the foot motions keeping time with the rattle. Men and women partners frequently alternate in the line. According to Deskáheh, "it was formerly danced by warriors to strengthen them against enemies and to serve as medicine to shield the warriors before going to invade an enemy's country," corresponding with the idea of a "war dance." So, being for an evil purpose, it was condemned by Handsome Lake, who opposed violence. Nevertheless, vigilance has so relaxed in the Sour Springs Long House that this dance may occur as a request rite on the third day of the Midwinter Ceremony in connection with a cure, as it did on February 1, 1936, when it took place as next to the last rite of the day, over sixty persons participating. It lasted for about twenty minutes.

Notation on this dance can not be passed by without reference to a legend narrated in 1946 by Deskáheh. The legend points to a different and evidently older source of origin than that given above.

It refers to a period in the formation of the Iroquois confederacy when it was being extended to embrace hostile peoples west of the Alleghenies—the Shawnee in this instance. In abstract the legend runs as follows. Delegates came from the Shawnee to the Iroquois council to invite its chiefs to meet their council and explain the principles of peace. The Iroquois feared that they would be betrayed but agreed to send a delegation of chiefs. With them was to go as interpreter a young adopted Shawnee married to an Iroquois woman. He cautioned them against treachery on the part of his people. He claimed to have had a vision before they reached the Shawnee settlement and warned them to prepare to defend themselves by camping at night on a hill above the village and to surround their camp with sharpened stakes. These precautions were taken, and just before daybreak the Shawnee encircled the camp and attacked it. The Iroquois warriors fought the attackers off, while the chiefs, whose status as such did not permit them to engage in conflict, joined hands and performed a circling dance while the young Shawnee chanted a victory song. The words of his song predicted that the peace mission would be successful. The Shawnee gave up when they could not overcome the Iroquois party and agreed to join the confederacy. The dance performed by the chiefs on the occasion is believed by some Cayuga authorities to have been the Clasping Hands Dance.

It may be of interest to note that when, in the course of research in ceremonies of the eastern woodlands, a series of Cherokee song records was played over for Cayuga informants, they noticed at once the resemblance of the Cherokee Beginning Dance (of the night's social performances) to the Clasping Hands Dance. Cayuga tradition points out that this dance was introduced to the Seneca at one time. At the Seneca Long House, incidentally, it is not permitted, as I was told by one of the officers there.

The Crocodile Dance (Degâ'nǫdǫt'kyā)

In the Crocodile Dance the men start the movement. The singers sitting on the bench in the middle of the floor use the water-drum and horn rattles. The dancers join in the song at a point when the leader sings *yohobiha*.[2] After several turns around the benches the

---

[2] With this occurrence of the bilabial *b* and *m*, the only instance in the author's recordings of Cayuga, arises the question of the source from which the song text as well as knowledge of the alligator ("crocodile") may have been derived. Aside from the speech of Algonkian tribes adopted into the Iroquois confederacy, Tutelo (Siouan), also an adopted tribe from the South, lists the bilabials *b* and *m*. The only people to the southward reporting an Alligator Dance are the Creeks of the Gulf coast area.

women who so desire join in, choosing men as partners and moving beside them on the outside, making a double file. At the syllables *yu hemen* (intervals in the song) the men turn, swinging their partners. There are two songs. The singers commence the song alone, then the rest continue it. This dance can be continued as long as it is desired. Its purpose is not medicinal.

The Delaware, or Skin Beating Dance (Ganéhwai)

The Delaware Dance gets its name from the Delaware type of drum which was originally introduced with the dance. The Delaware drum was a dry deerskin folded, and bound in several instances with thongs holding in place two wooden slats on opposite sides, the whole measuring about 32 inches across.[3] It was struck with carved and painted wooden beaters.

At the present time, however, no drum is used when this dance is performed at Sour Springs, but the singer beats upon the bench where he sits with a baton of wood shaped something like the Snapping Turtle shell rattle. The dancers, all men, circle around the singer contraclockwise, making short steps and occasionally bending down. The song is a short one and the dance is vigorous. It has been incorporated into the Six Nations series with full understanding of its Delaware origin, and it is especially enjoyed by the Delaware descendants in Iroquois communities who may attend the festivals. It is not a medicine rite in any respect. It celebrates the incorporation of the Delawares into the Six Nations in the middle of the 18th century. The dance is evidently that known among the Delawares as the Men's Dance.[4]

The One-side Male, or Chicken Dance (Skā'tekadji'na)

This dance was introduced among the Cayuga by one of the members of their tribe who went to Kansas and returned. It corresponds to the Stirrup Dance (the Delaware Stirrup Dance).[5] The first part is in slow time and the second part is in fast time. The dancers imitate roosters crowing at the end of each song. The movement is in single file, men and women alternating as partners. Women dance the first three songs in slow time, contraclockwise.

---

[3] See Harrington (1921, p. 94), and Speck (1931, pp. 67, 70; 1945b, pp. 44-6).
[4] Speck (1945, pp. 71-2).
[5] The description corresponds precisely, also, to a common Cherokee round dance, as performed by the band resident in North Carolina.

For the second part men choose partners and turn, one going forward and the other backward. It is similar in form to the Fish Dance. The woman puts her foot on her partner's instep at a certain point in the song and they continue to dance around for a short space. In the Cayuga dance the women in choosing partners must choose their "cousins," that is, men from the opposite moiety. The water-drum and the horn rattles are used.

The Drunken Dance (Gātci·'hayā)

The Drunken Dance, the title of which is not a translation of the Indian name, is known to be of Seneca origin. It is only performed outside the Long House and details of the procedure are lacking. Heavily condemned by Handsome Lake, it is now only carried out at night, surreptitiously. Handsome Lake saw in a vision while he stepped from one canoe to another that the Evil Spirit was singing it.

Before it was condemned they sang and danced this dance when partly intoxicated, being furnished with whiskey during the performance. The dancers performed in the middle of the Long House, closely bunched in a circle, swirling. Men and women participated. It was a favorite dance among the Tuscarora.

The Garters Dance (Atcį't'acra)

The name of the Garters Dance could not be explained by the informant. He suggested that it is quite possible that it refers to clustered shell leg-rattles similar to those worn by the Cherokee women dancers. The singing leader and assistant carry horn rattles, and the dancers proceed behind them in single file. At intervals during the songs the women turn and face their partners dancing backwards then face forward again. The dance was introduced in 1931. The story is that the dance came recently from the Seneca at Cattaragus. It is purely social. The Cayuga also call it deye''yot'há' kadā'trot, "partner kadā'trot."

The Sharpened Stake Dance (Wano'ki'yǫ)

No explanation of the name of this dance is offered. After the serious part of a ceremony has been performed, an officer, one of the chiefs who has been appointed for the occasion, decides upon and announces the social dances to be performed. He appoints the leaders and singers. The water-drum and horn rattles are used by the singers, who occupy the benches in the middle of the floor. The participants dance around the benches. The dance, in "fast time," is similar to the *Kayo'wa* (Fish Dance), though the songs are different. There are twelve songs, and the duration of the dance is about fifteen or twenty minutes. This dance is still performed by the Cayuga. It was brought to Six Nations about 1880, "over a generation ago," from Missouri, by a group of Cayuga of the family name of Jacobs. They also brought the Crocodile Dance at the same time. It was supposedly borrowed from some western tribe, possibly the Shawnee.

The Reversing Dance (Deswadényǫˤ)

"Reverse dance," as the Indian title is translated, is very seldom danced now. Two lines of dancers move in opposite directions, each line composed of men and women. The water-drum and horn rattles are used. In the first part of the dance there are six songs, and then the formation changes to a single line and swings into the Round Dance, or *Kadā'trot*. In this part of the dance the two files alternate by doing one turn around the Long House inside the other file, then one turn outside. When the two leaders going in the opposite directions meet they change places, the leader who has been around on the outside line takes the inside file and stops singing, leaving the other man on the outside to continue singing. Thus only the leader of the outside line sings. No singers know this song now at Sour Springs, so far as one can learn.

The Robin Dance (Djiˑckogo'kyɛ')

The Robin Dance consists of three songs. The instruments used by the singers are two horn rattles; there may be also the clapping of hands. The leader at the head of the line with the horn rattle leads the dancers in a circle, contraclockwise. The dancers, men and women, face sideways and dance sideways until the leader says *ho ho*, then the dancers reverse, right-about-face, and continue until the next *ho ho*, when they right-about-face again. The Robin Dance is a social dance, but it is sometimes requested by one who feels that it would do him good.

The Shawnee Dance (Sā'wanohonǫkyɛ')

In the Shawnee Dance no instruments are used; there is only the stamping of feet. The participants form lines behind two leaders.

In the first part (*ho wa hi yo* being the song burden) the two leaders go in opposite directions. Each time they meet, the leader on the outside takes the lead and sings, alternating. After the first part, the song runs into *Kadā'trot* (Table 3, Group C). In the second part all go in one direction and one singer leads the column. There is no specific medicinal purpose. This dance is one known to have been taken over from the Shawnee "a long time ago."

The Shivering Word Dance (Gāehọdā'tǫ)

The Indian name *Gāehọdā'tǫ* means "word shivering, vibratings." The instruments used are the drum and one or two horn rattles. The dancers, only women, go in single file, contraclockwise. The "orchestra" of men sings the first half of each song and the women sing the second half. There are about twenty verses to the entire song. It is very old and the significance of the name is not known, unless it referred to the swaying bodies and unsteady voices of the dancers. This unrestricted medicine dance was condemned by Handsome Lake and is not now celebrated. It was used for a disease when requested. The dance was considered immoral by reason of the implications of its words. There were possibly licentious, "immoral," actions or motions which contributed to its condemnation. It was associated with drunkenness, as its name indicates, and a bottle of whiskey was a requisite for its celebration.

The Mouth-on Dance (K'sóhā)

In the Mouth-on Dance the singers sit on the bench in the middle of the Long House. The instrumentalists consist of a drummer and two singers with horn rattles. The men form a single file abreast, on one side of the bench facing the singers, while the women face them, lined up on the opposite side. At the half verse they turn around, backs to each other. They dance contraclockwise around the bench very slowly until the last verse. Then in conclusion they all go around faster and the women catch up to the men, closing up the space separating the two rows.

The Fishing Dance (Dat'nyóha)

In the Fishing Dance there are two singers, and the instruments used are the horn rattle and one drum. The women stand on one side before the singers seated upon the bench, while the men go around dancing contraclockwise. At every half verse the men choose female partners. At the end of the verse, they drop the woman partners where they are standing. No curative purpose is specified.

The Tormentor's Dance (Ganugɛ'yǫ)

The Tormentor's dance, the title of which is not a translation, is considered to be an invocation to the Tormentor spirit, the evil one. It is considered a very old song and dance, one of those definitely condemned by Handsome Lake. A singer sitting on a bench furnished the music, using a horn rattle. The dancers, men and women in single file, follow a leader dancing contraclockwise. The singer chants the first part of each song stanza then stops while the dancers chant the second part.

The Cherokee Dance (Wiya·tàkehonǫ)

In 1936 a new social dance was brought to the Cayuga by Chancey Isaacs. Its Indian name means "Cherokee People." It is referred to vulgarly as the "Snake Dance." It is claimed by Chancey Isaacs, who frequently visits the bands in Oklahoma, that there are Tuscarora there. He talked with and understood them. They impressed him as being good singers and dancers. In this dance, one leader with a horn rattle circles contraclockwise and winds up the line into a tight huddle. Then another leader at the rear end reverses the motion and unwinds the line. At Sour Springs they do not follow this movement but dance it in the same manner as they dance the Kadā'trot.

XIII

FAMILY CONDOLENCE RITE OF THE SOUR SPRINGS BAND

WHEN a member of the Sour Springs Long House group dies, those of the opposite moiety perform a Family Condolence Rite ten days after the burial of the deceased. On this day the spirit departs for the realm above, traveling over the Milky Way. The condolence is given in the bereaved home or in the Long House. It is often postponed from the summer time owing to the belief that a frost might ensue by invoking the "chill" of a ghostly presence.

The purpose of the rite is to console the family of the deceased, preparing them to take up life's duties which they have been unable to perform during their bereavement. This rite is of much shorter duration than that of the League Council Condolence, recited after the death of a civil chief.[1] The speeches of the two rites vary in length but only slightly in the manner of address, the difference being that in the Council Condolence the deceased is referred to as "our cousin" (*agadǫni'ˑ'sǫ*), in the Family Condolence as "our brother (or sister)" (*kyédád'ekɛ̨q*).[2] Thirteen strings of wampum are used in the ritual at Sour Springs, they are known as "notes" and serve to remind the speaker of the parts of his speech. A ceremonial cane about three feet long is also used in the family condolence (see wampum reproductions, Pl. XVI, A, and cane, B).

It has been previously noted that members of the opposite moiety condole their "brothers" who have sustained the loss.[3] Thus if a member of the Wolf moiety dies, the condolers will be of the Turtle moiety.

The following is an outline of the procedure at Sour Springs.

[1] The full text of the extended ritual used in the League Condolence Council "for condoling deceased federal chieftains" is given in a beautiful translation by Hewitt from the Onondaga of Chief John A. Gibson (see Fenton, 1944).

[2] See Beauchamp (1907), Scott (1912, p. 334), and Hewitt (1933-34, pp. 6-7).

[3] See page 20 ff. for functions of the moieties. Another obsequial duty of the opposite moiety may be mentioned; the preparing of a fire ("bon-fire") and depositing of food at the grave the first night after burial to "give comfort to the deceased." In olden days the fire was made every evening until the tenth day. Food is now set aside for the departed spirit at every meal-time by the bereaved family until the tenth day.

(Deskáheh has observed some difference between this and other Long House condolence rites on the Six Nations Reserve.)

The members of the condoling party gather at the home of a neighbor of their deceased "brother." Any man who has the ability to speak and who knows the ritual by memory is chosen to be the leader, and two assistants are appointed. The ritual is rehearsed, and then they depart for the home of the bereaved family. Each member of the party carries one or two strings of wampum and one carries the cane. Upon entering the house the assistant takes two chairs and places the cane across them, an end resting on each chair. Then he lays the strings of wampum over the cane in the order in which they are to be used by the speaker. The second assistant takes his place on the opposite side of the room near the mourners. Now the speaker is ready to begin. He starts his speech by referring to the great loss sustained and the great sorrow of the mourners. The assistant hands him a wampum string (No. 1, Pl. XVI, A). The speaker continues, taking one string after another as he intones the message associated with each, in the following order, passing them to the assistant near the mourners.

No. 1 "Now when a person is in deep grief the tears blind his eyes and he cannot see. By these words we wipe the tears away from your eyes that you may again see." He passes the string to the assistant on the opposite side of the room who has the bag in which the strings are placed. The symbolism consists in the use of beads for "words": one dark bead alternating with one light bead represents eyes clouded with tears (dark) and then cleared (light).

No. 2 "When a person is mourning the loss of a loved one his ears are stopped and he cannot hear. By these words we remove that obstruction so that you may again hear." Symbolism: one dark bead and two light beads, alternating, representing ears stopped with grief (dark) and cleared (light).

No. 3 "When a person is mourning his throat becomes stopped so that he cannot breathe well nor can he consume the food which the Creator has given him to eat. By these words we remove that obstruction so that you may breathe and enjoy your food." Symbolism: two dark beads and two light beads, alternating, representing throat choked with grief (dark) and cleared (light).

No. 4 "In your grief your entire body has become very uncomfortable. We now remove all discomfort." Symbolism: three dark beads and one light bead, alternating, representing the body afflicted (dark) and relieved (light).

No. 5 "Your bed is uncomfortable and you cannot rest well at night. We now remove all discomfort from your resting place." Symbolism: six dark beads and one light bead, alternating, representing discomfort and restless grief at night (dark) and relieved (light).

No. 6 "During your grief you have been in darkness. We now restore the light." Symbolism: string half dark and half light, represents darkness replaced by light.

No. 7 "You have lost the sight of the sky. We remove the cloud so that you may regain sight of the sky." Symbolism: string half dark and half light, represents clouded sky cleared away.

No. 8 "You have lost sight of the sun. By these words we cause you to see the sun." Symbolism: string half dark and half light, represents sun obscured (dark) and cleared off (light).

No. 9 "The mourners are thinking of the two kinds of weather from which they must protect the grave of their loved one, the hot rays of the sun and the cold rain. So you throw grass on the grave to protect it from the hot rays of the sun and place a flat board on it to protect it from the cold rain." Symbolism: two sections of dark beads; representing the grave protected from sun and rain.

No. 10 The white portion represents the work of the Creator, or Great Spirit, which the deacons are carrying on. It applies in this instance to the female offices. The speaker now condoles those officers.

No. 11 This string is used in condoling the chiefs. The white beads symbolize the position and functions of the chiefs as leaders and "clean," honest men.

No. 12 "During your sorrow you have allowed your minds to dwell on the great loss which you have sustained. You must not let your minds dwell on this loss lest you suffer from a serious illness (insanity)." (Dark beads on one end denote this.) "During your sorrow your fire has gone out. The logs have become scattered. By these words we now rekindle your fire so that you may resume your duties." (Blue and white beads alternating symbolize the scattered fire logs.)

No. 13 "Since our brother has died the light has dropped from the sky. We now lift up the light and replace it in the sky." (The 13th string is missing from the original set.)

When all of the strings have been placed on the mourners' side, the speaker says, "We think that you have now accepted our message of condolence. We will now put our backs to the woods" (leave the house). The members of the condoling party are expected to make a move to go and the mourners quickly rise and say, "Will you stay awhile?" They sit down and then the leader on the mourners' side says, "You, too, have sustained a loss. We will now condole you." The speaker goes through the ceremony in a few words for each string as he places it in the pouch. The pouch with the strings is then returned to the custodian and the formal part of the ceremony is concluded. A feast is now served by the members of the family of the deceased. Any kind of food may be served at a Family Condolence feast, but corn and beef soup and bread are prescribed as the ceremonial foods at a Council of Condolence for a chief.

If a member of the tribe dies during the Thanksgiving Festival it is customary at the present time to have the body of the deceased brought into the Long House and for the speaker of the day to recite the condolence ritual in brief. This is referred to as "partial condolence."

During the ceremony observed by the writer in the Sour Springs Long House in 1933, partial condolence rites were held for two members of the tribe on the afternoon of the Fifth Day (February 3) of the festival. The Long House was crowded, there being about 250 people, as nearly as could be estimated. The opening speech was made by the speaker for the Wolf moiety followed by two chiefs, Jacob Isaac (Oneida) and Deskáheh, who divided the recitation of the condolence rite between them. The Great Feather Dance was then performed, and afterward the feast of corn soup, beef, bread, and berry juice was served by the attendants. The afternoon session was given over to the funeral rites for two members of the tribe who had died the day before. At two o'clock the body of a three-year-old girl was brought in at the Wolf moiety door and the casket was placed on the bench in the center of the Long House. The prayer was chanted by Chief Jacob Isaac of the Turtle moiety, following which all present in the Long House filed past the casket. The bearers took the casket out the same door, and then some friends followed the mourners to the burial-ground near by. The rest kept their seats throughout a long intermission, during which there was only an occasional whisper to be heard in the Long House. The second corpse to be brought in was that of a middle-aged man, Henry Hen Hawk. The prayer was chanted by Thomas Aaron, a leader of the Wolf moiety. When he had finished, the people filed past the casket, and then the body was taken out the Wolf moiety door. The speaker of the day then "directed the minds of the people" to the program for the following day which would be the sixth day of the ceremony, when tobacco would be burned and the *Adǫwa* rite performed. That concluded the ceremony for that day.

The salutary effect of the foregoing beautiful phrases of the consolation address upon the poignant emotions of the bereaved surely call for more than just passing thought. To a sophisticated reader of these accounts it seems superfluous to point out the psychopathic value they possess for the individual, and still more so to analyze the whole procedure in respect to its benefit to the family as a restorative to normalcy in the cycle of domestic and social life. We can sense the profound understanding of human psychology that prompted the original composers of the ritual to put it in words so appropriate to assuage grief.

FINAL THOUGHTS AND COMMENTS
IN RETROSPECT

THE account of the rites of the Canadian Cayuga Indians as performed at the Sour Springs Long House is herewith brought to a close. And now we pause to consider what remains to be said concerning the subject matter treated.

To a discerning student of native backgrounds of American culture history the study should suggest much that is significant. The natural developments of human social and religious thought, as yet so little known, appear revealed here in the examination of what has been achieved in the adjustment to life's needs by a people even so obscure in the great mass of mankind as one of eastern North America's ethnic groups.

The cultural background of the Iroquois people is indeed so complex in quality, so vast in content, that it is not yet understood in full by its students, as they do not hesitate to admit. This is not the time, therefore, to draw conclusions but to point out lines of advance into the understanding of the forces at work in its history.

These rites, mysteries to the early missionaries and travelers who contacted the Iroquois, are still mysteries even to those who may convince themselves that their fundamental nature is understood. None of us can be sure that we completely understand them.

To the ethnologist indulging in the intimate process of probing corners and likely hiding places of fact, surprises seem destined to appear at nearly every move. The contemplation of possibilities involving theory combined with the Baedeker of a trait list, leads to the uncovering and at least greater understanding of the make-up of habits and customs of an unfamiliar ethnic group.

An unbiased judgment on the creed of the Cayuga in its entirety would bear the stamp of its highly socialized thought and performances in respect to its purposes and measures of behavior in the life of any average civilized people, provided one could regard it aside from his own religious traditions.

To the ethnologist who has enjoyed intimate association with the upholders of such creeds as we have described, it is difficult not to sense its virtues, provided his judgment has been kept in balance by combined objective criticism and yet sympathetic understanding throughout the course of study in the field. To confess a weakness in this respect is to mitigate to a degree the distortion that it may cause. It seems easy for one who has witnessed and attended the rites described, by participation oftentimes, to magnify its qualities of prayer, music, and poetic imagery. It arouses admiration, but it would require the word power of a romanticist to express adqeuately the higher feelings of wonder and admiration for the form and beauty they actually evoke in a mind unprejudiced by channeled theological traditions. And is there not a slow, measured dignity running through it all? Even more, one despairs of representing such feelings to cold readers who have not seen their beauty and greatness in disguise, and never will. In beholding any and all alien religious rites, sacred to groups of men, one has to shut his eyes to certain crudities in the procedures as they might seem to him. Here also, were an estimate to be made in a treatise like the preceding, reasons could be brought forth by reformers in the name of education of social and political assimilation which would result in their being written off the records of mankind struggling to interpret the spiritual universe in terms of his own life, environment, and needs sensed through centuries. The annihilation of the achievements of an ancient people along lines of moral idealism, music, poetical imagery, and deep-sense meaning might result, in the case of the Iroquois, in the loss of their heritage through assimilation with Europeans, as has happened in the history of so many native tribes. It is the conviction of many, in short, that to change one set of superstitious beliefs for another under the force of a dominant civilization has resulted in so mournful a situation that frustration and unhappiness have taken place.

Here I quote a gem, a spontaneous expression of native appreciative feeling for religious symbolism and imagery written in 1888 by Chief John Buck of the Lower Cayuga Long House, Fire Keeper of the Six Nations of Canada, to George S. Conover of Geneva, New York. It was published in the *Daily Advertizer*, Auburn, New York, April 26, 1888, and brought to my attention by Edmund S. Carpenter. The epistle evidently refers to one of the society dances, possibly the Ghost Dance Rite which has been previously discussed. Chief Buck was, however, a tribal representative of the Tutelo tribal contingent adopted into the Six Nations in the mid-eighteenth century, so his allusion may have had reference to the Tutelo Spirit

Adoption Ceremony treated in a monograph at length by the writer (Speck, 1942).

> I am John Buck's messenger [referring to a wampum string]. Therefore, listen; John Buck says in olden times of my forefathers was able to recall their departed relatives to see them again, the living ones will make one accord whatever their number may be will get a feast at a certain house for the dead ones, and when the living ones will assemble at the appointed place will take a sliver off their bark door where it turns . . . and enter noiselessly in the house where the feast is spread out for the dead, and they will now all set down next to the wall of the house on the ground . . . and one is appointed to address the Great Creator at intervals he would throw Indian tobacco on the fire, he would ask the Creator to send their dead relatives, for they are desirous to see them again, and when he ends it, his speaking, he will sit down again, and they will let the fire go down till the light ceases, so that the house becomes dark and no one is allowed to speak or make any noise, and in a little while they will hear pepole coming outside, and they will enter the house and will set themselves around the spread feast, and the assembled living ones will wait till the dead ones are about done eating then the living ones will kindle the slivers of bark which they have brought with them, and the dead ones are now seen through this light. [In the preceding quotation I have added some punctuation and made a few grammatical alterations to make the sense of the letter clearer.]

And, one may ask, what have the Iroquois to entitle them to be cited even as possessing and maintaining the rudiments of a civilization, or shall we better say a culture? Would it be anything to assert that they have a logical understanding of such abstractions existing as the order of the universe, the rulings of land ownership, exploitation and conservation of resources, rulings of conduct, respect for others' rights, a recognition of prestige, a system of economic social and economic coöperation in place of competition, belief in a future existence, in a Father-Creator, a profound sense of sympathy for women, children, and the aged, a conscious aversion toward theft and deceit in words, and intimate experience in the natural history of animals, plants, and star-beings? Though they only possess many of the beauties of simple-minded civilizations, they lack the hideous growths and horrors of the civilizations of magnitude—those so colossal as to be nearly beyond control. Why should the professional ethnologist hesitate to say that his inferences through research do and will continue to offset the conventional conception of the Iroquois as a crude barbarian?

After some thought as to the best place in which to present an epitome of the causes lying within the animal realm as believed by the Cayuga to affect the physical welfare of man, I have decided to reserve a significant statement of Deskáheh until now. His statement explains the purpose of the animal and spirit medicine societies. The following gives the evidence of the close link between mankind and the faunal life of the country which has been proverbially assumed by the writers on the subject of Indian religion in general without having specific native authority for its existence. To put it somewhat as Deskáheh did, the idea is as follows:

The Iroquois have been natives of this, their country, for so long that they have developed associations with the native animals and with spirit forces (ghosts, dwarfs, and the like) so deeply rooted that now, when the animals and nature phenomena are put so far back out of mind and so reduced, they have become lonesome for their lost intimate associations with man. This estrangement between the human and the animal realm has motivated the desire to be feasted and to be invited to join the company of their former human companions of the almost vanished forest era. The effects of man's neglect of this long interwoven association are the causes of afflictions introduced among mankind through the agency of the offended forest creatures.

Deskáheh in one of our sessions referred to the White Otter and the White Buffalo as "super animals." His remarks seem to indicate that the conception of these creatures represented supernatural aspects which controlled the destinies of their kind on earth. Details of their functions in Cayuga religion have not yet been made the subject of study. Considerable significance may, however, lie beneath the surface in the allusions, since they reflect a condition of spiritual control of the owners of game animals comparable to the beliefs in this respect existent among the Algonkian hunting groups of the coniferous forest zone. We find, in looking over the category of medicine society ceremonies, that the otter is invoked as a potent and important source of nervous disorder and as a cure for the same when appealed to by members of the Otter or Fish Eating Society Rite (p. 65), and the White Buffalo in a tutelary of another equally important medicine society ritual (the White Buffalo Society, p. 67) which relieves the spasms of zoömanic victims. These connections have yet to be probed.

One can even think of Thoreau, who once proclaimed himself
a "mystic, transcendentalist and a naturalist to boot," in connection
with some of the points brought out in the procedures described.
The spiritual values which the Cayuga believe in have been waning
in the thoughts of modern man of the West. This indeed, is not
exceptional as one regards the fate of traditional creeds of religion,
as Philip Wylie sees it, the world around in an age of science which
is also one of dread and fear.

Some thoughts now present themselves on non-material aspects
of the Cayuga religious system.

It would not be easy to find a better-ordered system of socialized
religion among men than the Iroquois economy, so well balanced
between plant and animal food resources, *well-seasoned with spiritual
nourishment,* and all shown in accented proportions in the cycle of
rituals.

Inasmuch as the writing of this conclusion has occupied part of
the time of an academic Christmas recess, it might be apropos to
refer to the courteous but unrequited sentiment of the Cayuga people
toward Christianity in ruling that the great annual festival of the
Midwinter Ceremony of the Long House be held off until the new
moon phase of January. For they say that, during the Christian
festival of the birth of Jesus at the end of December, Christians are
shadowed by the anticipation of the crucifixion of their Messiah,
and their sensitivities might be aroused at seeing the Indian keepers
of the pagan faith rejoicing as they do in the Long House Ceremony.

Soul immortality is implied in every phase of Cayuga religion.
One might rather refer to this form of immortality as continuity. It
is not a soul-saving creed. That issue is taken care of in the Handsome Lake gospels. In them the moral issues are emphasized without
being made deciding factors of soul destiny.

Another feature of the subject matter is dual deism, recounting
the conflict in the Iroquois genesis myth between opposed forces of
good and evil as dominators of man's existence and of nature. The
subjugation of personified evil by the personified principle of good
has an exceptional significance in that the evil forces when overcome
in the myth of genesis leave their scar in the realm of man's life and
of nature, without, however, continuing the role of fiends bent upon
vindictive reprisal. In regard to this point, Cayuga mythology coincides with that of the Iroquois in general, as is known to most students of the people.

A strong religious keynote struck is that of father-offspring relationship, as one of affection without immediate concern regarding arbitrary or moral law from the Creator of all life, man, animal, and plant. It seems to be the easy-going natural balance of relationship transferred from the human life-pattern to the hierarchy. Father-Creator is a kind guardian, but he leaves his children in a situation where they must adjust themselves to natural laws and their governing spirits. Nor are the latter all benevolent or beneficient; so man is left to his own devices in respect to them. And here come the adjustment performances, the varied rituals of the medicine societies.

It is obviously shown that one of the main purposes underlying these developments is that of securing and maintaining health and sanity through spiritual science of the particular Iroquois brand. Does it mean anything that so many of the ailments of people are mental ailments; that so many of the cures are mental regulators? All other objectives in prayer-rite, wish, and performance, both spiritual and "scientific," are intended in their philosophy to be secondary to the welfare drive for health.

In Iroquois (Cayuga) ceremonial dances, psychotherapeutic influences stand out in high relief. The performances are more specifically to benefit an individual or a small group of sufferers while laying only a general "blessing" upon the community. And the performance results in a group-cult working for the welfare of an individual.

Not to be overlooked among the pattern elements of the Cayuga religious tapestry is the resort to confession as a purge from the position of sin. Confession in the case of the Cayuga appears as a social and psychotherapeutic device for the regulation of moral conduct and means of health preservation through an approach to the Creator and to the human associates of one guilty of wrongdoing or wrong thought for rectification and complete forgiveness. Confession is a prerequisite to participation in the blessings conferred upon the faithful by the Creator. The summary of confession in North America recently written by Dr. W. LaBarre does not overlook the Iroquois cases of treatment of social wrong by open confession which incidentally, he does not accredit to Jesuit influence.

Cayuga religion is definitely deistic, as the Indian people themselves define it for outsiders, in respect to those elements of thought and performance directed in worship to the Creator or High God;

polydeistic as directed to the spirit-forces of the lower pantheons, those above and on the earth.

The configuration of Iroquois religion, upon examination from the point of view of comparison with so-called primitive types, impresses one as being the development of a lengthy process of formalization and codification in memory. Its stress upon ritual formality, of the health-preserving or medicinal functions of religion, and its organized hierarchy denote age and the working of a directive influence of a discipline associated with a religion as old as any native creed in North America. Were its formalities glorified by panoply and enacted amid the architectural splendors of a mound-building or even a Central American culture the scene would stand complete. Its concepts point to a milieu of a civilization of a senior character, not to that of wandering semi-nomads of fortune. Its rites move under direction of a tradition possessing a naïve rationale, with moral obligations which assume a character modern rather than archaic, as for instance we find it among the Algonkians of the northeast. The semblance of simplicity has been dissolved through the evolution of a systematized spiritualistic logic. The forces of religious compulsion have pervaded civil and political life, making priests, so to speak, out of social chiefs as well. That the concepts of the Iroquois were accomplishing a kind of spiritual conquest over some alien, adopted tribes to a degree commensurable with the extent of political expansion of the League is apparent to some from certain indications. It is not a matter to be settled by analogies in rites alone. We must pause just now, however, at the threshold of such a consideration.

Let us glance at its internalities. For every problem of existence, for every phenomenon of nature, there is a fitting application. The attitude of supplication by direct appeal to spirits is present and is expressed in rites characterized by the gesture of self-subordination, and the accompanying feeling of reconciliation to it all whatever may come. There is no note of complaint or of beseeching as a beggar for relief, but the buoyant voice of those who expect tribulation, who accept it without remorse and who yet feel that all is right from a non-human sense of judgment and can be borne with equanimity in confidence that the Creator loves them as a father does his children. This is the attitude of response to and satisfaction with the forces of nature which pervades the reception of the litanies even in the ear of one to whom the compositions are not natively familiar themes.

To such a one, again, the sense of plurality of forces invoked is strong, the panoramic host of visions of source and spiritual influences from without is overcomingly present. One could hardly stop to think who might have composed them or even of one to whom they may be ascribed. One thinks of multitudes of scenes of living things, of imaginary things, yet unseen but felt to exist somewhere in the unknown alcoves of experiences yet to be explored as life expands and develops. These are pluralized sensations of force with vistas so many and varied, reminding one of nothing more (allowing a distant but possible comparison) than the varied emotions and memory evoked by one of Tchaikovsky's symphonies. One can think of the stars collectively, but seldom does a vision of a single ruling star, the sun for example, come to mind. It is the constellation groups which come into the mental picture aroused in both phases of music and ritual—both of them great in the height and breadth of their conceptional grasp. As the natural philosopher again comes to his analysis, ordinarily it is the great galaxy of forces at work silently and cogently in the affairs of life of man, animal, and plant which arise. The singers of chants do not compose, they settle the turmoil of thought resulting from the conventional human attempt to ascribe the workings of the universe to a single entity. Music of this character is, to say the least, consistent with the emotions and meditations of two minds—the scientifically ignorant mind of the aborigine and the scientifically informed mind of the philosopher. Impressions of a rolling on in the physical universe, of a continuity not concerned with the individual but with the genus and race come uppermost into the mental picture, and we know this is true of the aboriginal bearers of these chants. Here then is where the spirit of thanksgiving flows into the song invocations addressed to the higher spirits. It becomes clear that the world view, religious fundamentals, and ceremonial cycle all constitute in Cayuga a unified organism. The idealized conception of the Cayuga universe combines in its system the tangible and the intangible, the animate and the inanimate, the living and the dead.

This brings up a brief mention of another trait in the religious complex of the Cayuga; the spirit of thanksgiving ritually expressed for the blessings of nature and the universe of life on and above the earth. Emphasis on this sentiment of thanksgiving—the beatitudes of the faithful—is mysteriously marvelous in the overtone of worship by a people like the Iroquois. It cannot fail to impress us as deserving a degree of attention which it has never received by essayists in the field of religious psychology. A fair estimate of the proportion of time in the Long House program devoted to the extraordinary rites of rejoicing over bounteous blessings bestowed on mankind compared with those begging the Creator and his spiritual subordinates for benefits would, I am sure, reveal that the former outweigh the latter. In the Iroquois system are there not lessons of deep import for us to ponder over? A number of its most intimate students indeed have come to think so!

The final section of the book gives an account and verbatim translation by Deskáheh of "comforts" recited with wampum strings as testimonials of loving sympathy to the bereaved family in the condolence of religion. Measure these by their social values! Where can a better instance be found which probes the depths of the psychology of grief and its alleviation than the Condolence Ritual to restore mental equilibrium to the bereft?

One outstanding mark of vitality in the Cayuga national faith is that it has survived three or four crises arising to stop its existence. Each of them has witnessed an assault upon the stronghold of Iroquois culture by the grim aggression of European military and ecclesiastical forces. We may wonder, forsooth, if the Cayuga have been favored by the Creator. The invisible spirits of the realm beyond seem to have favored them also in giving them an inwardly-felt assurance of permanency of their support. For epochal changes in economic and material ways of life have not extinguished the ardor of Cayuga Long House religious beliefs and practices, or forced the creed and its tenets to the wall as has happened in the changing environment of other tribal groups about them. To be sure, substitutions of modern inventions and ceremonial furnishings for native ones have been necessitated as times changed, yet the Long House conservationists seem never to have balked or rebelled against those substitutions permitting the continuation of their actions.

An awakening of self-consciousness among Indian peoples of the New World is one of the noticeable outgrowths of the last few years. These movements have taken form under wise direction extensively in Mexico and South America. It would not be fair to say that in North America neither the tribal Indians nor their white friends and helpers have been indifferent to the awakening movement because it has been going on so quietly during the past two decades. No one need be disappointed in the quality of what is being done by several Indian organizations in the field of education, and in research in history and ethnology, nor have such efforts lagged in advancing the spirit of tolerance and sympathy with the past, present, and future of native American peoples whose background is different from that of Europeans but nevertheless possess the qualities of promise in their future.

The awakening of the spirit of self-consciousness among Indian groups is bound to increase the adjustments and the happiness of life of both the Indian people and broad-minded leaders in public office. The Indian people are here to stay, and their leaders have finally come to know that they have an exceptional cultural background. They have still much to contribute to the newer aspects of American life and they are ready to do it.

And so we leave the Cayuga account of religious belief and performance. In retrospect we see the Cayuga Iroquois in whose bosoms the conviction of intimate communion between the living people, the sensitive spirits of the dead, and the realm of plant and animal spirits is their most irreplaceable quality; one, as Henry Beston has expressed it, which shows their religious relation to the beauty and mystery of the American earth.

APPENDIX I

THE following is a list of the Long House ceremonies performed by the Sour Springs Cayuga during the year 1933. On the pages following this the Midwinter Ceremony as then performed is detailed in notes taken by the author.

Midwinter Ceremony		
(New Year's Festival)	January 30 to February 5	(daily attendance) 75-400
Maple Sap Ceremony	February 12	75(?)
False Face Traveling Rite	April (last week)	125-150
Corn Planting Ceremony	May 7	75
Thunder Ceremony	May (first week)	150
Sun Ceremony	May 18	75
Strawberry Ceremony	June 15	150
Raspberry Gathering		
Ceremony	July 9	50
(Green Bean Rite)	July 27	50
Corn Ripening Ceremony		
(Green Corn Dance)	August 31	100
Thanksgiving Ceremony	September 13	125
Recitation of Code of		
Handsome Lake	October 29	300(?)
Harvest Ceremony	November 11	50

In 1934 the ceremonial year began with the Midwinter Ceremony on February 18th. In 1935 it began on February 8th, and in 1936 on January 29th.

Delegates from the Sour Springs Long House went with other Long House delegates to Cold Spring, New York, on October 7th to hear the Code of Handsome Lake recited.

NOTES ON THE MIDWINTER, OR NEW YEAR, CEREMONY OF THE SOUR SPRINGS DIVISION OF THE CAYUGA, SIX NATIONS RESERVE, ONTARIO, JANUARY 30-FEBRUARY 5, 1933

FIRST DAY

Stirring Ashes Rite

January 30th (Monday)
Time: 11:30 A.M. to 1:00 P.M.
Number present: 37 Turtle moiety (12 females)
28 Wolf " (14 females)

Procedure: The ceremony was formally opened by the Wolf moiety. The speaker, George Bumberry, repeated the Thanksgiving Prayer directed to the Spirit Forces (see Tabulation I). The second speaker, Jacob Isaac, of the Turtle moiety, directed the attention of the people to the deep religious significance of the rites about to be performed. The two head chiefs, Thomas Aaron, of the Wolf moiety, and Alexander J. General (Deskáheh), of the Turtle moiety, were appointed by the "deacons" to lead the Stirring Ashes Rite. The assistant gave each of the two chiefs a ceremonial paddle. They moved to the east, or Turtle moiety, fire, the singer (A. General) chanting.

The assistants had opened the stoves and raked down the ashes.

At the fire, the speaker offered a short prayer and both assistants slowly stirred the ashes with the paddles, holding them in one hand. Then they walked slowly to the west, or Wolf moiety, fire, the singer chanting as they walked. At the Wolf moiety fire both stirred the ashes after a short prayer had been offered by Aaron. Now they returned to the east fire and performed as before and then went back to the west fire. Having stirred the ashes twice in each fire, the chiefs took their seats. The assistant on the Wolf side chose a leader and gave a paddle to him and to nine other members of the Wolf moiety, starting on the women's side of the house. The group followed the leader out of the west door, went around the Long House, entered the east door, and formed a semicircle before the fire of the Turtle moiety. While the leader chanted and prayed, the nine people stirred the ashes with their paddles. Then they went to the west, or Wolf moiety, fire and stirred the ashes. The assistant took the paddles and

the members of the group went back to their seats. The assistant on
the Turtle side then chose a leader and gave out the paddles, Turtle
moiety paddles, to ten individuals in his moiety. They went out the
east door, entered the west door, and formed a semicircle in front
of the Wolf moiety fire. This group performed the same as the first;
after stirring the ashes of their own fire they went to their places.
The members of the opposite moiety performed. This group procedure was continued until all present had performed the rite. The
first speaker resumed the Thanksgiving prayer, followed by the
second speaker, who spoke of the importance of participation in the
rite. The meeting was adjourned at this point.

SECOND DAY

Stirring Ashes Rite
    Time: 11:00 A.M.
    Number present at opening: 44 Wolf   moiety (14 females)
                               46 Turtle   "   (26 females)
                               Increased to 140 by afternoon

Procedure: The opening prayer was by Jacob Isaac, of the Turtle
moiety. The second speaker, George Bumberry, of the Wolf moiety,
announced the program for the day and spoke of the importance of
the rite. Chief Thomas Aaron spoke next and urged the chiefs and
deacons to be more united. Then the assistant of the Turtle moiety
gave out the paddles, as on the previous day, and the group stirred
the ashes of the Wolf moiety fire and then their own. This procedure
kept up until all present had stirred the ashes. Then the two chiefs
who had opened the ceremony went to the Wolf fire and stirred the
ashes, and the speaker thanked the people on behalf of the chiefs for
taking part in the rite. Then they went to the Turtle moiety fire and
performed as at the Wolf fire.

They performed twice at each fire. This was followed by "lifting
up the paddles." The two chiefs went to the Turtle moiety fire, and
they were followed by the deacons (male and female) and other
chiefs, who formed a semicircle in front of the fire. The women
stood on the north side. The assistant gave each one a paddle. A
young boy who is a "runner" for Chief Norman General took part
in this ceremony.

At this time the singer and the speaker represented the Great Spirit.

The speaker thanked the people for performing his (Great Spirit's) ceremony, and the singer sang a song which was to represent the Great Spirit rejoicing. The group stirred the ashes of each fire twice. This is called "lifting up the paddles." George Bumberry again directed the attention of the people to the performance of the societies' dances, which were to begin after a brief luncheon period. The deacons brought in water, and those who had brought a light lunch ate it in their places.

Societies Dances

Time: Afternoon to about 4 o'clock

1. Wooden False Face Dance for Jesse Green, Wolf moiety. 1 singer, 1 masked dancer, both from the Turtle moiety.

2. The same performance for a girl member of the Wolf moiety. The dancer rubbed ashes from both fires on the heads of the patients. When the dancer ended the performance he was given False Face mush.

3. Wooden False Face Dance (partial performance), in which members of all the False Face Societies represented took part. Requested by George Bumberry, of the Wolf moiety.

4. *Adǫ́wa* Rite for Bumberry, led by Chief John Davy, an Onondaga, of the Turtle moiety. Bumberry walked with each singer. The second to sing *Adǫ́wa* was Chief Jacob Isaac, an Oneida, of the Turtle moiety. The third to chant was Chief Alexander J. General, who conducted Bumberry back to the Wolf moiety. Then Sam John, of the Wolf clan ("Real Wolf"), of the Wolf moiety, sang *Adǫ́wa*, followed by William Johnson and Ernest Jamieson, also of the Wolf moiety. Bumberry walked with the singers, and the last singer took him to his seat.

5. Bear Dance requested by Lucy Hill, Head Deacon, of the Turtle moiety.

6. Duck Dance for the same woman.

7. Buffalo Dance for Mrs. David Jacob, a Mohawk, of the Turtle moiety. Following the performance Chief Jacob Isaac spoke to the people, telling that there were two visitors among them who had come from afar.

8. Woman's Dance (*Skā`nye*) for Mrs. Jerry Aaron.

9. Closing speeches by the speakers of the day. At this juncture the two visiting investigators were called as guests to the center of the floor, where standing between the two stoves they were formally introduced by Deskáheh and responded with a few words. Then they were asked to face to the north and the people passed by in line and greeted them, shaking hands individually, led by the chiefs and officers, followed first by the women and then by the rest of the men present. This was in accordance with an old custom, it was said.

A collection was afterward taken up to help defray the expenses of the ceremonies.

THIRD DAY

Societies Dances

Time: 11:30 A.M.

The opening speech by Jacob Isaac was the Partial Condolence Ritual, recited for the families of two deceased members of the group (a man and child who died on January 31st). This delayed the performance of the societies dances, scheduled to start at the beginning of the day's program.

1. Bowl Game for Mrs. Jerry Aaron, Wolf moiety. The first time, her opponent was a member of the Turtle moiety. In the second round, women from both sides played against her.

2. Wooden False Face and Husk Mask Dance. Three women were seated on the bench. Eight men wearing wooden False Faces and carrying large turtle-shell rattles danced around the women and rubbed ashes on their heads. They also blew on them. Four small boys wearing corn-husk masks entered when the False Faces had finished, and they danced around the women. They also blew on their necks.

3. (Fish Dance) *Kayówa*. All took part. Two benches were occupied by the eight singers. A drum and a horn rattle were used.

4. Bear Dance. Three women and one boy were seated on the bench. At each end of the bench was a man (one from the Wolf moiety and one from the Turtle) with a pail of berry juice and a cup. As the members of the society danced past they were given a drink of the berry juice, some of which they swallowed and the rest of which they blew in a spray on the heads of the patients. Mush and

peanuts were also passed to the dancers. "The bears like nuts," the informant said. The berry juice must not be washed off. The boy, in this instance, had been ill, and it was decided by his family that he needed "a ceremonial friend" (see Ceremonial Friendship, p. 135). It so happened that the "friend" chosen was a member of the Bear Society. After the formal rites of the society have been performed anyone in the house may join in the dance. The performers do not partake of the ceremonial foods on this occasion.

5. Clasping Hands Dance. All present joined in this dance. They danced around both fires.

6. (Women's Dance) *Skä`nye*. All participated.

7. Eagle Dance for a woman, a member of the Wolf moiety. The woman sat on the bench with two singers and two assistants. Four dancers carrying shell rattles squatted and sang as they advanced toward the singers' bench. The woman failed to provide the feather wands for the dancers, but she did have a basket of gifts which were distributed by the speaker at the conclusion of the rite. The gifts included a chicken, biscuits, apples, and tobacco.

8. False Face Dance (Partial, see page 87).

9. Bear Dance.

10. False Face Dance (Partial).

11. Stirring Ashes Song (*Ganahawi'*), requested by a member of the Wolf moiety, for the continuation of the blessings of the Great Spirit throughout the year. This was sung by Alexander J. General, of the Turtle moiety, and William John, of the Wolf moiety. They walked slowly on the south side of the Long House between the two fires as they chanted.

12. False Face (informal without masks).

13. False Face (partial).

14. Feather Dance, led by Charlie Hill, of the Wolf moiety, and Levi Baptiste, of the Turtle moiety, as second leader.

15. Bear Dance. Three patients were seated on the bench. The procedure was the same as before.

16. *Adǫwa*, requested by Timothy General, of the Turtle moiety. The first singer was Oscar Johnson, of the Wolf moiety; the second singer, Jerry Aaron, of the Turtle moiety.

17. Feather Dance, in part, led by Levi Baptiste, of the Turtle moiety.

18. Feather Dance, in part, led by William John, of the Wolf moiety.

19. False Face Dance (Partial).

20. (Round Dance) *Kadátrot*. All participated. Closing speech by Chief Jacob Isaac, telling of the program for the following day.

FOURTH DAY

Rituals and Feasting

Time: 11:00 A.M.

Food spirits were addressed, and thanks given to the Great Spirit. The women changed their seating on this day. The Turtle moiety women took seats with the Wolf women on the west side of the house.

The Thanksgiving prayer was led by Jacob Isaac, of the Turtle moiety. The response was by George Bumberry, of the Wolf moiety.

A cauldron of corn soup was brought in by assistants and placed on the south side of the Wolf moiety stove.

The Feather Dance was led by a boy about ten years of age wearing a costume. The dance lasted twenty minutes. Between the songs Jacob Isaac recited portions of the Code of Handsome Lake.

The Deacon of the Wolf moiety served the corn soup. Each one brought a container, which he placed near the stove, and when the corn soup had been put into all pails and dishes, the people went forward and claimed their containers. The assistants passed biscuits and corn bread by hand to the people. Berry juice was passed to the chiefs.

The Wolf and Turtle moieties were represented by speakers, who told of the program for the following day. Deskáheh announced that the ceremony would start at an earlier hour on account of the funeral services for the deceased members of the group, which would be held in the Long House on the following afternoon. The meeting was adjourned at 2:30 P.M.

FIFTH DAY

Sacred Dances

Time: 10:00 A.M.

The Long House was filled to capacity in a short time. It was estimated that there were about 350 persons, many standing in the east end of the house. The opening speech was by George Bumberry, of the Wolf moiety, followed by Jacob Isaac and Alexander J. General, of the Turtle moiety, officiating in the Partial Condolence Rite. The Feather Dance was announced, and then the cauldron of corn soup was brought in. The dance was performed in honor of the food, "our nourishment." Charlie Hill led the dance, and there were nine men and six women in costume. There was an intermission during which Deskáheh addressed the dancers. The dance was repeated, this time led by William John. Nearly everyone present took part, and double lines were formed going around both fires.

Following this the feast was served. Meat was served for the first time, in addition to the usual foods such as corn soup, corn breads, and berry juice. When the corn soup had been served to the people on both sides of the house, the cauldrons were taken to the Wolf and Turtle men, and they scooped out the soup using ceremonial wooden spoons which they keep for such occasions. At two o'clock the body of the three-year-old child was brought in and placed on a bench in the center of the Long House.

The head was toward the west. The partial Condolence Ritual was recited by Jacob Isaac, of the Turtle moiety. All viewed the body and the casket was taken out; some of the people went to the grave a few hundred yards away. A long intermission followed. The people kept their seats and a profound silence fell over the group. Possibly three quarters of an hour passed before the body of the man was brought in. The ritual was recited by Chief Tom Aaron, Wolf moiety. Following the speech the members of both groups viewed the body. Some went to the grave. The meeting was adjourned at about 4:00 P.M.

SIXTH DAY

Burning Tobacco Rite
   Time: 10:00 A.M.

About 185 people were present, including men, women, and children. The opening prayer was led by George Bumberry, of the Wolf moiety, followed by Jacob Isaac, of the Turtle moiety. Then six men (chiefs and deacons), three from each moiety, formed a semicircle in front of the east fire. The prayer (see p. 131 for details) was chanted by Tom Aaron, of the Wolf moiety, and Jacob Isaac, of the Turtle moiety. This prayer was directed to the Spirit

Forces above and on the earth (see Tabulation I). Two cauldrons of corn soup were brought in. Jacob Isaac spoke to the people, urging the men to take part in the *Adǫ́wa* rite. Tom Aaron spoke, representing the Great Spirit, urging the people on earth to take part in his (Great Spirit's) ceremony, *Adǫ́wa*. Then he offered his personal appeal to the Great Spirit and the spirits who are guiding us and begged them to spare us to witness another ceremony.

Those singing *Adǫ́wa* were: Timothy General, George Bumberry, Robert Isaac and son, Tom Aaron, George Nash, Oscar Johnson, and Mannie General.

Bumberry carried a male child and sang *Adǫ́wa*. The speaker announced the name given the child. *Adǫ́wa* is not sung for a female child when given a name ceremonially.

The name *Saų́hyes*, "long sky," was given Mannie General.

Jerry Aaron sang *Adǫ́wa* and had a friend walk with him.

Names were given one girl, a young man, and a small boy.

Levi Baptiste, Jacob Isaac, David Jacob, Jacob Jacob, Simon Jonathan, and George Aaron sang their individual *Adǫ́wa* songs.

The Skin Dance was performed. It lasted forty minutes. The Feather Dance followed and lasted 25 minutes. Men were appointed to collect stakes for the Bowl Game. The speaker called attention to the significance of this rite. The feast was served.

SEVENTH DAY

Bowl Game

Time: 11:00 A.M.

Assistants paired stakes collected by runners for the bowl-game "sacrifice" before the meeting was opened. Women of the Turtle moiety took seats on the Wolf side of the Long House as on the first three days. Opening speeches were made by Tom Aaron, Levi Baptiste, and George Bumberry.

In the Bowl Game the chiefs play first, followed by the assistants, then the other men and women. On this occasion the game was won by the Wolf moiety in about two hours. The Feather Dance was performed by way of rejoicing at the completion of the Great Spirit's ceremonies. Stakes were distributed to the winning side.

Then the chiefs spoke, thanking the people for having taken part in the ceremonies and telling them to carry on their work as before and to love one another. The speaker transferred the ceremonies of the ensuing portion of the year to the women, who in turn decided to defer the performance of the Forest Dance until the following Sunday. The feast was partaken of, and the ceremony ended about 3:00 P.M.

Listed below are the names of the officers and active participants in the 1933 rites of the Sour Springs Long House. The sib affiliations where known are given in small type, the moiety in capitals, thus: Heron, WOLF. The tribal identities of the individuals are Cayuga unless otherwise noted.

Leaders

Sodjε'hes, "Long Fire," George Bumberry.

Hǫwa'ʿtcʿhadèʿhǫ, "Somebody burying him," Jacob Isaac, Oneida Council Chief living with the Cayuga, Bear, TURTLE.

Takahε'dro, "Several things leaning over," Thomas Aaron, Heron, WOLF.

Desga'heʿ, "More than eleven, in the teens." (Chief's title) Alexander J. General, also known as *sǫhyówa,* "Sky great" (personal name), Young bear, TURTLE.

Toʿwεga'ʿkwε, "He has picked up the wood," Norman J. General, Chief, WOLF.

Djïʿ'gragǫ, "In the clouds," George Aaron, Head Deacon, Heron, WOLF.

Tųʿwεdjo'was, "Earth splitter," Timothy General, Head Deacon, Young Bear, TURTLE.

Senayïʿ'hwas, "Name undiscovered, not found," Maggie General, wife of Timothy General, Head Officer, Heron, WOLF.

Assistants Who Distributed Paddles

Dagǫʿhyu'tǫ', "The sky stood up," Ezekiel Hill, Eel (Onondaga).

Gaų'yatā`se, "Sky surround" or "Sky wound around," Oscar Johnson, Heron, WOLF.

Taųhayaïʿcro, "Beating the sky," Charlie Hill, WOLF.

Sadegą'hes, "Equal height of trees," Jeremiah Aaron, Deer, TURTLE.

Hahǫwadïʿ'ho, "Resting canoe on something," Eli Jacobs, Snapping Turtle, TURTLE.

Ta'tᶜkᶜtᶜǫs, "The man that looks around," John Davy (Onondaga Chief).

Hǫunⁱsᶜɛᶜᶜte, "Carried a long time," Samuel John, Wolf, WOLF.

Twⁱᶜhwą́ndon, "Leading off the word," Ernest Jimerson, descendant of Tutelo.

Ha'snogaᶜ, "Saw the bark," William Johnson.

Gą̄́hawas, "Tree shedding," Lucy Hill.

Kai'hᶜnɛs, "Dropping bundles," Mrs. Jeremiah Aaron.

Sagwⁱehwa'ᶜtᶜa, "He awakens them," William John, WOLF.

Sau̜'hyes, "Long sky," Mannie General, WOLF. (Name given ceremonially.)

APPENDIX II

The following list made by Deskáheh of male family heads gives a cross-section of the group make-up of the Sour Springs Long House communicants. There is no enrollment or membership affiliation beyond cooperation and participation in the activities of the Long House: all is free-will. The list affords a crude sampling of tribal identity of an unselected average among the Cayuga conservatives in 1933. Out of 21 family heads listed it will be seen that 13 have Cayuga lineage, all have Iroquois ancestry, 4 classify as Mohawk, and 3 trace Tutelo descent, 2 Nanticoke, 1 Delaware, and 1 Shawnee.

Family Constituency and Tribal Extractions

Family Head	Mother's Tribal Identity	Father's Tribal Identity
Oscar Johnson	Cayuga	Cayuga-Mohawk-Tutelo
William Isaacs	Oneida	Cayuga
George Bumberry	Nanticoke	Cayuga
Ernest Jimerson	Tutelo	Cayuga-Mohawk
Norman General	Cayuga	White
Norman General	Nanticoke	Cayuga-Oneida
Jerry Aaron	Mohawk	Cayuga
Tom Aaron	Mohawk	Cayuga
James Johnson	Cayuga	Shawnee
David Jacob	Delaware-Cayuga	Cayuga
William John	White	Onondaga-Tutelo
Aleck General	Cayuga-Oneida	Cayuga-Oneida
Timothy General	Cayuga-Oneida	Cayuga-Oneida
Ernest Davis	Mohawk-?	
Lawrence Davis	Mohawk-?	
John Montour	Mohawk-?	
Charley Davis	Oneida-White	
Reginald Martin	Mohawk-?	
Robert Henhawk	Onondaga-Mohawk	
John David	Onondaga-?	
James Henry	?	Cayuga

BIBLIOGRAPHY

BARBEAU, C. M., 1912. "On Iroquoian Field-Work, 1912," *Summary Report of the Geological Survey, Canada, for the calendar year 1912,* Sessional Paper No. 26, 454-460.

BEAUCHAMP, W. M., 1907. "Indian Councils and Ceremonies," *Bulletin* 113, New York State Museum, Albany.

1922. *Iroquois Folk Lore,* Onondaga Historical Ass'n., Syracuse, 247 pages.

BOAS, FRANZ, 1909. "Notes on the Iroquois Language," in *Putnam Anniversary Volume,* 427-460.

BOYLE, DAVID, 1899. In "Archaeological Report, 1899," Appendix to the *Report of the Minister of Education,* 1900.

BRODHEAD, JOHN ROMEYN, Edited by E. B. O'Callaghan, 1855. *Documents Relative to the Colonial History of the State of New York,* Vol. VI, Albany, "Onondaga conference," 808-15.

CLARK, J. V. H., 1849. *Onondaga.* 2 vols. Syracuse.

DODGE, E. S., 1949 (MS), "A Cayuga Bear Society Curing Rite."

FENTON, WILLIAM N., 1936. "An Outline of Seneca Ceremonies at Coldspring Long House," *Yale University Publications in Anthropology,* No. 9, 1-23.

1937. "The Seneca Society of Faces," *Scientific Monthly,* Vol. 44 (March), 215-238.

1944. "The Requickening Address of the Iroquois Condolence Council," by J. N. B. Hewitt, late ethnologist, Bureau of American Ethnology, *Journal of the Washington Academy of Sciences,* Vol. 34, No. 3 (March 15), 65-85.

1940. "Problems Arising from the Historic Northeastern Position of the Iroquois," *Smithsonian Miscellaneous Collections,* Vol. 100 (whole volume), Essays in Historical Anthropology of North America, 159-251.

1941 a. "Masked Medicine Societies of the Iroquois," *Smithsonian Report for 1940,* 397-430.

1941 b. "Tonawanda Longhouse Ceremonies: Ninety Years After Lewis Henry Morgan," Smithsonian Institution Bureau of American Ethnology *Bulletin* 128, 140-166, *Anthropological Papers,* No. 15.

1942. "Songs from the Iroquois Longhouse: Program Notes for an Album of American Indian Music from the Eastern Woodlands," (From records in the Archive of American Folk Song, The Library of Congress) Smithsonian Institution Publication 369. 34 pages.

GOLDENWEISER, A. A., 1912. "On Iroquois Work, 1912," *Summary Report of the Geological Survey, Canada, for the calendar year 1912.* Anthropological Division Sessional Paper No. 25, 464-475.

1914. "On Iroquois Work, 1913-1914," *Ibid.,* 1914, 365-372.

HARRINGTON, M. R., 1909. "Some Unusual Iroquois Specimens," *American Anthropologist*, Vol. 11, No. 1, 85-91.

1921. "Religion and Ceremonies of the Lenape," *Indian Notes and Monographs*, Museum of the American Indian, Heye Foundation. New York.

HAWKINS, BENJAMIN, 1848 (Posthumous). "A Sketch of the Creek Country," *Collections of the Georgia Historical Society*, Vol. 3, Part 1. 88 pp.

HEWITT, J. N. B., 1916. Account of his field studies for that year in "Exploration and Field-Work of the Smithsonian Institution in 1916," *Smithsonian Miscellaneous Collections*, Vol. 66, No. 17, 121-129.

1918. "A Constitutional League of Peace in the Stone Age of America," *Annual Report*. Smithsonian Institution, 527-545.

1933-34. *Fifty-first Annual Report*, Bureau of American Ethnology, 6-7.

1944 (Posthumous). "The Requickening Address of the Iroquois Condolence Council" (Ed. Wm. N. Fenton), *Journal of the Washington Academy of Sciences*, Vol. 34, No. 3 (March 15), 65-85.

KEPPLER, JOSEPH, 1941. "Comments on Certain Iroquois Masks," *Contributions from the Museum of the American Indian, Heye Foundation*, New York, Vol. XII, No. 4.

KINIETZ, W. V., 1940. "The Indians of the Western Great Lakes." University of Michigan Press, Ann Arbor, 427 pages.

LA BARRE, W., 1947. "Primitive Psychotherapy in Native American Cultures; Peyotism and Confession," *Journal of Abnormal and Social Psychology*, Vol. 47, No. 3, 301-7.

LEDERER, JOHN, 1672. *The Discoveries of John Lederer, in three several marches from Virginia to the West of Carolina*. London. (Cited by Mooney.)

LLOYD, H. M. (editor) 1901. *League of the Ho-De-No-Sau-Nee or Iroquois*, by L. H. Morgan. 2 vols. New York.

MICHELSON, TRUMAN, 1932. "Notes on the Fox Wapanowiweni," Smithsonian Institution Bureau of American Ethnology *Bulletin* 105.

MOONEY, J., 1894. "Siouan Tribes of the East," Smithsonian Institution Bureau of American Ethnology, 71.

MORGAN, L. H., 1901. *League of the Ho-De-No-Sau-Nee*. Ed. H. M. Lloyd. 2 vols. New York.

OLSON, RONALD L., 1933. "Clan and Moiety in Native America," *University of California Publications in American Archaeology and Ethnology*, Vol. 33, No. 4, 351-421.

PARKER, ARTHUR C., 1909. "Secret Medicine Societies of the Seneca," *American Anthropologist* (n.s.), Vol. 2, No. 2, 161-85.

1912. "Certain Iroquois Tree Myths and Symbols," *American Anthropologist* (n.s.), Vol. 14, No. 4, October-December, 608-620.

1913. "The Code of Handsome Lake, the Seneca Prophet," New York State Museum *Bulletin* 163, Education Department Bulletin No. 530, University of the State of New York, Albany, November 1, 1912. 148 pages.

1916. "The Origin of the Iroquois as Suggested by Their Archaeology," *American Anthropologist* (n.s.), Vol. 18, No. 4, October-December, 479-507.

SCHOOLCRAFT, H. R., 1846. *Notes on the Iroquois*. New York. 498 pages.

SCOTT, DUNCAN C., 1912. "Traditional History of the Confederacy of the Six Nations," prepared by A Committee of the Chiefs, *Transactions of the Royal Society of Canada*, Vol. 5 (third series, 1911), Section 2, 195-246.

SNYDERMAN, G. S., 1948. "Behind the Tree of Peace, A Sociological Analysis of Iroquois Warfare," *Bulletin of the Society for Pennsylvania Archaeology*, Vol. XVIII, Nos. 3-4, 93 pages.

SPECK, FRANK G., 1931. "A Study of the Delaware Big House Ceremony," *Publications of the Pennsylvania Historical Commission*, Vol. 2. Harrisburg. 192 pages.

1942. "The Tutelo Spirit Adoption Ceremony, Reclothing the Living in the Name of the Dead." (Transcription and Analysis of Tutelo Music, George Herzog.) *Publications of the Pennsylvania Historical Commission*, Harrisburg. 125 pages.

1945 a. "The Iroquois, A Study in Cultural Evolution," *Bulletin* No. 23, Cranbrook Institute of Science, Bloomfield Hills, Michigan. 94 pages.

1945 b. "The Celestial Bear Comes Down to Earth, The Bear Sacrifice Ceremony of the Munsee-Mahican in Canada as Related by Nekatcit." (In collaboration with Jesse Moses.) *Scientific Publications* No. 7, Reading Public Museum and Art Gallery, Reading, Pennsylvania. 115 pages.

SPECK, FRANK G., SPECK, FRANK S., and HERZOG, GEORGE. (Unpublished) Songs of the Sour Springs Cayuga, transcribed recordings.

SPECK, F. S., 1941. "The Cayuga Indian Snow Snake Game," *The General Magazine*, University of Pennsylvania, Vol. XLIII, No. 1111, 416-9.

SPIER, LESLIE, 1935. "The Prophet Dance of the Northwest and Its Derivatives: The Source of the Ghost Dance," *General Series in Anthropology*, No. 1, 1-74.

WALLACE, PAUL A. W., 1946. *The White Roots of Peace*, University of Pennsylvania Press, Philadelphia. 57 pages.

WAUGH, F. W., 1913. "On Work in Material Culture of the Iroquois, 1912," *Summary Report of the Geological Survey, Canada, for the Calendar year 1912*, Sessional Paper No. 26, 476-480.

WITTHOFT, J., MS. on Cayuga hunting fetish.

INDEX

Acculturation, in ceremonial paraphernalia, 40 n.; in Confession Rite, 52; damage in loss of cultural heritage among Iroquois, 165

Adǫ́wa Rite, 131-38

Algonkian beliefs, compared with Cayuga, 1-2, 167

Altruism, in curing rituals, 26, 169-70; toward people in general, 134-35; toward Christian beliefs, 168

Animals, as food spirits, 30; as tutelaries of Medicine Societies and objects of thanksgiving, 32; as neglected spirit forces causing sickness, 63, 103, 167; associated with mask spirits, 91

Art objects, headdress, 24-25; carved drumsticks, 44; feathers, face paint, costume, 45; paddles in Stirring Ashes Rite, 53

Ashes, in consecration of masks, 77; as purifying agency, 94; rubbed on patients' heads, 177, 178

Baptiste (Bateese), Levi, 104

Bear Society Rite, 64-65

Bezoar stone, 113-14

Blowing of medicine on patients' heads in curing treatment, 65, 68, 80, 87-88, 110, 178

Bowl Game Rite, 141-45; sacrificial character, 141; Deskáheh's explanation, 142

Buck, John, 96, 165-66

Buck, Mrs. John L., 71 n., 74, 95-96 n., 131

Calendar of ceremonial rites, 174

Cane used by leaders of masking groups, in spring rites, 94-95, Pl. XI, D, in Eagle Dance, 112, in Thunder Rite, 118, in War Dance, 119, in Condolence Rite, 159-60

Catawba, similarity between Horse Dance and Cayuga Striking Stick Dance, 119

Cayuga, vitality of native beliefs, 4

Cherokee, introduction of "pig" mask, 106; similarity of eagle belief to Cayuga, 113; similarity in music of Beginning Dance and Cayuga Clasping Hands Dance, 153; of round dance with Cayuga Chicken Dance, 154 n., 155, of Horse Dance and Cayuga Striking Stick Dance, 119 n.

Chicken Dance, 119-20, 154

Chipmunk Rite, 44, 116

Choctaw, 116 n.

Christianity, 170

Clasping Hands Dance, 152

Communion between spirits and people, 50

Condolence Ritual, 159-63

Confession of misdeeds, 52, 170

Corn Dance, 148

Corn-husk Mask Society, 88-99; associated with vegetation, 95, 98; origin myth, 96; associated with females, 98

Corn Planting Ceremony, 35

Corn soup, 41

Creator, concept of, 29, 30; signal cries to, 139; as father of mankind, 169-70

Creator's words quoted in Long House ceremonies, 55, 133, 177

Crocodile Dance, 153

Dark Dance, 109-11

Dekanawidah and Fatherless Boy legend, 3

Delaware, contacts and relationships with Cayuga, 1-2, 4; adoption by Iroquois, 16, 18; influences on Cayuga mask rites, 75

Delaware Dances, introduced into Cayuga series, 154; similarity of Stirrup Dance with Cayuga Chicken Dance, 154

Deskáheh (Alexander General), 6-7

Dichotomy, in moiety and sex activities, 34. *See also* Moities, Sex distinctions

Disease, exorcism of, by mask rituals, 93-94

Dog Sacrifice Rite, 143, 145-46

Dolls, corn-husk, 99-100

Dreams, cause of illness, 122 (*see also* Psychiatry); cured by guessing spirit causes, 122

Drum, water drum, 44; Delaware folded skin drum, 154

Drunken Dance, 155

Duck Dance, 151

189

PLATE I

A

B

A. Sour Springs Cayuga Long House, Six Nations Reserve, Ontario (October 1944). View look-
   ing westward showing the old cook house. (Photograph by E. S. Dodge, Peabody Museum,
   Salem, Massachusetts).
B. Deskáheh, Alexander General, in ceremonial garb.

PLATE II

A famous Cayuga Ceremonialist and Healer, Isaac Doctor (Tᶜéta' atᶜų, "Runner") and his four sisters. He died about 1890 at over ninety years of age. (From an old photograph).

PLATE III

A. Chief Alexander J. General and his wife in formal Cayuga costume and pose. As civil chief
   representing the Young Bear Clan of the Cayuga Turtle Moiety, he holds the title and office
   of Deskáheh in the Six Nations Council.
B. Mother of Deskáheh. (From a daguerreotype).
C. Jeremiah Aaron (Sadegáhes, "Equal Height of Trees"), Cayuga Long House Official.
D. Wife of Jeremiah Aaron (Háiht'nes, "Dropping Bundles").

PLATE IV

A

B   C

A. "Food! Blessings of the Creator!" Corn braided in strings on shucks and hung on poles to dry for winter use. (November 1936). At the home of Alexander General, Deskáheh.

WOODEN MASKS OF THE MEDICINE MEN'S SOCIETY

B. Represents spirit of smallpox and measles.

C. Represents spirit of fever.

PLATE V

A. and B. Cayuga False Face Society Members in formal garb as appearing in the Long House in the Midwinter Ceremonial January 30-February 7, 1933. Note the ragged clothing, turtle rattles and staffs.
C. and D. Cayuga Masks painted half red (right side) half black (left side) representing the whirlwind
spirit, to be suspended on a tree before the house to avert an approaching storm. The mask on the left is
in the collection of the Peabody Museum, Salem, Mass. The mask on the right has a movable tongue.

PLATE VI

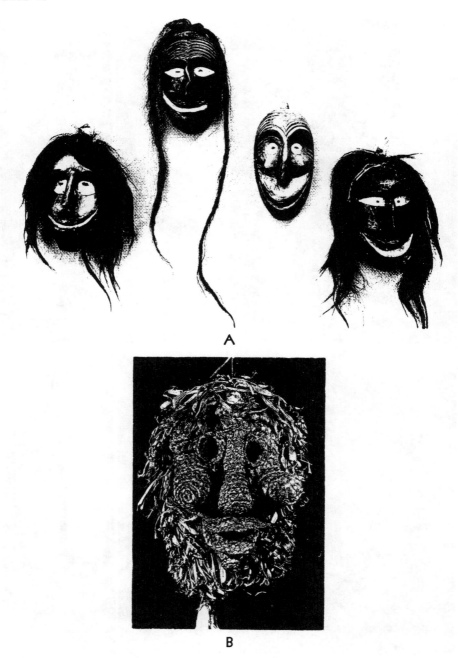

A

B

A. Group of four masks representing Thunder Beings, worn in convocation rites and known as the four mystery men since they do not remove masks or disclose their identity. (Lower Cayuga and Seneca. Masks at left and second from right, red; upper center and right, black). (Denver Art Museum, Denver, Colorado).

B. Corn-husk Mask with exaggerated features denoting age. Worn by "Leader" of Corn-Husk Mask Society. (Collection of Mr. Robert Riggs).

PLATE VII

CAYUGA MASKS USED IN SOCIETY RITES

A. Uncolored wood mask with red nose and pig tusks, used by doctor in Medicine Men's Society rites. This is known as a Pig Mask and has mythical associations.

B. Variation of Pig Mask with black upper face and uncolored snout, with pig teeth, movable tongue, and horse hair.

C. Black mask with corn-husk hair, representing the "Crooked Face", used in Wooden False Face Society rites.

D. Red mask used in same society rites as C. Wrinkles shown in white paint and protruding moose teeth symbolize old age.

(Museum of The American Indian, Heye Foundation, N. Y.)

PLATE VIII

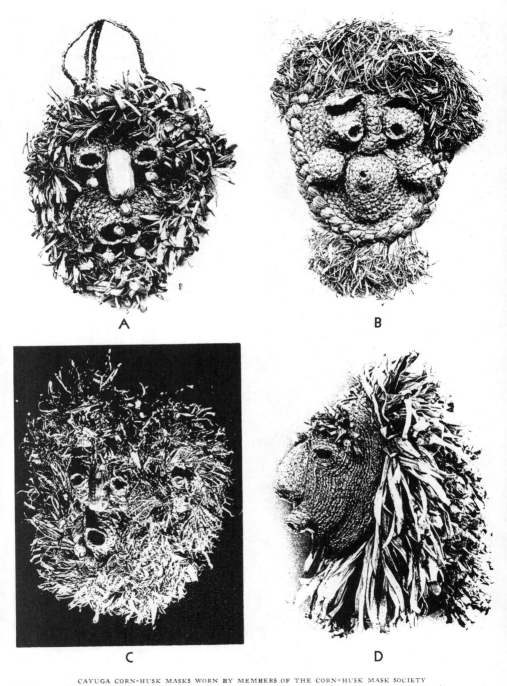

CAYUGA CORN-HUSK MASKS WORN BY MEMBERS OF THE CORN-HUSK MASK SOCIETY

A. Image with six medicine powder bags under eyes, nose, and mouth (tears, mucous and saliva) representing the Six Nations.

B. Corn-husk mask with puffy eyes, cheeks, and mouth for blowing medicine, and chin beard.

C. Bushy mask with minature corn-husk mask in upper left-hand side representing "vanishing spirit".

D. Corn-husk mask of helmet type covering entire head, with puffy lips for blowing medicine.

PLATE IX

CAYUGA MINIATURE MASKS, TWO-THIRDS NATURAL SIZE. USED IN DREAM GUESSING RITE IN THE LONG HOUSE.
A. and B. Black images of wood with horse hair. (Length 2″).
C. Small shell image with yarn for hair (Collection of Mr. Robert Riggs). (Length ¾″).
D. Corn-husk image (Museum of the American Indian, Heye Foundation, N. Y.). (Length 3 inches).
   (18/4743)
E. and F. Red images, E with horse hair; F with gray fox hair. (Length 2″, 1¾″).

PLATE X

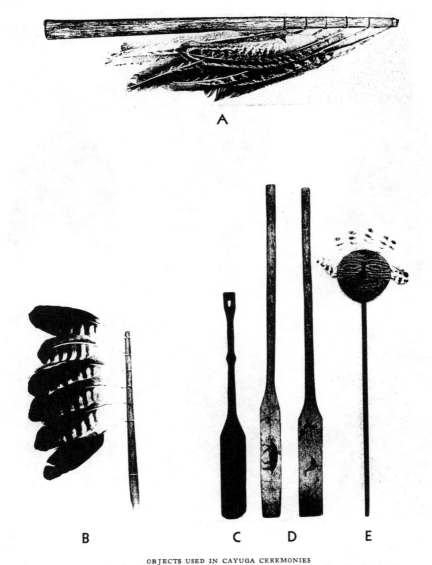

A

B   C   D   E

OBJECTS USED IN CAYUGA CEREMONIES

A. and B. Feather wands, two of which are held in hands of dancers in the Eagle Dance: upper of
pheasant feathers, lower of hawk feathers. (Length 12″, 14″). (18/4749)

C. Stirring Paddle for food in feasting cauldron, also carried by member of Corn-husk Mask Society. (Length
36″). (18/3734)

D. Paddles used in Stirring Ashes Rite. Note clan emblems burnt into blades, representing wolf and
turtle on opposite sides, deer and heron (specimen at left) on opposite sides of the other (at right).
They also represent moiety emblems. (Length 49″). (18/4732-3)

E. Sun disk wand symbolizing sun and rays of warmth and light, carried by man in Sun Rite while chanting
his Thanksgiving Song (Adǫwa). (Length 40″). (18/4738)

Museum of The American Indian, Heye Foundation, N. Y.

PLATE XI

OBJECTS USED IN CAYUGA CEREMONIES

A. Wooden bowl (Seneca, N. Y.) used in Bowl Game Rite, peach pit dice and bean counters (Sour Springs Cayuga). (Width 8¾"). (18/4755,18/4751)

B. Woven corn-husk basket for burnt sacrifice of tobacco in Thunder Rite. (Height 2"). (18/4746)

C. Ceremonial wooden spoon with bird carved on handle, used by men in Long House feasts. (Length 6¾"). (18/4735)

D. Walking-stick with face image on handle carried by leader in spring rites of Wooden False Face Society when entering Long House. (Length of face 2½").

Museum of The American Indian, Heye Foundation, N. Y.

PLATE XII

A

B

C

OBJECTS USED IN CAYUGA CEREMONIES

A. Deer-skin robe with head in place and cow horns attached, worn with wooden mask (Plate VII D.) by member of Wooden False Face Society (see Plate V B). (Length 52″). (Museum of The American Indian, Heye Foundation, N. Y.) (18/4743)

B. Sun disk, with down glued on margin, carried by reciter in Thanksgiving Rite (Adǫwa) (Onondaga Long House, Six Nations Reserve). (Length 12″).

C. Cayuga clan matron, Mrs. Jeremiah Aaron.

PLATE XIII

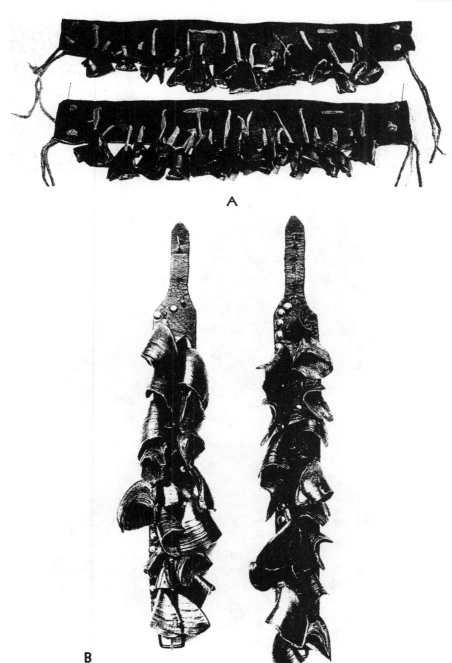

A

B

CAYUGA MUSICAL INSTRUMENTS

A. Garter rattles made of deer hoofs, worn by men dancers in Feather Dance and other costume rites. (Length 14″).

B. Same, made of pig hoofs. (Length 15″). (18/4749)

Museum of The American Indian, Heye Foundation, N. Y.

PLATE XIV

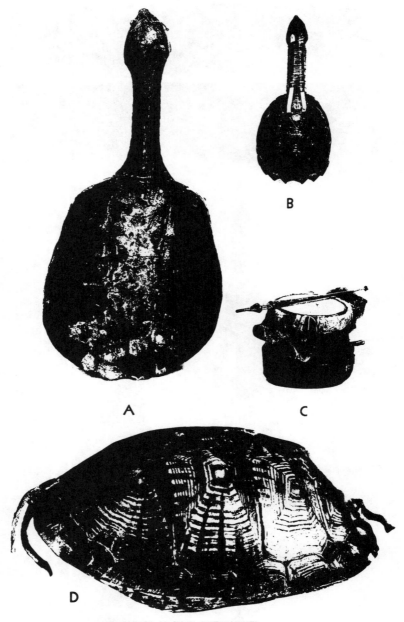

CAYUGA MUSICAL INSTRUMENTS

A. Full grown snapping-turtle rattle used by members of Wooden False Face Society in formal rites. (Length 23″). (18/4727)

B. Half-grown snapping-turtle rattle used in Woman's Song Rite. (Length 10″). (18/4728)

C. Water-drum and drum beater used in ceremonial rites of societies and social dances. (Height 4″). (18/4748)

D. Box turtle shell rattle formerly used in Woman's Song Rite. The specimen is said to have survived from the Cayuga migration from New York State, having been retained by the Long House officers at Sour Springs. It is now replaced by the small snapping-turtle shell rattle (B above).

PLATE XV

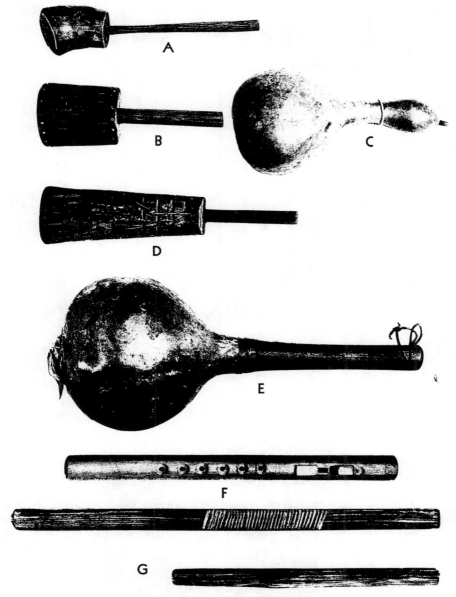

CAYUGA MUSICAL INSTRUMENTS

A. Cow horn rattle used in the majority of rites and dances, usually accompanying the water-drum. (Length 11"). (18/4729)

B. and D. Short and long elm-bark rattles of an old type; traditional prototype of A. (Length of D. 14"). (18/4730-1)

C. Entire pumpkin rattle with seeds dried inside used in planting and harvest ceremonies. (Length 10"). (18/4750)

E. Pumpkin rattle with wooden handle inserted and peach pits inside, used as is C. (Length 18").

F. Flageolet of hollowed cedar used for musical purposes but never associated with ceremonies. (Length 17").

G. Notched resonator or rasp and stick, used in Chipmunk Dance. (Length 24"). (18/4747)

Museum of The American Indian, Heye Foundation, N. Y.

PLATE XVI

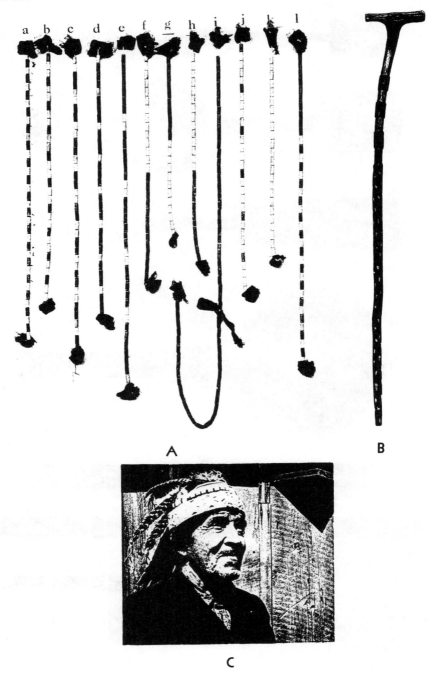

a b c d e f g h i j k l

A

B

C

A. Reproduction of set of wampum strings used in Family Condolence Rite of Sour Springs Cayuga. (18/4737)
B. Ceremonial cane, part of equipment used with wampum strings in the rite. (Length 36″).
   Museum of The American Indian, Heye Foundation, N. Y.
C. Chief Jacob Isaac, civil chief and ritual leader of Sour Springs Long House.